BREAKING BREAD

TAPER, SEED

↓

AFTER SEEDS, PLACE ON
COUCHE.

BREAKING BREAD

A

BAKER'S

JOURNEY

HOME

IN

75 RECIPES

MARTIN PHILIP

PHOTOGRAPHY BY JULIA A. REED

HARPER WAVE

An Imprint of HarperCollinsPublishers

HarperCollins books may be purchased for educational, business, or sales promotional use. For information, please email the Special Markets Department at SPsales@harpercollins.com.

FIRST EDITION

DESIGNED BY LEAH CARLSON-STANISIC

PHOTOGRAPHY BY JULIA A. REED

ILLUSTRATIONS BY MARTIN PHILIP

Library of Congress Cataloging-in-Publication Data

Philip, Martin, author; Reed, Julia A., photographer.

Breaking bread : a baker's journey home in 75 recipes / Martin Philip; photography by Julia A. Reed.

Includes bibliographical references and index.

p.   cm

ISBN 978-0-06-244792-0

1. Philip, Martin—Travel—United States. 2. Cooking (Bread). 3. Bread. 4. Bakers and bakeries.

TX769.P49 2017

641.81′5—dc23   2017011318

17 18 19 20 21 LSC 10 9 8 7 6 5 4 3 2 1

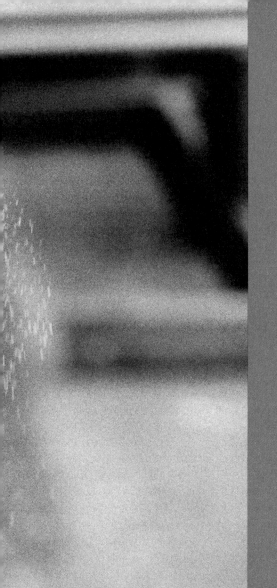

FOR THE BENT-KNUCKLED AND CALLOUSED,
WRINKLED, AND FORGOTTEN;

FOR THE KNEADING, AND TENDING, CRADLING,
AND EMBRACING;

FOR THE NEWBORN, THE GRASPING, THE REACHING,
AND HOLDING; FOR THE HANDS.

And the world cannot be
discovered by a journey of
miles, no matter how long,
but only by a spiritual
journey, a journey of one
inch, very arduous and
humbling and joyful, by
which we arrive at the
ground at our own feet, and
learn to be at home.

Wendell Berry
The Unforeseen Wilderness

CONTENTS

BREAKING BREAD

AUTHOR'S NOTE

I began this book with no plan, no structure, no writing experience, and no sense of my skill or lack thereof. In every imaginable endeavor this predicament might have resulted in disappointment or worse. But in hindsight I see that an empty space was the most fortunate beginning as I was free of expectations, free of confines, an open field ready for sun, rain, darkness, and time to transform and to grow. And so, it was here that I began, planting words and waiting to see what would take. What came out was something winding. If sentences and paragraphs were trees, we'd see their beginnings, roots twisting through red clay soil rising upward into burls, knots, and limbs before leaves and seeds fall, returning to dirt, journeying homeward.

In this structure the book abandons the traditional form of a cooking or baking book. Recipes are not grouped by dough type or method. Rather, they grow into the manuscript organically, introduced in the same order in which they made their way to my life, my hands, and eventually, my own mixing bowl and oven.

Some of you may wish to bypass the narrative sections; I understand. Dinner needs to be on the table in thirty minutes and words don't fill bellies. For ease we've listed recipes with page numbers for quick reference. Also, you may find yourself directed to the Method section of the book for specific skills and technical content; this mostly relates to the bread recipes, which tend to be more involved.

The details of this story are mine but they are not unique. We all have tales, lives with beginnings, heartache, happiness, movement, and endings. I hope that you find yourself inspired to bake your own narrative, to connect the lines of your experience to your own environment, your family, and those around you, for baking and giving are truly acts of love.

Happy baking,
Martin

Part 1

RECIPES
AND STORIES

BREADWRIGHT

Bread: Old English bread "bit, crumb, morsel; bread," cognate with Old Norse *brauð*, Danish *brød*, Old Frisian *brad*, Middle Dutch *brot*, Dutch *brood*, German *Brotbrot*. According to one theory [Watkins, etc.] from Proto-Germanic *brautham*, which would be from the root of *brew* [v.] and refer to the leavening.

Wright: Old English *wryhta*, *wrihta* [Northumbrian *wyrchta*, Kentish *werhta*] "worker," variant of earlier *wyhrta*, from *wyrcan* "to work" [see work [v.]]. Now usually in combinations [wheelwright, playwright, etc.] or as a surname. Common West Germanic; cognate with Old Saxon *wurhito*, Old Frisian *wrichta*, Old High German *wurhto*.

My name is Martin Rainey Philip.

"Martin" for Martin Chamberlin of Shortsville, New York, a cooper who made barrels and drained them with equal skill; dead of cirrhosis, 1919. "Rainey" for Thomas Rainey, who left countless Scotch-Irish Raineys and the gray skies of County Armagh, Northern Ireland, for work as a bleachery foreman in the toxic woolen mills of Central Falls, Rhode Island; dead of influenza, 1944. And "Philip" from George Rennie Philip of Aberdeenshire, Scotland, a journeyman stonecutter who traded Scottish granite for Vermont granite and worked himself to death in Barre, Vermont; dead of exhaustion, 1915.

To gain a name is an easy thing—a mouthlong chain of consonants and vowels cut and stamped. With a sharp pen stroke one can carve on a family tree for eternity. Census documents hold forests of these trees and branches and you can climb around in them, moving past a spot of ink here, a correction there, the antique curling scripts counting lives, and livelihoods, as they wind through centuries of occupations and births. There once was a time when lives were linked to tangible trades and physical connections—the crush of a hammer between arm and stone, palms on spinning bobbins of cotton warp, fingers dragging across fresh-sawn staves in a cooperage, a baker's arms bent at the dough trough, pulling and kneading—once, we lived at the intersection of our hands and our materials.

And if men's names make paternal ladders with lineage and crests, and Jr. and Sr., what of the women? Frances Harriet Chamberlin, occupation, blank. Carolyn Rainey Harris, occupation, blank. Cora Isabelle King, occupation, blank. While men passed down names in direct lines, matriarchs lived in round forms moving from knitting circles to mixing bowls, a wrap of arms around a child. Through these connected, embracing forms, they have sewn, baked, tended, and grown those parts of us which shape, rather than name. My grandmother, Carolyn Harris, or "Oma" as we called her, was a quilter. Her quilting frame, her foundation, hand-cut and smoothed by years of use, was constructed by her long-deceased son. In cold months the frame was assembled in the living room, equidistant from bed and board where she worked, her face bent close to the frame. This quiet play of hands and material, whether in a bowl of flour, in a bucket of bulbs, or quietly pulling a needle and thread at the dimming of day, was her connection, her evensong of fingers and heart; her handcraft was the outward representation of her soul craft.

Oma passed this connection to my mother, Frances Philip, through will or environment. And what emerged in Mama was an entirely alternative form. Where Oma was precise and traditional and classical, my mother blew everything to the moon, scattering scrap quilts cut from colorful bikinis along the way. If Oma was control and adherence—delicate angel food cake for every birthday—Mama was hollering "Chinese fire drill" at a stoplight with a car full of kids. I'm thankful for the contrast, for Mama's ability to improvise, to roll with it, to encourage a baking adventure to never-never land even in the face of an empty pantry. And I miss Oma—the precision, the formality, the pecan pie with a splash of whiskey, blond brownies spiked with black walnuts, orange-glazed angel food cake adorned with fresh flowers—treats held in the soul's memory.

These two distinct lines—the men, handing names and a connection to trade; and the women, living through example, nurturing with linens, layettes, and food—made their way to my lap as I, attempting to cross-stitch, sewed my pants to a cloth napkin as I sat on the couch next to my mother. Heritage is stamped within and without. There are jewels and there are scars. On my arm, the faded white of two holes where I was impaled running in a thicket, the sticks entering my arm and later yanked out under running water by my brother. Despite decades of fresh skin and new memories, the scars still look back at me, bearing witness to a time and place where stick punctured arm. So it is with craft and lineage, hearts, and names.

Today I reach down through grass and dirt to grasp the roots of this lineage. My wife Julie and I left New York City to bring our family back to Vermont, where the first Philips settled when they came from Scotland. We live at the confluence of rivers and rusty train tracks in a railroad town. It is here that, daily, I embrace handcraft, trade, and round forms, milling flour on circular stones, mixing doughs, and baking bread at King Arthur Flour for my family and communities of happy eaters, which encircle us. If today is *my* day to be counted, to climb and take a place on the family tree, to lay down my roots or make the last journey, it is a good day as I am proud of my listing—I'm in the right line, in the right place to receive and also give. I am a baker, and flourishing.

My path to this good place hasn't been straight: I've been lost; I've moved from roots, heritage, and home before heading back again. And this journey, all of it, began with drop biscuits.

I grew up in the creases of the Ozark Mountains, learning to speak with soft mouth and even tones to the night calls of whip-poor-will and chuck-will's-widow. I was the third of six children and we were a mixture of old ways and hippie new ways. We had Foxfire books on the shelf, comfrey in the garden, and cures, which favored hair-tying for deep scalp wounds, garlic pills for blood clots, and cider vinegar for everything else. Our diet had no meat, preservatives, food coloring, additives, white sugar, or anything else multisyllabic on a label. When we could afford it, my mother would place a bulk order with the food co-op for tubs of tofu, fifty-pound bags of rolled oats and pinto beans, buckets of blackstrap molasses, and bags of brewer's yeast.

Those days were not gentle imprints or glancing marks from casual use; they were dents and patina, weathered paint on hardwood boards, and their impressions remain, forty years on. I see steam vents rising from oatmeal in a house with frost on inside windows, cornmeal-crusted sunfish fried in cast iron, twisted inside-out, tails pulled through mouths. And my mother's ragged drop biscuits, flecked with whole wheat flour. They were not lofty or light; they weren't brushed with butter or made with lard. They were simple, they were cheap, and they were dinner. Flour in the bowl, baking powder—enough to cover the small dip between her palm's heart and life lines—and a thimbleful of salt. In my mind's eye, she was near the stove, framed by a greasy fox pelt and cast-iron corn pone pans hanging on a brick chimney. She hand-mixed the dry ingredients, then made a well, filled it with water, and floated enough oil on top to cover the liquid surface. Stir, stir, scoop, drop, bake, and serve with honey or brewer's yeast gravy.

Biscuits for dinner, folk medicine made with the eye's measurement. We all have these memories, recollections, which, when summoned, can transport us. Food traditions have a way of leaving marks, indelible ink the whiff of which yanks us whirling and swirling to lands beyond and long gone. But could I re-create these biscuits with my own palms? Would I, in some attempt to go back, use these warm forms as a means of travel to an old house in Arkansas? What is it about biscuits that brings weight beyond the measure of ingredients? Over my years as a baker I have given innumerable loaves to friends, family, and strangers, and, while each loaf carries something and was passed along in earnest, I cannot say there is a more tender act than the sharing of biscuits. This gift, this simple mix of flour, milk, butter, salt, and leavening, when eaten warm from the oven, contains me, my heritage, my home, my upbringing—all that I am. And the biscuits have changed as I have—when I make them today I fuss some, perhaps as Oma would, gently incorporating layers of cold butter and folding the dough before cutting it into small rounds. When no one's looking I might even make them without measuring anything, as Mama would. During baking, moisture in the butter expands, pushing upward before setting and transitioning—toasting to golden. Small hands can break them, separating tops from bottoms easily, each half ferrying butter or jam or simply riding sidecar to a bowl of beans. I don't know what the old home would feel like today—but I do know that my heart is here, in this very moment when I have biscuits.

BUTTER BISCUITS

INGREDIENTS	METRIC (GRAMS)	VOLUMETRIC (APPROXIMATE)
All-purpose flour	355	3 cups
Salt, fine	6	1 teaspoon
Baking powder	4	1 teaspoon
Baking soda	2	¼ teaspoon
Butter, unsalted, cold	113	½ cup (8 tablespoons)
Buttermilk	240	1 cup + 1½ teaspoons

PREPARE

Position an oven rack on a rung in the top third of the oven.

Preheat the oven to 425°F.

Lightly grease a 13 by 18-inch sheet pan, or line it with parchment paper.

Cut the butter into ⅛-inch-thick slices. Chill until use.

Weigh and chill the dry ingredients.

MIX

In a medium bowl, whisk together the flour, salt, baking powder, and baking soda.

Add the cold butter and toss to coat with the dry ingredients. Then press the butter slices between your thumb and forefinger into small flat pieces or "leaves."

Add the buttermilk all at once and mix gently until the mixture is just combined. The dough should be firm and barely cohesive (some dry bits are OK).

SHAPE

Transfer the dough to a lightly floured work surface and pat into a ¾-inch-thick rectangle. The dry bits will incorporate in the following steps.

Fold the dough in thirds as you would a letter and gently roll or pat it into a rectangle. Repeat this fold-and-roll process once more if the dough isn't cohesive.

Lightly flour the top of the dough and cut the dough into circles with a sharp 2-inch biscuit cutter, or square the sides and edges and cut into 8 to 10 even squares using a chef's knife.

BAKE

Place the biscuits on the prepared sheet pan.

Bake for 16 to 18 minutes, rotating after 14 minutes, until the biscuits are golden.

Cold Butter

There are a couple of key points to remember in making biscuits, scones, and pie crusts. Ingredients should be kept cold until use. Keeping them cold will ensure that the butter will have no opportunity to melt until it reaches the oven. Melting butter releases moisture, which supports the development of gluten (too much of which will make the crust tough); and once the butter is melted, there will be no separation between it and the flour within the dough. This separation is what creates flake and tenderness and supports a puffy, crisp pastry.

After adding the liquid to your dough be careful not to overwork it with too much kneading or mixing. Mechanical action will develop gluten and toughen pastries. Just mix until the ingredients are combined and then stop. Additional incorporation of a dry bit here or there will be handled when the dough is rolled or shaped.

There are things that are no longer homemade, and the list seems to keep growing. At Oma's house a sandwich prepared with store-bought bread would be served only with a side of apology. These days, spotting a committed home baker is not unlike that spring afternoon when cedar waxwings migrate through our yard—it's worth a trip to the window. You and I can change that with a few ingredients and a little time, but before we get to that, let's bring back another staple that will reward our attention and our mouths.

I don't know where store-bought butter comes from, I picture a windowless lab with white walls and an expensive instrument, the lauded "flavor extractor," which purifies, beats, and stabilizes the formerly flavorFUL cream and renders it entirely tasteless but shelf stable (whee, who cares!). If you follow labels you will even notice that butter is often made with the addition of natural flavoring . . . because butter needs more flavor? Let's stop this insanity; butter is damn easy and quick to make. What do you need? Cream. The stuff from the store in the wax carton will work, but if you can find your way to a local farm that sells directly, or find a source at a local food cooperative (look for the glass bottles), the experience will be even richer.

FRESH BUTTER

Yield: **227 grams (1 cup)**

INGREDIENTS	METRIC (GRAMS)	VOLUMETRIC (APPROXIMATE)
Heavy cream	465	2 cups
Ice water, for rinsing the butter	465	2 cups
Salt, fine	3	½ teaspoon

PREPARE   Chill the bowl of your stand mixer and the whisk attachment.

Put the cold cream in the bowl of the stand mixer fitted with the whisk attachment.

Cover the mixer with a tea towel to minimize the spatter of cream, or use a splatter guard if your mixer has one.

Turn the mixer on high and beat the cream until it thickens like whipped cream, a few minutes.

Continue beating past this point until the fat separates from the buttermilk and the butter clumps on the whisk.

Remove the bowl from the mixer, pour off the buttermilk, then return the bowl to the mixer.

MIX   Add 1 cup of the fresh ice water to the bowl and set to high speed for 1 minute. Remove the bowl from the mixer and pour off the cloudy rinse water.

Return the bowl to the mixer, add the second cup of ice water, and beat the butter and water on high speed for an additional minute.

Remove the bowl from the mixer, pour off the cloudy water, and knead the butter briefly in the bowl by hand to remove as much of the remaining water as possible. The rinse water should appear mostly clear, not milky.

Add the salt and knead/mix by hand in the mixing bowl to incorporate.

The butter can be chilled and kept, refrigerated, for a week, or frozen for up to a month.

If made well, jam is a season in a jar—fruit remains intact and the sunshine of summer can express its purity. And amendments can be added to heighten, surprise, or leave a question mark on a palate, which will encourage knives and hands to return for seconds. This refrigerator jam pairs good plums with a natural match, port wine, and adds star anise as an accent, elevating the plums.

PLUM PORT JAM

Yield: **681 grams (3 cups)**

INGREDIENTS	METRIC (GRAMS)	VOLUMETRIC (APPROXIMATE)
Plums, whole, fresh	900	2 pounds
Star anise	8 intact "stars"	8 intact "stars"
Sugar	360	1¾ cups
Port wine	120	½ cup
Lemon juice, freshly squeezed	14	1 tablespoon

DAY ONE

PREPARE

Pit and quarter the plums.

Wrap the star anise in cheesecloth and tie it with a piece of kitchen string for easy retrieval.

FIRST BOIL

In a wide medium nonreactive pot, combine the plums, star anise, sugar, port wine, and lemon juice.

Bring to a full boil, stirring occasionally.

Remove from the heat, cover the pot, and let the mixture sit at room temperature for at least an hour, or as long as overnight.

DAY TWO

FINAL BOIL

Remove the pot lid. Set the jam mixture over medium-high heat, and bring it to a medium boil.

Cook, stirring occasionally, until the jam thickens.

The jam is ready when it reaches a temperature of 220°F and passes the plate test: Freeze a plate and drop some jam onto it; if the jam wrinkles when gently pushed after cooling, it is ready.

This jam will hold well, chilled, for up to 2 weeks.

NOTE: For larger batches and greater yield you may double all amounts and proceed with the method as written.

Checking Temperatures

A candy or probe thermometer is the most accurate way to test the set of a jam or jelly. During testing we found that the infrared thermometer did not accurately read the boiling jam. At sea level, full set should occur at or just below 220°F. As water leaves the boiling liquid, progress toward this temperature will slow.

Once the boil reaches 212°F to 215°F, keep a very close eye on it, as it can burn quickly. I personally do not mind a jam that is somewhat loose; so depending on how it looks, I will often turn it off right around 215°F.

As an alternative to the thermometer you may also use the plate test. Before beginning the final boil, place a ceramic or glass plate in the freezer. When the boiling mixture forms glassy bubbles the size of marbles and seems well thickened, place a teaspoon of jam on the plate and return it to the freezer for 2 minutes. While waiting for the mixture to set, lower the heat under the jam pot, or remove it from the burner. After the 2 minutes, remove the plate from the freezer and push gently on the jam, checking to see if it wrinkles. If it is set and wrinkles with pressure, the jam is ready. If it is not set, return the pot to the heat and cook the jam for 1 or 2 minutes longer, then repeat the test.

LEMON-BLACKBERRY JAM

Yield: **681 grams (3 cups)**

INGREDIENTS	METRIC (GRAMS)	VOLUMETRIC (APPROXIMATE)
Blackberries, fresh or frozen	900	3 pints
Sugar	360	1¾ cups
Lemon zest	6	1 tablespoon
Lemon juice	14	1 tablespoon

DAY ONE

PREPARE

Wash and clean the blackberries. If you are using frozen berries, thaw them and keep all the juice.

FIRST BOIL

In a wide medium nonreactive pot, combine the blackberries, sugar, lemon zest, and lemon juice.

Bring to a full boil, stirring occasionally.

Remove from the heat, cover the pot, and let the mixture sit at room temperature for at least an hour, or as long as overnight.

DAY TWO

FINAL BOIL

Remove the pot lid. Set the jam mixture over medium-high heat and bring it to a medium boil.

Cook, stirring occasionally, until the jam thickens.

The jam is ready when it reaches a temperature of 220°F and passes the plate test: Freeze a plate and drop some jam onto it; if the jam wrinkles when gently pushed after cooling, it is ready.

This jam will hold well, chilled, for up to 2 weeks.

NOTE: For larger batches and greater yield you may double all amounts and proceed with the method as written.

There is comforting, there is belly-warming, there are old rituals and new traditions, there is delicious, and there are hoecakes. This corny staple, found in cultures from central America to the Caribbean and north to the United States, is the obvious product of water, coarse cornmeal, and hot fat. We amend ours with eggs, a little leavening, butter, and salt. We didn't cook ours on a hoe over an open fire as they may have been made formerly; our cast iron works plenty well. Southerners have endless access to grits . . . in Vermont I have to search a little but can usually find them. I like the yellow ones for their color and prefer "Regular" over "Instant" as Regular are crunchier. You may use what you like! And, for a nice variation, try them "savory," garnished with shredded chicken, roasted salsa, fresh avocado, cilantro, and lime juice.

CORN GRIT HOECAKES

Yield: **Ten to twelve 3- to 4-inch hoecakes**

INGREDIENTS	METRIC (GRAMS)	VOLUMETRIC (APPROXIMATE)
Water, boiling	160	¾ cup
Grits, instant or regular	160	1 cup + 1 tablespoon
Butter, unsalted	28	2 tablespoons
Cornmeal, yellow	28	heaping 3 tablespoons
Sugar	28	scant 2 tablespoons
Baking powder	4	1 teaspoon
Salt, fine	3	½ teaspoon
Egg, large	50	1
Buttermilk	125	½ cup + 1 tablespoon
Butter, for greasing the pan or griddle		

PREPARE

Combine the boiling water, grits, and 2 tablespoons butter in a bowl and stir thoroughly.

While the grits soak up the water, gather and measure the remaining ingredients.

MIX

In a small bowl, whisk together the cornmeal, sugar, baking powder, and salt.

In a medium bowl, whisk together the egg and buttermilk, then add the soaked grits and butter mixture. Stir until smooth.

Add the dry ingredients and stir until smooth.

Set the batter aside to rest while you preheat an electric griddle to 350°F, or heat a frying pan over medium heat.

COOKING

Rub a small amount of butter over your griddle or frying pan. Use a paper towel to fully distribute it and remove any excess.

Using a scant ¼-cup measure, drop the batter onto the griddle or frying pan, spreading it into 3- to 4-inch circles with the bottom of the cup if necessary.

As there is no gluten, these cakes are very tender. Flip gently when the edges are set and the cakes hold their shape. Cook for an additional 1 to 2 minutes on the second side. Repeat with the remaining batter.

Enjoy with molasses, maple syrup, honey, or fresh jam!

Molasses, that blackstrap sugarcane sweetener, dark as pitch and rich with iron and minerals, may be an acquired taste. Its unsavory history in this country goes back to a triangle of trade, which moved slaves from West Africa to the Caribbean where ships took on molasses bound for Boston for use in making rum. Booze-laden, they then completed the route, returning to Africa, leaving the drink, and taking humans. A by-product of sugar production, molasses was cheaper than white sugar and, before World War 1, led the sweetener market in the United States along with maple syrup. In Arkansas the lazy Susan on our kitchen table always spun with a jar of molasses *and* a jar of honey—set to please the tastes of two camps, one preferring oatmeal with molasses and the other choosing honey. It isn't a subtle taste—these days most homes keep a dusty jar in the cupboard for molasses cookies or gingerbread. But at my house the jar lives on—sticky sides ensuring a firm grip during transport from cupboard to table, its journey on a cornbread boat ending with passage from a child's hand to waiting teeth. It can also be made into my favorite pie.

When shelves are empty, cupboards bare, no cream in sight or hoard of chocolate, there is molasses. And, if there are molasses and eggs from our hens, a little flour and butter, there can be pie. I have a few of Oma's recipe cards, cup measures written with cursive curls and tips in the margin. It could be that the magic of her molasses pie can be found on this card but I'm guessing her experience, that place beyond the margins where craft lives, is where the secrets lie. If I had known, as a child I would have reached a small hand upward, past the counter, over the edge of a cool bowl to pinch-test the consistency of her pie dough, to watch as ingredients were carefully combined. My children have come to know my own molasses pie, perhaps believing that maybe I have some magic of my own.

If molasses is a new taste for you, you might begin with the lighter variety as it is more sweet than strong. And then I encourage you to move, armed with fresh whipped cream, along the spectrum toward dark or even blackstrap.

MOLASSES PIE

INGREDIENTS	METRIC (GRAMS)	VOLUMETRIC (APPROXIMATE)
Eggs, large	150	3
Molasses, light, dark, or blackstrap	329	1 cup
Salt, fine	Pinch	Pinch
Vanilla extract	5	1 teaspoon
Pie crust, unbaked, 9-inch		1

PREPARE   Preheat the oven to 375°F.

MIX   Beat the eggs well.

Add the molasses, salt, and vanilla and stir to combine.

Pour the filling into the unbaked pie crust.

BAKE   Bake the pie at 375°F for 20 minutes, then reduce the oven to 350°F and bake for another 30 minutes, until the filling is set. During baking, the pie will dome some and then settle.

Serve when cool. Garnish with softly whipped cream.

RECIPE for   *Molasses Pie*

from the kitchen of   *Carolyn Harris*

Beat three eggs well and add
1 to 1¼ cup molasses depending on
size of pie pan. Give it plenty of
room as it puffs up
but will go down. Add
a pinch of salt and 1 teaspoon
Vanilla. Pour into your
baked crust. When baking
these pies it helps to have
the oven hotter at first to
let the crust start cooking
(over)

MOLASSES PIE **PAGE 21**
OMA'S PIE CRUST **PAGE 24**

OMA'S PIE CRUST

Yield: **Two 9-inch crusts; enough for 1 double-crust pie, or 2 single-crust pies**

INGREDIENTS	METRIC (GRAMS)	VOLUMETRIC (APPROXIMATE)
All-purpose flour	300	2½ cups
Salt, fine	3	½ teaspoon
Butter, unsalted	200	¾ cup + 2 tablespoons (14 tablespoons)
Water, iced and strained	80 to 100	6 to 7 tablespoons

PREPARE

Measure and combine the flour and salt, and chill until use.

Cut the butter into ⅛-inch-thick slices. Chill until use.

MIX

Add the cold butter to the dry ingredients and toss to coat with the flour mixture. Then press the butter slices between your thumb and forefinger into small flat pieces or "leaves."

Rub this mixture briefly between your palms and fingers, 10 to 15 seconds. It should be the texture of cornmeal with many larger pieces of flattened butter still intact in some places.

Add ice water, a tablespoon at a time, tossing to combine. Stop adding ice water as the mixture comes together but before it is a homogeneous mass. A handful of the pie dough should hold its shape when squeezed together, with a few dry bits in the bottom of the bowl.

Transfer the dough onto a work surface and knead gently to combine, just until the mixture comes together. The dough should be flecked with visible pieces of butter.

Divide the dough into 2 pieces and shape each into a disk about ¾ inch thick. Wrap the disks in plastic wrap and place in the refrigerator for 20 minutes, or up to 24 hours, before rolling. You may freeze one for later use.

RECIPE CONTINUES

Remove a disk of dough from the refrigerator and allow it to soften slightly before rolling, 10 to 15 minutes.

SHAPE

On a lightly dusted surface with a sheen of flour on the top of the dough, roll from the center out, working in all directions until the crust is 10 to 11 inches in diameter for a 9-inch pan. If the dough sticks, use a bench knife to release it, and also push some bench flour under the dough. You may invert your pie pan over the dough to check the diameter; add an extra inch all around to allow for a crimped edge.

The rolled crust can be crimped and placed in a standard 9-inch pie pan and chilled, covered, until use, up to 24 hours. The unbaked crust can be well wrapped and frozen for up to 1 month.

RECIPE for *Pecan Pie*

from the kitchen of *Carolyn Harris*

3 beaten eggs
1 cup brown sugar
1 cup corn syrup

1 cup pecans
1 t. vanilla
pastry

Beat eggs, add sugar & beat well. Add syrup, nuts & vanilla. Pour into pastry lined pan.

Faye sent this to my mother here in Fayetteville before your mother was born. Fall, 1944.

PECAN PIE

Yield: **One 9-inch pie**

INGREDIENTS	METRIC (GRAMS)	VOLUMETRIC (APPROXIMATE)
Eggs, large	150	3
Brown sugar	255	1¼ cups
Corn syrup (dark or light), or brown rice syrup	312	1 cup
Pecan halves	100	scant 1 cup
Vanilla extract or whiskey	14	1 tablespoon
Pie crust, unbaked, 9-inch		1

PREPARE

Preheat the oven to 350°F.

MIX

Whisk the eggs together until smooth.

Add the sugar and whisk together.

Stir in the syrup, pecans, and vanilla or whiskey.

Pour the filling into the prepared shell.

BAKE

Bake for 45 to 50 minutes until the pie is set and the crust is nicely browned. During baking, the pie will dome some and then settle.

Serve when cool. Garnish with freshly whipped cream.

At our house, bread making was a ritual, reliable and grounding in its weekend occurrence, something to be repeated, revisited, and awaited. It would happen on Saturdays when there was time to spare; the bread was begun and then tended when a moment allowed. Occasionally, it was forgotten, but bread tolerates life and interruptions relatively well. It is not egg whites in a mixer or pastry cream on medium heat; it is a process of waiting, sprinkled with bits of activity. Mix, then wait. Shape, then wait. Load the oven, then wait. In a corner of our kitchen at a counter with an east-facing window gathering light and illuminating puffs of flour as a wooden spoon moved in circles, my father or mother was the baker. Twenty-five pounds of dough at a time were mixed in our largest wooden bowl. As with the biscuits, the recipe was variable; but, in broad terms, it was a blend of all-purpose white flour and coarse whole wheat flour, spring water, oil, honey or molasses, salt and dry yeast. Sometimes even the leftover oatmeal from the morning would be dumped into the batch if it hadn't been fed to the dog. The dough was mixed with a wooden spoon before being hand-kneaded until a piece pulled from the mass sprang back. In summer, encouraged by southern heat and humidity, the dough might grow enough to spill over the counter, expanding in all directions, unrestricted, leaving its mark to be scraped off cupboards at some point, or never. A benefit of a lengthy rise (what bakers refer to as fermentation) is that flavor is given time to develop—I didn't know any of this as a child but, passing the large, bran-flecked mound of dough scantily clad with embroidered dish towels on the counter, I would reach under to pinch a piece of dough, leaving the mark of two fingers and hole. And what a flavor, gently sweet, slightly acidic and yeasty, a delicious preview of wheaty things to come. It was weighed into two-pound pieces, shaped, and put in pans for the final rise, then baked until browned and hollow to the thump. What does bread baking smell like in heaven? It smells like bread baking. How could the afterlife possibly improve on the aroma of 540

identified volatile chemical compounds that defy scientific imitation creating the most universally accepted and loved smell in the world? These days I've learned to wait until this aroma calms and the bread has cooled before slicing. Cutting it hot releases moisture into the air, prematurely halting the process during which starches settle and the loaf temperature equalizes. Waiting is similar to allowing a chicken or steak to rest before slicing. But did we wait as kids? Hell no. We would saw through an entire loaf straight from the oven, stacking cut slices wedged with butter between them so that it would melt quickly. We gobbled the first slices with garlic on them—our savory course—and then we'd slather them with honey for dessert.

But, while this bread sustained us at home, it was shameful in the school lunch box. Sitting at the lunchroom table, surrounded by classmates and their blue or red milk choices, I would have given a kidney for that 1970s staple: crustless Wonder bread with Skippy and Smucker's grape jelly glue. I would have gladly sported an orange mouth ring of Cheetos crumbs and devoured a frosted Hostess cake in order that their chemicals could swirl kaleidoscopic in my gut. Not only are those foods designed for deliciousness, but carrying them in my lunch box would have been a ticket to belonging, an escape route from the requisite explanation of why I had rugged wheat bread slices spackle-bound with homemade peanut butter. Life in the chicken coop of elementary school is tough on young birds; spots are pecked, blemishes highlighted. Even today I find myself compensating where I can, giving care to my children's lunches in order that they might survive. I like to imagine them opening their lunch boxes to envious eyes rather than teasing mouths. Carefully wrapped fresh muffins, crusty baguettes with butter, soups made from scratch, rich pastas in heated containers, a bonanza in every lunch box. And, while I may have decried that bread, even hidden it, years later I have turned things around. I've headed back to this form, which is entirely more delicious and healthy than plump factory loaves pumped with chemicals ranging from azodicarbonamide (also used in floor mats) to potassium bromate (known carcinogen). Supermarket aisles are proof that if you add enough high-fructose corn syrup, preservatives, and stabilizers, people will still eat the packaged stuff months after it is produced. And, I would argue, meeting the bar of being edible isn't enough, not anymore. Bread deserves more, food deserves more, and most important, *we* deserve more. And we can have it quite easily. We are in the midst of a baking renaissance; more and more of us are using food as an opportunity to connect ourselves to our environment through eating, to handcraft through mindful ingredient choices and traditional methods. If you are new to bread making I encourage you to begin here, with this basic loaf. You can find, or return to, your own connection with this timeless staple, as I did.

MAMA'S BREAD

Yield: **Two 9 by 5-inch pan loaves**

INGREDIENTS	METRIC (GRAMS)	VOLUMETRIC (APPROXIMATE)	BAKER'S %
All-purpose flour	516	4¼ cups	50%
Whole wheat flour	516	4¼ cups	50%
Water	659	3 cups	64%
Salt, fine	21	1 tablespoon + ¾ teaspoon	2%
Yeast, dry instant	10	heaping 1 tablespoon	1%
Butter, unsalted	52	¼ cup (4 tablespoons)	5%
Honey	26	1 tablespoon + ¾ teaspoon	2.50%
Butter, unsalted, for brushing the crust (optional)			
	1,800		174.50%

PREPARE

Melt the 52 grams (¼ cup) of butter.

Calculate temperatures. See Setting Temperatures, page 320, for instructions. Desired dough temperature: 76°F

MIX

In a large mixing bowl, whisk together the flours, salt, and yeast. Add the water, melted butter, and honey. Mix with your hand or the handle end of a wooden spoon until the dough forms a shaggy mass. With some doughs you may have to knead for a few strokes in the bowl to incorporate everything. If you find it easier, after some stirring, scrape the dough out of the bowl with a plastic scraper onto your work surface and knead briefly with your hands just until the dough comes together. Resist the urge to add more flour. Scrape the dough off the work surface and return to the bowl for bulk fermentation.

BULK FERMENTATION

Scrape down the sides of the mixing bowl and allow the dough to rise, covered, for 2 hours at room temperature, folding as directed below.

FOLD

Fold after 30 and 60 minutes, then leave untouched for the second hour. See Folding, page 327.

RECIPE CONTINUES

DIVIDE AND PRESHAPE

Divide the dough into 2 pieces weighing about 900 grams each. See Dividing, page 328, for instructions.

Preshape as tubes. See Preshaping, page 329, for instructions.

Cover and let rest for 5 to 10 minutes.

SHAPE

Spray or lightly grease two 9 by 5-inch loaf pans.

Shape the dough as pan loaves. See Shaping, page 331, for instructions.

Place the dough in the prepared loaf pans, seam side down, pressing with your knuckles to evenly fill the pan.

PROOF

Cover and proof until the dough is 1 to 1½ inches above the top of the pan, 1 to 1½ hours.

BAKE

Toward the end of the proof, preheat the oven to 400°F.

Bake on the middle rack for 40 to 45 minutes, rotating after 30 minutes, until the top and sides are firm and the loaves are a deep golden brown.

Remove the bread from the pans and place on a cooling rack. For a softer crust, rub butter directly on the crust after baking, while the bread is still warm.

Bread pudding is a scrap quilt of baking. Pieces salvaged from this or that, a remnant that hardened before I got to it. With a few handfuls of raisins, sugar, some milk, and eggs, dessert is on the way. If we twist it slightly, remove the sugar, substitute stock for milk, and add sautéed garlic and fresh pear, onion, sausage, and sage, we can turn the dial to stuffing. For this recipe we will stick to sweet and make a sauce with whiskey, butter, and sugar, which would probably be good on just about anything.

50% fresh milled Turkey
5% fresh milled Emmer Farro
5% fresh milled Rye

Fresh milled ... 20%
preferment ... stiff
salted

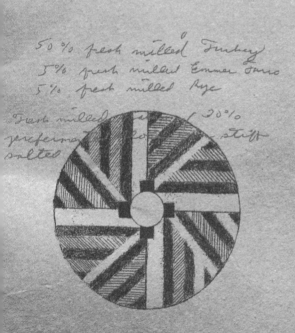

BREAD PUDDING

Yield: **One 9 by 13-inch pan**

INGREDIENTS	METRIC (GRAMS)	VOLUMETRIC (APPROXIMATE)
Milk, whole	976	4¼ cups
Stale bread, cut into 1-inch chunks	454	7½ to 8 cups
Eggs, large	150	3
Vanilla extract	28	2 tablespoons
Sugar, granulated	300	1½ cups
Raisins (optional)	150	1 cup
Butter, for greasing the pan		

PREPARE

In a large bowl, combine the milk and stale bread, and allow to stand for 1 to 2 hours, or until the bread is tender and the milk has been mostly absorbed.

Apply a generous, even coating of butter to a 9 by 13-inch baking pan.

When the bread is tender, preheat the oven to 350°F.

MIX

Mix the eggs, vanilla, and sugar. Gently fold into the soaked bread and add the raisins, if using.

Pour into the prepared pan, spreading evenly if necessary.

BAKE

Bake on the middle rack of the oven for 50 to 60 minutes.

The pudding is done when the crust is crisp in spots and springs back when pressed.

WHISKEY SAUCE

INGREDIENTS	METRIC (GRAMS)	VOLUMETRIC (APPROXIMATE)
Butter, unsalted	85	6 tablespoons
Milk, whole	28	2 tablespoons
Salt, fine	Pinch	Pinch
Confectioners' sugar	113	1 cup
Whiskey or half the amount of vanilla extract	42	3 tablespoons

SAUCE

While the pudding cools, make the sauce.

In a small pot over low heat, melt the butter with the milk and salt, then whisk in the confectioners' sugar.

When the mixture is smooth, stir in the whiskey or vanilla.

Serve the pudding warm with the sauce on the side, or pass it in a gravy boat.

LEAVING

I left Arkansas in 1988. It was time and I was ready. Homes and starting places of all sizes, shapes, and spaces lie and wait for the leaving. As a parent I know it is coming—I watch and hold on with hurting heart as my own children, nestled today in an embrace, slowly outgrow my arms and lap in order to jump out, away from me. I, too, grew and flew, leaving limestone caverns, chicken houses, and roots in search of something different.

A tale of leaving is a rich weave, for, in the midst of change, movement, and parting of all sorts, there is will. A need unfulfilled, a calling, an avoidance, so many choices to change a course.

And, in this place where heart is used, stories are found. As we pack bags, we cull and categorize; this pile for the journey, this one for discard. Here, wings for flight. Here, a chrysalis holding a shape from before, now useless. In this winnowing we define ourselves, stripping off layers to go in the direction of the new.

My leaving path had begun years before when I joined a children's choir at church. Over time and years I learned to be a cantor, leading evensong services, and singing baritone solos in Handel's *Messiah.* In high school I saw a poster from Oberlin Conservatory—a nighttime picture taken from outside a practice building, the camera spying on multiple floors of illuminated students. There were singers, violinists, brass players, and pianists—focused faces with hearts working at the intersection of hands and mind. To see this was to crave it, I yearned to live in that space, far away from Hemmed-In Hollow and the rest of my native experience. And, with luck and to my great surprise, I arrived on that very campus on northern plains with unobstructed sunset views over flattened earth. And was struck dumb.

In that space I was allowed, able, and encouraged to hold music closely, to live within the sonorous walls of my own heart. Walking practice hall passages, I could overhear concertos and cadenzas, sonatas and arias, a front-row stroll through a cacophonous blender of Western art music. Or I could sit for multiple concerts a day, orchestra rehearsals, or dance recitals—all options, endless access to a space where time stops, where the gaps of silence between last notes and clapping hands are full and flowing. But the music is not the point, not necessarily the part that survives today. That which I've held on to is the proximity that I felt, the closing of a distance between passion and existence, I was able to live with what moved me and not as a casual partner; the connection was there to stay. This was a gift of that place, but not the only one.

Life happens collectively in small schools where student lounge becomes main drag, city square, saloon, and even flophouse. It was there that I met a girl, a soprano named Julie from a small village in upstate New York. Brown hair, gray-blue eyes, and real—no airs or affectation—honest, and beautiful. She was a year ahead but constantly appearing next to me. And I reciprocated, finding ways to forever bump into her. Casual turned to regular with notes, study dates, and endless pursuit. Whatever amount of time we spent together, it wasn't enough.

Stories of life in different states and the exchange of histories led to talk of food, upbringing, and connections. And, if you spend that many moments together, you will eventually cook for each other, serving identities as the main course.

Perhaps predictable but at least consistent, the first card I played was the only one I held; black-eyed peas with cornmeal biscuits and molasses. It wasn't a recipe I knew by heart. As I stirred dry ingredients and summoned guidance from below the Mason-Dixon Line, I felt my way through the process, turning the bowl, moving my hands in mock forms to imitate what I had seen, hoping the recipe on the container of cornmeal would produce a crunchy contrast to soft beans and bittersweet molasses. As we ate the ragged dropped forms, alternating with bites of beans from unmatched bowls, quiet settled. This wasn't the first time that love was served on a baking sheet. Humans have always sat in circles, feeling the nourishment of fire, taking shelter from cold as food passed from mother to child, baker to stranger, or cook to company since the beginning of time. Each circle offers a chance to love anew, saying: Come, eat. In this spirit I made this simple meal, hoping she would accept these gifts of me, my edible history.

BLACK-EYED PEAS

Yield: **One big pot of beans**

INGREDIENTS	METRIC (GRAMS)	VOLUMETRIC (APPROXIMATE)
Black-eyed peas, dried	454	2½ cups (about 1 pound)
Water for cooking	1,800	approximately 8 cups
Bacon, raw	143	6 to 7 slices (less if thick)
Onion	156	1 medium
Garlic	18	2 large cloves
Salt, fine	8	scant 1½ teaspoons
Black pepper, ground	6	2 teaspoons
Cider vinegar or hot sauce to taste	2	½ teaspoon
Water or stock to thin the beans after cooking, if needed	227	1 cup

PREPARE Rinse the beans, and remove any stones or debris.

PROCESS Put the beans into a medium stockpot and cover by 2 inches with cold water. Bring to a boil.

Reduce the heat to medium and cook until the beans are tender when you bite one, 1 to 2 hours. Add more water as needed so the beans are always covered while cooking.

While the beans cook, dice the bacon into ¼-inch pieces, chop the onion, and mince the garlic.

In a small sauté pan, cook the chopped bacon over low heat until the fat has rendered. Add the chopped onion and garlic and sauté until softened and translucent.

Add the bacon mixture to the beans. Season to taste with salt and pepper.

Just before serving, add the cider vinegar or hot sauce to balance the natural sweetness of the beans.

There are meals that satisfy in both their frugality *and* their flavor. With tenderloin or fresh fish the bar is as high as the price tag but, with this lowly legume pressure swaps with enjoyment for a simple, happy mouth filled of peas, biscuits, and molasses.

If biscuits are quick and easy, these are even easier. Whereas I fret a little, looking for layers with a traditional rolled and cut biscuit, with these I worry less. Cornmeal is a non-glutenous flour, it adds tenderness as well as gorgeous color and flavor. The yellow crumb of these biscuits with a pat of butter and the black of molasses running off the side is enough. Simply enough.

CORNMEAL DROP BISCUITS

Yield: **12 to 16 small drop biscuits**

INGREDIENTS	METRIC (GRAMS)	VOLUMETRIC (APPROXIMATE)
All-purpose flour	200	1¾ cups
Cornmeal, yellow	138	1 cup
Salt, fine	5	scant 1 teaspoon
Baking powder	12	1 tablespoon
Baking soda	3	½ teaspoon
Butter, unsalted, very cold	113	½ cup (8 tablespoons)
Milk or buttermilk	250	1 cup + 2 tablespoons

PREPARE

Position an oven rack in the top third of the oven.

Preheat the oven to 425°F.

Lightly grease a 13 by 18-inch sheet pan, or line it with parchment paper.

Measure the dry ingredients and chill until use.

MIX

Combine the flour, cornmeal, salt, baking powder, and baking soda.

Grate the butter into the dry ingredients. Toss to combine.

Add the milk or buttermilk. Mix until barely combined.

SHAPE

Drop the biscuits from a large spoon onto the prepared sheet pan.

BAKE

Bake for 18 to 22 minutes on the top rack, rotating after 14 minutes, until they are lightly golden and firm to the touch.

Cornmeal

As we've tested recipes and compared flavor, texture, and even weight per cup of volumetric measure we have found more variance in cornmeal than in any other dry ingredient. The most common national brand, sold in a round paper canister, has a sandy, homogeneous grind that feels and tastes nothing like the fluffy, color-flecked variety that my mother used to buy right off the millstone at Johnson's Water Mill in Johnson, Arkansas. Looking for nationally available options that taste and perform better than the sandy stuff, I consistently prefer cornmeal labeled "stone ground," especially meals from local sources that still retain the character of this beautiful grain. Look around: you are in for a treat.

Through this and many other meals we bonded—breaking bread in an oasis where our present selves—bumps and blemishes included—were acceptable and good enough for each other.

In the shelter of that meal space we could push back the crush of conservatory criticism and self-inspection and connect with each other, free of striving and pressure. A ramshackle house Julie shared with friends had shag carpets and wood paneling, and in its linoleumed kitchen a copy of James Beard's *Beard on Bread*. That book, as well as an oil-stained spine-broken copy of *The Joy of Cooking*, was enough to get us making and baking. My first attempt at a chicken soup was prepared in a giant glass mixing bowl set directly on a glowing orange electric burner. While the liquid heated I confidently threw in leftover rice and chopped vegetables, then put my feet up as my masterpiece transformed itself. And change it did, with an ear-popping crack and geyser steam hiss, a full gallon of flavor concentrated itself on the heating element of the stove.

We began our baking with Beard's Caccia Nanza and looked quizzically at the instructions, wondering if we could actually make it work. I had seen bread made many times, but there was a territory between the land of watching my mother add ingredients in intuitive amounts and that place where I would go it alone. Caccia Nanza is a flat, focaccia-like bread, studded with garlic clove spears; rubbed with olive oil, rosemary, and salt; and baked in a hot oven. As it happens, focaccia was an auspicious place to begin. *Panis focacius*, as the Romans called it, has roots that extend to the Greeks or Etruscans in the West, or, I would argue, back to our earliest relationship with grains and baking, irrespective of locality. In simple terms *focacius* can be translated as "from the ashes," and is related to the Latin word *focus*, which means "hearth," or "place for baking." Soon after grains could be gathered, sprouted, brewed, crushed, or even milled, they were baked, but not in ovens. A dough was mixed, patted into a thin flat disk, then placed atop ashen coals, and turned to bake on both sides, or simply covered with more hot coals. So, I put my own hands into this earliest of baked forms in order to be transported back, to eat fresh bread and thus begin my own path with leavening. When I make this bread today, more has changed than not, but in those early moments perfection wasn't as important as the soul-warming movement of ingredients to mouth.

As a novice baker, I had a hard time seeing the forest for the trees. It took time and mistakes to learn what was critically important and what was secondary. I was unsure where to concentrate, wholly unaware of dough hydration, flour choices (pastry, bread, white, whole wheat), baking surfaces (baking stone or baking sheet), mixing techniques, or length of fermentation, all of which have impact. I took the recipe as a prescription, like directions to a place where I'd never been. Carefully following it, I found some success when, reaching into the mass of kneaded dough after an initial rest, I felt that it had begun to rise slightly, becoming soft and silky, lively, and air-filled against my hand. I very clearly remember touching the dough with a shocked response, "It worked!" We baked that dough on a flimsy baking sheet, so cheap that it bowed and buckled with heat.

Today when I bake, I see this bread within a context; it is more than starches bound by protein chains and filled with gas from yeast's activity—it is like a word, with roots in languages and cultures. It has a history in addition to its crunch, salt, oil, and herb.

FOCACCIA

Yield: One 13 by 18-inch pan (half-sheet pan) or two 9 by 13-inch pans (quarter-sheet pans) of focaccia

INGREDIENTS	METRIC (GRAMS)	VOLUMETRIC (APPROXIMATE)	BAKER'S %
All-purpose flour	740	6 cups + 1 tablespoon	100%
Water	502	2¼ cups	68%
Salt, fine	15	2½ teaspoons	2%
Yeast, dry instant	6	2 teaspoons	0.75%
Olive oil, extra virgin	37	3 tablespoons	5%
Olive oil, for greasing the pan			
Prepared toppings, as desired			
Total Weight	1,300	All	175.75%

Calculate temperatures. See Setting Temperatures, page 320, for instructions. Desired dough temperature: 76°F

MIX

In a large mixing bowl, whisk together the flour, salt, and yeast. Add the water and extra virgin olive oil. Mix with your hand or the handle end of a wooden spoon until the dough forms a shaggy mass. With some doughs you may have to knead for a few strokes in the bowl to incorporate everything. If you find it easier, after some stirring, scrape the dough out of the bowl with a plastic scraper onto your work surface and knead briefly with your hands just until the dough comes together. Resist the urge to add more flour. Scrape the dough off the work surface and return it to the bowl for bulk fermentation.

BULK FERMENTATION

Scrape down the sides of the mixing bowl and allow the dough to rise, covered, for 2 hours at room temperature, folding as directed below.

FOLD

Fold after 15, 30, 45, and 60 minutes, then leave untouched for the second hour. See Folding, page 327, for instructions.

Alternatively, after the 4 folds, the dough may be chilled for up to 24 hours. If using this method, allow the dough to rest for 1 to 2 hours at room temperature before proceeding to the dividing step.

RECIPE CONTINUES

DIVIDE

Leave the dough undivided for a single half-sheet pan or divide the dough into 2 pieces weighing about 650 grams each for quarter-sheet pans. See Dividing, page 328, for instructions.

Do not preshape or fold the dough. Any rough handling will make stretching the dough more difficult.

Gently place the dough on a well-oiled sheet pan. Turn it once to coat both sides and then allow it to relax, covered, for 15 to 30 minutes.

After the rest, dimple the dough in the pan with your fingertips, distributing it evenly to the corners and sides. If the dough resists being stretched into place, allow it to relax a little longer before proceeding.

Variation: For a crustier, even more rustic version of focaccia, place the dough on parchment paper and bake it directly on a preheated baking stone rather than on a sheet pan.

TOPPING

Position an oven rack on a rung in the lower third of the oven.

Preheat the oven to 450°F.

Drizzle the dough with olive oil, and garnish with coarse salt, fresh herbs, roasted onions, hard cheese, cherry tomatoes, or anything else that suits your fancy, and allow to rise for 10 to 15 minutes.

BAKE

Bake the focaccia on the lower rack for 22 to 24 minutes, rotating after 15 minutes. After 22 to 24 minutes, turn the oven to broil and move the pan to an upper rack to brown the toppings for 1 to 2 minutes, keeping a close eye on it! The focaccia is done when the bottom crust is golden and the toppings are well colored.

Remove from the pan and cool on a wire rack. If the focaccia is left in the pan to cool, the crust will become soggy.

SIZING OPTION

Mini-focaccia are also an option. Portion the dough in rough squares weighing about 65 grams each. As with the larger pans of focaccia, any rough handling will make the dough more difficult to stretch. Place the divided pieces on a well-oiled sheet pan, about an inch apart, turning once to coat.

It is especially to important to aggressively dimple the mini-focaccia, pushing your fingers almost entirely through the dough. This will keep the dimpled surface; otherwise, it will dome too much.

For the mini-focaccia, check at 16 to 18 minutes, then move them to an upper rack and broil for 1 to 2 minutes, watching closely.

TAPENADE

Yield: **725 grams (about 3½ cups)**

INGREDIENTS	METRIC (GRAMS)	VOLUMETRIC (APPROXIMATE)
Bell peppers, 2 to 3 fresh, for roasting, or one 12-ounce jar, drained	130	1½ cups
Garlic, fresh	9	1 large clove
Anchovies, oil-packed, drained (2-ounce tin)	32	2 tablespoons
Olives, green, manzanilla or similar, drained (5.75-ounce jar)	120	1¼ cups
Olives, kalamata, drained (10-ounce jar)	171	1⅓ cups
Capers, drained (3.5-ounce jar)	65	¼ cup
Olive oil, extra virgin	198	1 cup
Minced fresh basil, oregano, marjoram, or mint, for garnish (optional)		

PROCESS

IF YOU ARE ROASTING YOUR OWN PEPPERS

Place 2 or 3 large, clean bell peppers over an open flame and char, turning occasionally, until well blackened.

Place in a paper bag or a bowl. Close the bag or cover the bowl, and let the peppers cool.

Rub off most the blackened skin, then seed and stem. Reserve until use.

TO MAKE THE TAPENADE

Place the garlic and anchovies in a food processor fitted with the cutting blade. Pulse to puree.

Add the olives, capers, and reserved bell peppers and pulse briefly, 5 to 10 seconds. Pause to scrape down the sides if necessary. The texture should be coarse, not pureed.

Stir in the olive oil and garnish with fresh herbs.

efore Food Network, before "EVOO" and "Bam!" entered the stockpot of our lexicon, and well before the cult of celebrity replaced the cult of capability, there was a series on PBS called *Great Chefs*. Narrated by Mary Lou Conroy in her inviting southern drawl, the shows were the best thing before food TV and have remained the greatest thing since. Episodes were built around cities and their great foods, focusing tightly on technique, flavor, and craftspeople. They were a gateway drug that led me to *Baking with Julia*, Jacques Pépin, and beyond. It is no exaggeration to say that I received my informal culinary education in thirty-minute chunks. Following Julia, I found a French bread recipe, published in the *New York Times* magazine, which I hoped would approximate the flavor of loaves we could buy at the West Side Market in Cleveland. It was my first attempt at a hand-shaped artisan bread.

crust is my copilot

BASIC FRENCH DOUGH

Yield: **2 boules or bâtards, or 4 baguettes**

TOTAL FORMULA

INGREDIENTS	METRIC (GRAMS)	VOLUMETRIC (APPROXIMATE)	BAKER'S %
All-purpose flour	478	4 cups	85%
Whole wheat flour	85	scant ¾ cup	15%
Water	422	1¾ cups + 2 tablespoons	75%
Salt, fine	11	scant 2 teaspoons	2%
Yeast, dry instant	4	1¼ teaspoons	0.75%
Total Weight	1,000		177.75%

MIX

Calculate temperatures. See Setting Temperatures, page 320, for instructions. Desired dough temperature: 76°F

In a large mixing bowl, whisk together the flours, salt, and yeast. Add the water and mix with your hand or the handle end of a wooden spoon until the dough forms a shaggy mass. With some doughs you may have to knead for a few strokes in the bowl to incorporate everything. If you find it easier, after some stirring, scrape the dough out of the bowl with a plastic scraper onto your work surface and knead briefly with your hands just until the dough comes together. Resist the urge to add more flour. Scrape the dough off the work surface and return it to the bowl for bulk fermentation.

BULK FERMENTATION

Scrape down the sides of the mixing bowl and allow the dough to rise, covered, for 3 hours at room temperature, folding as directed below.

FOLD

Fold after 15, 30, 45, 60, and 120 minutes, then leave untouched for the third hour. See Folding, page 327, for instructions.

As you perform each series of folds, you'll begin to notice that the dough becomes smoother, stronger, and more cohesive.

DIVIDE AND PRESHAPE

For boules or bâtards, divide the dough into 2 pieces weighing about 500 grams each. See Dividing, page 328, for instructions.

Preshape as rounds. See Preshaping, page 329, for instructions.

RECIPE CONTINUES

Cover and let rest for 10 to 15 minutes.

DIVIDE AND PRESHAPE CONT.
For baguettes, divide the dough into 4 pieces weighing about 250 grams each. See Dividing, page 328, for instructions.

Preshape as tubes. See Preshaping, page 329, for instructions.

Cover and let rest for 10 to 15 minutes.

SHAPE
Shape as boules, bâtards, or baguettes. See Shaping, page 331, for instructions.

Place boules, seam side up, in a floured, tea towel–lined banneton or bowl, approximately 9 inches wide and 3½ inches deep.

Place bâtards and baguettes, seam side up, on a floured couche, and pleat the couche between the loaves to support the sides as they rise.

PROOF
Cover the loaves and proof for about 45 to 55 minutes.

BAKE
During the proof, preheat the oven to 450°F (for bâtards or boules) or 500°F (for baguettes) with a baking stone and steaming system in place. See Baking, page 349, for instructions.

Transfer the loaves to parchment paper or a baker's peel, gently inverting them so that the underside, which was against the dusted tea towel, linen, or banneton, becomes the top.

Score the bread prior to loading. See Scoring, page 339, for ideas and tips.

Slide the loaves onto the preheated baking stone.

For bâtards or boules, bake with steam for 35 to 40 minutes. After 20 minutes, carefully remove any steaming devices, lids, parchment paper, or bowls. Rotate the loaves on the stone.

At 35 to 40 minutes the bâtards or boules should be well colored. Turn off the oven, prop open the door a few inches, and allow the loaves to dry for an additional 10 minutes.

For baguettes, bake with steam for 22 to 25 minutes. After 18 minutes, carefully remove any steaming devices, lids, or parchment paper. Rotate the loaves on the stone.

At 22 to 25 minutes the baguettes should be well colored and feel light when picked up. Turn off the oven, prop open the door a few inches, and allow the loaves to dry for an additional 5 minutes.

In order to chip away at my student debt, I worked in dining halls, I waited tables, I did yard work and then eventually lucked into a job at a shiny pizzeria with a display kitchen near a mall outside Cleveland, Ohio. I arrived early in the day to gather hardwood logs from pallets near the Dumpster and stoke the wood-fired brick oven to over 1,000°F before letting it fall to around 800°F in order to bake pizzas in a few minutes. While the fire crackled, burning the oven's interior clean, I prepared doughs and toppings and waited with clean tools and a crisp apron for customers to arrive. And sometimes while waiting, I made myself a pie, my first food of the day.

Place the wooden peel, blackened from heat and use, on the counter and sprinkle evenly and generously with coarse cornmeal. Cornmeal keeps the dough from sticking and, once toasted, adds a nutty speckled crunch to the bottom crust. Stretch the dough thinly and evenly and gently place on the peel, carefully tugging it to form a perfect circle. Ladle a scoop of red sauce in the center and spread, spiraling outward in a nautilus shape, stopping just shy of the crust edge. Add whole-milk mozzarella and a small shower of grated smoked cheese. A couple of shakes of the peel will confirm that the pie isn't adhering before it is sent onto the hearth near licking flames. Loading a pie off the peel is a skill that takes time to master—it is a movement in two parts: a fling forward and a snap back, the timing of which requires practice and learning from mistakes. In the early seconds a well-heated oven will puff the edge crust, producing large, irregular dough bubbles. Then, as sauce, crust, and cheese superheat, ingredients boil, shimmering and pushing pipes of steam up, backlit by orange light, as the cheese darkens and the crust colors deeply. If something is missing at that moment, none of us waiting in the fire glow for pizza will care, for worries melt and hearts lighten. I had no hair on my arms that entire summer but did have the best pizza of my life and, most important, I was back to making things, using my hands, my nose, my mouth, and my smile.

I continue to love the simplicity of hot fire, dark crust, red sauce, and molten cheese—humans have been topping and baking flatbreads much longer than tomatoes or pastas have been in Italy. From Asia to Africa, South America to the Pacific Rim, many cultures have found their way through naan, roti, pita, and paratha to eat flat things both plain and topped. This vestigial connection between heart and hearth continues today even if much of the bread eaten in America isn't made with human hands. Both heart and hearth hold warmth and life force, each near the center of its structure. The words that relate to fireplace, the focus of a home, are endless and enduring and extend into our baking lives— even the floor of an oven is referred to as the sole. And, while the best of these pizzas are baked with live fire, great pizza can also be had from the home oven.

PIZZA NAPOLETANA

Yield: **Four 8- to 10-inch Neapolitan-style pizzas**

INGREDIENTS	METRIC (GRAMS)	VOLUMETRIC (APPROXIMATE)	BAKER'S %
All-purpose flour	579	4¾ cups + 1 tablespoon	100%
Water	406	1¾ cups	70%
Salt, fine	12	1 tablespoon	2%
Yeast, dry instant	3	1 teaspoon	0.60%
Oil, for greasing the containers			
Cornmeal or semolina, for dusting the baker's peel (optional but helpful)			
Total Weight	1,000		172.60%
Prepared toppings, as desired			

DAY ONE

Calculate temperatures. See Setting Temperatures, page 320, for instructions. Desired dough temperature: 76°F

MIX

In a large mixing bowl, whisk together the flour, salt, and yeast. Add the water. Mix with your hand or the handle end of a wooden spoon until the dough forms a shaggy mass. With some doughs you may have to knead for a few strokes in the bowl to incorporate everything. If you find it easier, after some stirring, scrape the dough out of the bowl with a plastic scraper onto your work surface and knead briefly with your hands just until the dough comes together. Resist the urge to add more flour. Scrape the dough off the work surface and return to the bowl for the bulk fermentation.

BULK FERMENTATION

Scrape down the sides of the mixing bowl and allow the dough to rise, covered, for 2 hours at room temperature, folding as directed below.

FOLD

Fold after 60 minutes, then leave untouched for the second hour. See Folding, page 327, for instructions.

DIVIDE AND PRESHAPE

Divide the dough into 4 pieces weighing about 250 grams each. See Dividing, page 328, for instructions.

Preshape as rounds and place in individual oiled plastic containers; recycled quart-size yogurt containers are perfect. Seal the lids and chill overnight, or up to 48 hours. See Preshaping, page 329, for instructions.

RECIPE CONTINUES

DAY TWO

Remove the containers from the refrigerator and let them warm to room temperature for 1 to 2 hours. A good trick for this is to flour your work surface, then take off the lids and invert the containers, letting the doughs gently fall and settle as they warm.

While the doughs warm, prepare the toppings and sauce.

About an hour before you plan to bake the pizzas, preheat the oven to 500°F with a baking stone or pizza steel placed in the upper third of the oven.

After the doughs have warmed, lift the inverted containers off the dough pieces and flour the top of the dough generously.

SHAPE Gently pat a piece of dough to remove any large air bubbles and stretch it into a small round, 4 to 5 inches in diameter.

Next, working with your fingertips and starting in the center of the dough, press down and move outward in concentric circles dimpling the gas from the dough, leaving an inch of rim untouched around the entire piece. Check periodically to see if additional flour is needed under the dough. If it sticks, release it gently with a bench knife and add more flour.

Holding only the outer rim of the dough and leaving the dough in contact with the bench, work around the perimeter, stretching gently, slowly coaxing the dough into a thin round 9 to 10 inches in diameter. If the dough resists being stretched, cover it and allow it to rest and relax for 20 to 30 minutes.

Turn the preheated oven to broil.

Generously sprinkle a wooden peel with semolina or cornmeal and place the dough on it, jiggling the peel forward and backward to ensure the dough isn't sticking.

Top the pizza with ½ cup of red sauce using a large kitchen spoon or an offset spatula. Then add a few slices of fresh mozzarella or any other topping desired, being careful to leave a ½-inch margin around the outside of the pizza with no toppings. Moisture that breaks this margin will adhere the dough to the peel every time!

BAKE If this feels daunting, try your first few pizzas on baker's parchment paper that has been cut to a diameter slightly larger than your intended pie. The crust will be almost as good.

Slide the pizza onto the preheated stone or pizza steel and set a 3-minute timer.

When the timer goes off, rotate the pizza 180 degrees and reset for 1 minute.

Be prepared with tongs and a plate, a cooling rack, or a cutting board to take the pizza out. The toppings should be well cooked and the dough around the edges should be dark.

Before loading the next pizza, check that the stone or steel is clean of the dusting cornmeal or semolina.

Red sauce for pizza can be as simple as a jar of good tomato sauce opened, spread thinly, and garnished with fresh herbs. Or, you may take the scenic route and sauté garlic, onion, celery, and carrots in olive oil; add fresh tomatoes; reduce; soften; and puree. Two roads to a happy place.

RED SAUCE

Yield: **850 grams (4 cups)**

INGREDIENTS	METRIC (GRAMS)	VOLUMETRIC (APPROXIMATE)
Olive oil, extra virgin	50	¼ cup
Black pepper, ground	3	1 teaspoon
Salt, fine	12	2 teaspoons
Onion, chopped	142	1 medium
Carrot, chopped	130	2 medium
Celery, chopped	50	1 medium stalk
Garlic, minced	9	1 clove
Tomatoes, fresh, cored and roughly chopped	900	2 pounds
Basil, fresh	3	¼ cup

PREPARE

Heat the oil in a medium pot over medium heat, then add the pepper, salt, onion, carrot, and celery. Sauté for 2 to 3 minutes, to soften the vegetables.

Add the garlic and sauté briefly, then set the heat to medium-low and leave untouched for 5 to 7 minutes, or until the vegetables begin to color slightly.

Reduce the heat to low, then add the tomatoes.

Add the basil and simmer over low heat until thickened. The time required will vary by tomato variety and relative moisture content. Beefsteak tomatoes have more liquid than plum (paste) tomatoes (such as Roma).

When the sauce reaches a consistency that is still pourable but not watery (it will lightly coat the back of a dipped wooden spoon), turn off the heat, taste, adjust the seasonings, and cool.

Puree before use.

We graduated from Oberlin and decided without discussion that we would stick together. We had auditioned for graduate programs, but rather than take different paths, we loaded our car beyond capacity and drove west to the Bay Area of California—a new life, a new coast; new voice teachers, taquerias, wine country, sunshine, and the endless cold ocean. We could sing in many languages; we had learned stagecraft and diction, Renaissance dance and European art song traditions, but what, of all of this, related to our roots? So much time spent acquiring the words and music of other cultures and centuries. For what? Art happens when we speak, when who and what we are is given expression by means of the tools and skills we acquire. I do understand the need for training—a young person needs skills—but, in retrospect, to spend too much time in this place, where you can visit everyone's home but your own, still leaves you homeless.

The summer after we landed in California we scraped together money for plane tickets to Europe to spend an extended shoestring-budget summer in Italy, bathing full body in culture, language, and music. We stayed at Julie's cousin Steven's flat in Rome, sleeping on a hide-a-bed, awakened daily by a grand piano as Steven practiced Tchaikovsky's epic Concerto No. 1 in preparation for a concert. We followed his directions to neighborhood markets. One for meat, selling rabbits with furry feet for the savvy consumer to confirm they weren't cats. One for bread with enormous dusty boulder loaves for sale by the kilo and thin cracker bread with olive oil and rosemary. Yet another sold vegetables—piles of artichokes, fresh figs, eggplants, and bright peppers—and there were many for pizza, sold *al taglio* in rectangular portions. Steven's country home was north of the city in a tiny hill town with fountains from the 1400s and a bread oven in his backyard, built into a rocky hillside. If in music one lives in a place where the heart is passionately connected to work, in Italy we saw this connection extend to our food; we witnessed a link, which wasn't at all a movement or trend—it was the only way. To sit and eat was to take a table-length walking tour, our mouths traveling around Bassano in Teverina, stepping from plate to plate, from winery to fruit tree, through tomato patches, past grazing goats. Handmade fresh ricotta, olive oil, and wine all brought in abundance from the kitchen of Steven's housekeeper. Crusty rosette rolls, eaten simply with a slice of pecorino Romano and pancetta; no big box stores, no freezers. The hill towns of Italy, rising from verdant plains, are built on rocks holding stacked fortress walls constructed of stones from underfoot a millennium earlier. These layers of earth, stone, and home are honest and resonate as fully and naturally as tones of a chord align and ring. The imagined world of Italy, which we'd lived between the flat covers of Puccini opera scores, was vibrant and breathing before our eyes in a way we could eat. The simplicity, and the sense of it all, changed me; there was no going back; there was only going closer.

South of Rome there is a town called Genzano da Roma. Many know Genzano for the annual flower festival, which blossom-paints its large central via in geometric patterns and perfumed flower portraiture. But I leave Rome for a different aroma, for this town holds more wood-fired bread ovens per capita than any other city in the world. Wine lovers have Bordeaux, for mariachi there is Jalisco, and for bread heads Genzano is legendary. Large loaves rolled in coarse bran are picked from superheated wood ovens daily, baked so dark you would swear the baker fell asleep. To make Pane Genzano, a wet dough with ample water and soft flour is mixed with sourdough culture and salt before fermenting. The loaves are then divided, gently shaped into either a *pagnotta* (a large round) or a *filone* (a tube), and laid on bran-lined baker's linen to proof. What exits the oven at the end of baking looks not that dissimilar from the wood used to fire the ovens. The dark crust—eggshell crisp and light—protects a crumb that is moist and glossy, perfumed with the acids from the sourdough culture and from the tobacco-dark crust itself.

Harpoon

PAUILLE

Rose
Ba
Dout
de
Coff

PANE GENZANO **PAGE 69**

PANE GENZANO

Yield: **1 large pagnotta, or 2 medium pagnottelle**

TOTAL FORMULA

PREFERMENTED FLOUR: 25%

INGREDIENTS	METRIC (GRAMS)	VOLUMETRIC (APPROXIMATE)	BAKER'S %
All-purpose flour	657	scant 5½ cups	100%
Water	494	2¼ cups	75%
Salt, fine	13	2¼ teaspoons	2%
Yeast, dry instant	3	1 teaspoon	0.50%
Sourdough culture	33	heaping 2 tablespoons	5%
Coarse wheat bran, for the crust			
Total Weight	1,200	All	182.50%

STIFF LEVAIN

INGREDIENTS	METRIC (GRAMS)	VOLUMETRIC (APPROXIMATE)	BAKER'S %
All-purpose flour	164	1½ cups	100%
Water	99	½ cup	60%
Sourdough culture	33	heaping 2 tablespoons	20%
Total Weight	296	All	180%

FINAL DOUGH

INGREDIENTS	METRIC (GRAMS)	VOLUMETRIC (APPROXIMATE)
Water	395	1¾ cups
Stiff levain	296	All
All-purpose flour	493	scant 4 cups
Salt, fine	13	2¼ teaspoons
Yeast, dry instant	3	1 teaspoon
Total Weight	1,200	All

RECIPE CONTINUES

DAY ONE:

STIFF LEVAIN

In a medium bowl, combine the tepid water (75°F to 80°F) and sourdough culture. Mix with your hands and fingers until the culture is broken up and well distributed in the water, then add the flour.

Mix briefly, then knead until smooth.

Cover and set at room temperature for 12 to 16 hours.

DAY TWO

MIX

Calculate temperatures. See Setting Temperatures, page 320, for instructions. Desired dough temperature: 76F

In a large mixing bowl, combine the final dough water and stiff levain. Mix with your hands until the levain is broken up in the water, then add the flour, salt, and yeast. Stir with the handle end of a wooden spoon until the dough forms a shaggy mass. If you find it easier, after some stirring, scrape the dough out of the bowl with a plastic scraper onto your work surface and knead briefly with your hands just until the dough comes together. Resist the urge to add more flour. Scrape the dough off the work surface and return it to the bowl for bulk fermentation.

BULK FERMENTATION

Scrape down the sides of the mixing bowl and allow the dough to rise, covered, for 3 hours at room temperature, folding as directed below.

FOLD

Fold after 15, 30, 45, 60, and 120 minutes, then leave untouched for the third hour. See Folding, page 327, for instructions.

As you perform each series of folds, you'll begin to notice that the dough becomes smoother, stronger, and more cohesive.

DIVIDE AND PRESHAPE

If making a single large pagnotta, preshape as a round. See Preshaping, page 329 for instructions.

Cover and let rest for 15 minutes.

If making 2 pagnottelle, divide the dough into 2 pieces weighing about 600 grams each. See Dividing, page 328, for instructions.

Preshape as rounds. See Preshaping, page 329, for instructions.

Cover and let rest for 10 to 15 minutes.

To make the bran crust, layer ¼ inch of bran on a rimmed sheet pan. On a second pan, place a well-moistened tea towel or dish towel.

Shape as boules. See Shaping, page 331, for instructions.

Press the top side into the moistened towel and roll the moist top in coarse bran, thoroughly and heavily coating the top of the loaf.

SHAPE

Place the large pagnotta, seam side up, in a banneton or towel-lined bowl, approximately 10 inches wide and 4 inches deep, that has been sprinkled with additional bran.

Place the two medium boules, seam side up, in bannetons or towel-lined bowls, approximately 9 inches wide and 3½ inches deep, that have been sprinkled with additional bran.

As this dough is quite wet, take the additional step of dusting the seam side of each loaf after placing it in the basket or couche.

PROOF

Cover and proof for 60 to 75 minutes at room temperature.

During the proof, preheat the oven to 500°F with a baking stone and steaming system in place. See Baking, page 349, for instructions.

Transfer the loaves to parchment paper or a baker's peel, gently inverting them so that the underside, which was against the dusted tea towel or banneton, becomes the top.

BAKE

Slide the loaves onto the preheated baking stone.

Bake with steam for 35 to 40 minutes. After 25 minutes, carefully remove any steaming devices, lids, parchment paper, or bowls. Rotate the loaves on the stone.

At 35 to 40 minutes the loaves should be well colored. If making a single large loaf, bake 10 minutes longer than the two medium loaves.

Turn off the oven, prop open the door a few inches, and allow the loaves to dry for an additional 10 minutes.

FILONE DI SESAME

Yield: **3 medium loaves**

TOTAL FORMULA
PREFERMENTED FLOUR: 25%

INGREDIENTS	METRIC (GRAMS)	VOLUMETRIC (APPROXIMATE)	BAKER'S %
All-purpose flour	465	3¾ cups + 2 tablespoons	100%
Water	364	1½ cups + 1 tablespoon	78%
Salt, fine	9	1½ teaspoons	2%
Yeast, dry instant	2	¾ teaspoon	0.50%
Sourdough culture	23	1½ tablespoons	5%
Sesame seeds	37	¼ cup	8%
Sesame seeds, for the crust			
Total Weight	900	All	193.50%

STIFF LEVAIN

INGREDIENTS	METRIC (GRAMS)	VOLUMETRIC (APPROXIMATE)	BAKER'S %
All-purpose flour	116	1 cup	100%
Water	70	¼ cup + 1 tablespoon	60%
Sourdough culture	23	1½ tablespoons	20%
Total Weight	209	All	180%

FINAL DOUGH

INGREDIENTS	METRIC (GRAMS)	VOLUMETRIC (APPROXIMATE)
Water	294	1¼ cups
Stiff levain	209	All
All-purpose flour	349	2¾ cups + 2 tablespoons
Salt, fine	9	1½ teaspoons
Yeast, dry instant	2	¾ teaspoon
Sesame seeds	37	¼ cup
Total Weight	900	All

DAY ONE

STIFF LEVAIN

In a medium bowl, combine the tepid water (75°F to 80°F) and the sourdough culture. Mix with your hands and fingers until the culture is broken up and well distributed in the water, then add the flour.

Mix briefly, then knead until smooth.

Cover and set at room temperature for 12 to 16 hours.

DAY TWO

PREPARE

Put the sesame seeds in a large heavy pan set over low to medium heat.

Toast the seeds, stirring and moving them around, until golden; they will often pop some as they toast. This toasting may also be done on a sheet pan in a 400°F oven, for about 10 minutes.

MIX

Calculate temperatures. See Setting Temperatures, page 320, for instructions. Desired dough temperature: 76°F

In a large mixing bowl, combine the final dough water and stiff levain. Mix with your hands until the levain is broken up in the water, then add the flour, salt, yeast, and sesame seeds. Stir with the handle end of a wooden spoon until the dough forms a shaggy mass. If you find it easier, after some stirring, scrape the dough out of the bowl with a plastic scraper onto your work surface and knead briefly with your hands just until the dough comes together. Resist the urge to add more flour. Scrape the dough off the work surface and return it to the bowl for bulk fermentation.

BULK FERMENTATION

Scrape down the sides of the mixing bowl and allow the dough to rise, covered, for 3 hours at room temperature, folding as directed below.

FOLD

Fold after 15, 30, 45, 60, and 120 minutes, then leave untouched for the third hour. See Folding, page 327 for instructions.

As you perform each series of folds, you'll begin to notice that the dough becomes smoother, stronger, and more cohesive.

DIVIDE AND SHAPE

To make the sesame seed crust, place the sesame seeds on a sheet pan. On a second pan, place a well-moistened tea towel or dish towel.

Turn the dough out onto a generously floured surface and gently stretch to a 9 by 12-inch rough rectangle.

RECIPE CONTINUES

	Divide the dough into 3 pieces, roughly 3 by 12 inches and weighing about 300 grams each. It's OK if you choose to divide them by eye rather than using the scale; keep them as even as possible. See Dividing, page 328, for instructions.
DIVIDE AND SHAPE CONT.	Set the top side of each piece on the moistened towel, then roll in sesame seeds and place on a lightly floured baker's linen (couche) or tea towel, top side down. Be sure to get as many seeds on the crust as possible. Pleat the couche between the loaves to support their sides as they rise.
PROOF	Cover and proof for 60 to 75 minutes at room temperature.
	During the proof, preheat the oven to 500°F with a baking stone and steaming system in place. See Baking, page 349, for instructions.
BAKE	Transfer the loaves to parchment paper or a baker's peel, gently inverting them so that the underside, which was against the dusted tea towel or linen, becomes the top.
	Slide the loaves onto the preheated baking stone.
	Bake with steam for 25 to 30 minutes. After 15 minutes, carefully remove any steaming devices, lids, parchment paper, or bowls. Rotate the loaves on the stone.
	At 25 to 30 minutes the loaves should be well colored. Turn off the oven, prop open the door a few inches, and allow the loaves to dry for an additional 10 minutes.

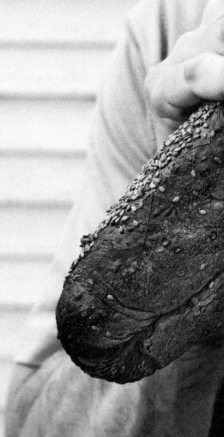

For a foreigner in a foreign country there are many benefits to association. The tourist, starving and blind, wandering, lusting for authenticity, is mostly lost unless guided by locals, especially where the native tongue is required. In Rome our "in" was Julie's cousin. Steven, an American expat, now a dual citizen, working for Rome opera as a coach and accompanist, could sing us a tune about where to go and was happy to come along. During the summer, Rome Opera set up outside in the Roman baths, the Terme di Caracalla, for *Aïda* with live elephants, *Turandot* with choral armies, and other crowning achievements of Italian opera, all framed by crumbling skyward columns of Roman brick. On Steven's coattails we could ride past ticket takers and find open seats five nights a week if we wanted. During intermissions the concessions would open and offer vino, gelato, sparkling water, and panini among other treats. The panini were a revelation in simplicity. A crusty roll or hunk of bread, a slice of cheese (pecorino Romano), and a piece of pancetta or prosciutto di Parma. *Basta così*—let's call it a day. This crusty loaf can be made at home, like many breads, with some time but little effort.

CIABATTA

Yield: **2 large loaves**

TOTAL FORMULA
PREFERMENTED FLOUR: 33%

INGREDIENTS	METRIC (GRAMS)	VOLUMETRIC (APPROXIMATE)	BAKER'S %
All-purpose flour	614	5 cups + 1 tablespoon	100%
Water	492	2 cups + 2 tablespoons	80%
Salt, fine	12	2 teaspoons	2%
Yeast, dry instant	2	¾ teaspoon	0.40%
Total Weight	1,120	All	182.40%

BIGA

INGREDIENTS	METRIC (GRAMS)	VOLUMETRIC (APPROXIMATE)	BAKER'S %
All-purpose flour	203	1¾ cups	100%
Water	122	½ cup	60%
Yeast, dry instant	Pinch	Pinch	0.10%
Total Weight	325	All	160.10%

FINAL DOUGH

INGREDIENTS	METRIC (GRAMS)	VOLUMETRIC (APPROXIMATE)
Water	370	1½ cups + 2 tablespoons
Biga	325	All
All-purpose flour	411	3¼ cups + 1 tablespoon
Salt, fine	12	2 teaspoons
Yeast, dry instant	2	scant ¾ teaspoon
Total Weight	1,120	All

DAY ONE

BIGA

In a medium bowl, stir together the room-temperature flour and yeast, then add the tepid water (75°F to 80°F).

Mix briefly, then knead until smooth.

Cover and set at room temperature for 12 to 16 hours.

RECIPE CONTINUES

DAY TWO

MIX

Calculate temperatures. See Setting Temperatures, page 320, for instructions. Desired dough temperature: 76°F

In a large mixing bowl, combine the final dough water and biga. Mix with your hands until the biga is broken up in the water, then add the flour, salt, and yeast. Stir with the handle end of a wooden spoon until the dough forms a shaggy mass. If you find it easier, after some stirring, scrape the dough out of the bowl with a plastic scraper onto your work surface and knead briefly with your hands just until the dough comes together. Resist the urge to add more flour. Scrape the dough off the work surface and return it to the bowl for bulk fermentation.

BULK FERMENTATION

Scrape down the sides of the mixing bowl and allow the dough to rise, covered, for 3 hours at room temperature, folding as directed below.

FOLD

Fold after 30, 60, 90, and 120 minutes, then leave untouched for the third hour. See Folding, page 327, for instructions.

As you perform each series of folds, you'll begin to notice that the dough becomes smoother, stronger, and more cohesive.

DIVIDE AND SHAPE

Turn the dough out onto a generously floured surface and gently stretch to an 8 by 12-inch rough rectangle.

Using a bench knife or chef's knife, cut the rectangle exactly in half along the long axis, and place on a generously floured baker's linen (couche) or tea towel. Pleat the couche between the loaves to support their sides as they rise.

PROOF

Cover and proof for 45 to 60 minutes at room temperature.

BAKE

During the proof, preheat the oven to 475°F with a baking stone and steaming system in place. See Baking, page 349, for instructions.

Transfer the loaves to parchment paper or a baker's peel, gently inverting them so that the underside, which was against the dusted tea towel or linen, becomes the top.

Slide the loaves onto the preheated baking stone.

Bake with steam for 32 to 35 minutes. After 20 minutes, carefully remove any steaming devices, lids, or parchment paper. Rotate the loaves on the stone.

At 25 to 30 minutes the loaves should be well colored. Turn off the oven, prop open the door a few inches, and allow the loaves to dry for an additional 10 minutes.

Pain rustique has nothing to do with pain; rather, it's the intersection of aromatic crumb and sturdy crust. *Pain*, as you may know, is the French word for "bread." A *rustique* is simply a rustic loaf, unshaped in the traditional sense. Sound like *ciabatta*? Yes, it is very similar but easier for the French to pronounce than "ciabatta." The rustique, like ciabatta, can handle a wide variety of amendments from simple herbs and olive oil to cured meat or dried fruits and nuts. Here is a favorite flavor marriage—good olives, olive oil, and fresh rosemary. At my house we pour olive oil on a plate and then pool some balsamic vinegar in the middle. Tear off a chunk of the bread and dip, picking up the fruity oil and the sharp vinegar and introducing them to olives and herbs in your mouth. And, of course, have a glass of prosecco or vinho verde.

OLIVE AND ROSEMARY RUSTIQUE

Yield: **2 large loaves**

TOTAL FORMULA

PREFERMENTED FLOUR: 20%

INGREDIENTS	METRIC (GRAMS)	VOLUMETRIC (APPROXIMATE)	BAKER'S %
All-purpose flour	499	4 cups + 2 tablespoons	100%
Water	358	1½ cups + 1 tablespoon	72%
Salt, fine	10	1½ teaspoons	2%
Yeast, dry instant	3	1 teaspoon	0.60%
Olives, Kalamata	110	¾ cup	22%
Olive oil, extra virgin	10	1½ teaspoons	2%
Rosemary, fresh	10	2 teaspoons	2%
Total Weight	1,000	All	200.60%

BIGA

INGREDIENTS	METRIC (GRAMS)	VOLUMETRIC (APPROXIMATE)	BAKER'S %
All-purpose flour	165	1¼ cups + 2 tablespoons	100%
Water	99	¼ cup + 3 tablespoons	60%
Yeast, dry instant	Pinch	Pinch	0.10%
Total Weight	264	All	160.10%

FINAL DOUGH

INGREDIENTS	METRIC (GRAMS)	VOLUMETRIC (APPROXIMATE)
Water	259	1 cup + 2 tablespoons
Biga	264	All
All-purpose flour	334	2¾ cups
Salt, fine	10	1½ teaspoons
Yeast, dry instant	3	1 teaspoon
Olives, Kalamata	110	¾ cup
Olive oil, extra virgin	10	1½ teaspoons
Rosemary, fresh	10	2 teaspoons
Total Weight	1,000	All

RECIPE CONTINUES

DAY ONE

BIGA

In a medium bowl, stir together the flour and yeast, then add the tepid water (75°F to 80°F).

Mix briefly, then knead until smooth.

Cover and set at room temperature for 12 to 16 hours.

DAY TWO

PREPARE

Pit and coarsely chop the olives.

Stem and mince the rosemary.

MIX

Calculate temperatures. See Setting Temperatures, page 320, for instructions. Desired dough temperature: 76°F

In a large mixing bowl, combine the final dough water and biga. Mix with your hands until the biga is broken up in the water, then add the flour, salt, and yeast. Stir with the handle end of a wooden spoon until the dough forms a shaggy mass. If you find it easier, after some stirring, scrape the dough out of the bowl with a plastic scraper onto your work surface and knead briefly with your hands just until the dough comes together. Resist the urge to add more flour. Scrape the dough off the work surface and return it to the bowl for bulk fermentation.

Place the olives, olive oil, and rosemary on top of the mixed dough and fold briefly to begin incorporation. It doesn't need to be homogeneous; these ingredients will fully incorporate during folding.

BULK FERMENTATION

Scrape down the sides of the mixing bowl and allow the dough to rise, covered, for 3 hours at room temperature, folding as directed below.

FOLD

Fold after 15, 30, 45, 60, and 120 minutes, then leave untouched for the third hour. See Folding, page 327, for instructions.

As you perform each series of folds, you'll begin to notice that the dough becomes smoother, stronger, and more cohesive.

DIVIDE AND SHAPE

Turn the dough out onto a generously floured surface and gently stretch to a 9 by 12-inch rough rectangle.

Using a bench knife or chef's knife, cut exactly in half along the long axis, and place on a generously floured baker's linen (couche) or tea towel. Pleat the couche between the loaves to support their sides as they rise.

RECIPE CONTINUES ❦

PROOF   Cover and proof for 30 to 45 minutes at room temperature.

During the proof, preheat the oven to 475°F with a baking stone and steaming system in place. See Baking, page 349, for instructions.

Transfer the loaves to parchment paper or a baker's peel, gently inverting them so that the underside, which was against the dusted tea towel or linen, becomes the top.

BAKE   Slide the loaves onto the preheated baking stone.

Bake with steam for 32 to 35 minutes. After 20 minutes, carefully remove any steaming devices, lids, or parchment paper. Rotate the loaves on the stone.

At 32 to 35 minutes the loaves should be well colored. Turn off the oven, prop open the door a few inches, and allow the loaves to dry for an additional 10 minutes.

Years of work, practice, striving, and singing passed. Our résumés grew with our pursuits, and high notes got higher. We continued to cook together, explore food, and grow our commitment, solidifying what we'd both known very early on. We were married on a soggy August day under soaring poplars in a simple ceremony, which wove together pieces of our histories and families. Mama was there, singing a lullaby from my childhood; Julie's parents read from prepared texts; and my father, speaking off the cuff, offered his heartfelt welcome to the union of our families and his neck-breaking embrace.

Eventually, signs suggested that a move to the East Coast was necessary for our careers. It was a long time in the making but we eventually leaped again with no jobs and no savings and departed in December, waving good-bye to nude beaches, the crush of fog banks on coastal ranges, sunburned Steinbeck hills, and the scent of eucalyptus.

NEW YORK

If you have a plan to pull up your Bay Area stakes and leave wine country, coastal red-woods, and sunny dispositions for New York City and arrive in the depths of winter, let me warn you that it is a bad idea in every way. Take my advice and wait until April, or even early May. Enjoy a few more West Coast months, have a taco, and watch the hills grow emerald as rains return heartbeats to golden grass. And then, when Central Park trees flower and explode blossom fireworks in celebration of lengthening days, take *that* as your cue to go.

Wintertime in daylight-saving New York, where subterranean tunnel travel moves humans to basement connections through stench passages and up traveler-choked es-calators, is a poor greeter. Wind off the Atlantic is compressed and released in avenue canyons. It pushed me uptown and downtown past blackened snowpack piles where the trash of winter waited for spring's melting release. After many travel days we arrived at this destination, double-parked the car, and unloaded it, leaning into the burning cold and wind as we schlepped the sum of our possessions up five flights of stairs to our new home. Two rooms, two windows, and one air shaft full of pigeons. The song goes, "If I can make it there, I'm gonna make it anywhere." The lyric seems appropriate and the crux is for each of us to find.

Our alarm, that muezzin of Manhattan, summoning the faithful to work, sounded early our first full day in frozen January, and we stumble-walked trash-strewn streets, side-stepping piles of dog shit in darkness, down into buzzing fluorescent corridors through pinching turnstiles onto overfull subway cars, heading downtown to look for a way to pay the bills while we practiced, auditioned, worked, and scraped our way toward a Big Apple life.

In time we found work at a temporary agency and were dispatched daily across the city to answer phones, type memos, keep a chair warm, or do data entry. But "temp work," can be feast or famine—on feast days you arrive early, sit in the waiting area until your name is called, and then head to your job. And when famine struck, I didn't mind playing hooky—I felt better outside, learning the city on foot, than sitting in a windowless office huffing Xerox fumes. In walking and looking, I found places that felt like oases, quiet spaces where the din of striving and surviving could fall away and yield to peace: St. Thomas's church in midtown, where incense fills the air in Kentucky sandstone arches, rising and framing stained-glass windows; the New York Public Library with endless board feet of dark wood and ceiling murals; Inwood Hill Park, ribbons of dirt trail and soaring tulip poplars; the Cloisters with medieval staircases and gardens. In those spaces I could take refuge; they were a buttress, a shield, a hedge against all the drawbacks of city life.

Every few months we returned to California for voice lessons and sun, and we made a special trip in 2001 to sing a benefit concert for an AIDS charity, lodging with retired benefactors who hot-tubbed every morning in the nude and carried nightcaps to bed. These were our people; they probably existed in New York . . . but not in our walk-up. Their Berkeley breakfast consisted of citrus from their trees, dark espresso, and homemade bagels. Now, coming from New York, a city that defines itself by its bagels, we believed we knew the bagelry gold standard set by H&H on the Upper West Side. H&H's garlic, onion, or everything bagel, dumped from a hot oven straight into your waiting bag, set a bar high above the mass-produced pucks sold in frozen eight-packs in the supermarket. But somehow, these Berkeley bagels blew the lid off our standards. They had the flavor of wheat and a slightly open crumb, a sign that they were hand-shaped rather than machine-made. The crust was shiny from a bath in boiling water and malt syrup, deep mahogany from the oven, and it tugged against my teeth when bitten. Just before being baked on a hot masonry stone they were garnished with coarse sea salt, dried onion, or sesame seeds. We ate them with rich cream cheese, lox, and fresh avocado. There are times when experience intersects with greatness and all one can muster is an openmouthed, incredulous laugh. If you garden, if you sew or knit, if you write poems, build rock walls, or bake for friends and strangers, you understand the meaning found in this space where making, sharing, baking, and giving are creative and love-filled. Eating these simple, delicious bagels was an act of prayer, a wish, a reminder of how close we are to a miracle—simple ingredients combining to create a space with so much good. I have made changes over the years, drying my own onion, adding seed blends to the outside; but in essence the dark, chewy, flavorful bagels remain unchanged, as they should.

Bagels are a zany, misfit member of the baked goods family. Prone to outlandish ties, wild hair, and loud laughing, they dance comfortably, albeit awkwardly, in front of others while pan bread and soft rolls, baguettes and shortcakes stand on the sidelines, too cool to engage. The process of making bagels may seem complicated—multiple steps spread across two days, a bath in boiling water before baking, what!?—but, once the schedule is understood it can be planned for, and the result is worth the work. On day one a poolish is mixed a few hours before the final dough. The dough rises for a bit and then is chilled overnight, covered, in the refrigerator before the dividing, final shaping, boiling, and baking on day two. If you are tentative, if you fear exposure or risk, I say jump in, put on your dancing shoes or your best ugly sweater, and try moon-walking; you might just be the life of the breakfast party.

BAGELS

Yield: **Twelve 4-inch bagels**

TOTAL FORMULA

PREFERMENTED FLOUR: 20%

INGREDIENTS	METRIC (GRAMS)	VOLUMETRIC (APPROXIMATE)	BAKER'S %
All-purpose flour	824	6¾ cups + 2 tablespoons	100%
Water	537	2¼ cups + 2 tablespoons	65%
Salt, fine	16	2¾ teaspoons	2%
Yeast, dry instant	3	1 teaspoon	0.40%
Barley malt syrup, for boiling the bagels	42	2 tablespoons	
Salt, for boiling the bagels	19	1 tablespoon	
Cornmeal, for dusting the pan (optional)			
Sesame seeds, coarse salt, dehydrated onion, or poppy seeds, for topping the bagels			
Total Weight	1,380	All	167.40%

POOLISH

INGREDIENTS	METRIC (GRAMS)	VOLUMETRIC (APPROXIMATE)	BAKER'S %
All-purpose flour	165	1¼ cups + 2 tablespoons	100%
Water	206	¾ cup + 2 tablespoons	125%
Yeast, dry instant	1	¼ teaspoon	0.75%
Total Weight	372	All	225.75%

FINAL DOUGH

INGREDIENTS	METRIC (GRAMS)	VOLUMETRIC (APPROXIMATE)
Water	331	1½ cups
Poolish	372	All
All-purpose flour	659	5½ cups
Salt, fine	16	2¾ teaspoons
Yeast, dry instant	2	scant ¾ teaspoon
Total Weight	1,380	All

RECIPE CONTINUES

DAY ONE, PART ONE

POOLISH

In a medium bowl, stir together the room-temperature flour and yeast, then add the tepid water (75°F to 80°F).

Mix until smooth.

Cover and set at room temperature for 2 to 8 hours. The broad time range for the poolish is for both convenience and flavor. More time will yield more flavor, but even a few hours will be enough to make a noticeable difference.

DAY ONE, PART TWO

MIX

Calculate temperatures. See Setting Temperatures, page 320, for instructions. Desired dough temperature: 76°F

In a large mixing bowl, combine the final dough water and poolish. Mix with your hands until the poolish is broken up in the water, then add the flour, salt, and yeast. Stir with the handle end of a wooden spoon until the dough forms a shaggy mass. If you find it easier, after some stirring, scrape the dough out of the bowl with a plastic scraper onto your work surface and knead briefly with your hands just until the dough comes together. Resist the urge to add more flour. Scrape the dough off the work surface and return it to the bowl for bulk fermentation.

BULK FERMENTATION

Scrape down the sides of the mixing bowl and allow the dough to rise, covered, for 2 hours at room temperature, folding as directed below.

FOLD

Fold after 60 minutes, then leave untouched for the second hour. See Folding, page 327, for instructions.

After 2 hours, place the dough in the refrigerator overnight, 8 to 12 hours.

DAY TWO

Remove the dough from the refrigerator and set it at room temperature for 1 to 2 hours.

DIVIDE AND PRESHAPE

Divide the dough into 12 pieces weighing about 115 grams each, and round tightly into balls. See Dividing, page 328, and Preshaping, page 329, for instructions.

Cover and let rest for 15 to 30 minutes.

SHAPE

To shape, poke a hole in the exact middle with a finger and gently, slowly expand the opening to 2 to 3 inches. The opening will close some as the pieces sit.

Place the shaped pieces back on the floured surface. Cover and let rest for 20 to 30 minutes before boiling. See below for an alternative method.

Bagels may be baked on a sheet pan or on a piece of parchment paper slid directly onto a baking stone.

PREPARE TO BAKE AND BOIL THE BAGELS

Cut 2 pieces of parchment paper to the size of your sheet pan or to fit your baking stone.

If using a sheet pan without parchment paper, dust it with semolina or cornmeal or lightly oil it to prevent sticking.

While the shaped bagels rest and proof, prepare the toppings. Spread a pan with sesame or poppy seeds, or have ready a small container of coarse salt. Dehydrated dry onion and garlic are also excellent choices.

Thirty minutes before you plan to bake the bagels, preheat the oven to 475°F.

BOIL

Put 4 inches of water in a 6-quart stockpot, then add the barley malt and salt. Bring to a medium boil.

Add the bagels, 3 at a time, to the boiling liquid. Using a slotted spoon, flip them after 30 seconds and remove them after another 1 to 1½ minutes.

For plain bagels, allow them to drip for just a moment before placing them on your parchment paper or prepared pan. For seeded bagels, allow them to drain briefly above the pot, then set top side down in the seeds. Place them seed side up on your sheet pan or parchment paper, leaving 2 to 3 inches between them. If baking 6 bagels at a time, distribute them as evenly as possible for best results.

Continue boiling until your parchment paper or sheet pan has 6 bagels (half the batch), then slide them into the oven.

BAKE

Bake the bagels for 15 to 20 minutes, rotating the pans or parchment paper halfway through the baking. They are done when the bottoms and sides are well colored and firm.

ALTERNATIVE METHOD

If you would rather bake the next day, the bagels may be refrigerated immediately after shaping, covered, on a sheet pan dusted with cornmeal or semolina.

On day two you may proceed with the recipe, adding the cold bagels directly to the boiling liquid and proceeding. The cold bagels will have a thicker crust.

On that same trip, Peter the bagel maker showed me a book that pictured large, dark French loaves, thick-crusted and dusty, ripping open where they had been cut with a razor before being baked in massive wood-fired ovens. I was drawn in by the images, I couldn't look away—it was as though they connected with something in a life I had lived previously. I saw stories with lines deeper than the bread's color and form. There is much in that combination of flour, water, salt, sourdough culture, and hot oven. A form rises to tell a tale that began in Mesopotamia when nomads collected grains from cereal grasses. Those grains, which were saved and resown—the ancestors of modern wheat—enabled humans to settle and form societies. Over time, the breads evolved from flat shapes to larger loaves; grain grinding evolved from hand-turned rotary cairns to water- and wind-powered gristmills; and masons learned to make domed bake ovens, which modern builders continue to copy. Civilization in an edible package, delicious in color and form, moved by hands from field to shape to baker's peel; I couldn't look away, I *had* to make those loaves.

I have to admit something about what happened next. I am not casual. I don't do things half-interested or part-time. When I started running, I leapfrogged marathons and went straight to super-distances. I suppose it's been this way for a while; work in classical music certainly reinforced the benefit of daily involvement and passion. The power of the heart muscle is undeniable.

I started by reading everything I could find on artisan baking. Baby steps and early questions . . . what the heck is the difference between a baguette and a bâtard? If at first I was a motorist, pleased to drive across a beautiful bridge, in time I developed the eyes of an engineer, seeing stanchions, guy wires, and footings, the structure and necessity of it all. I joined the largest bread trade organization in the United States, the Bread Bakers Guild of America, and found coursework in New York where I could supplement my reading. And I baked and I baked and I baked, keeping meticulous notes and eating the mistakes.

I baked my first sourdough loaves on terra-cotta quarry tiles at the hottest temperature possible in my tiny New York oven. I gently scored their raw skins with a utility razor and used an old piece of cardboard to slide them onto the smoking preheated tiles. I quickly steamed, pouring boiling water onto a pan in the bottom of the oven and slamming the door closed to retain as much moisture as possible on the expanding loaf. I checked its progress once too often and was rewarded by the bleeping scream of smoke alarms and the smell of overheated laminate cabinetry. The loaf rose well, jumping as it darkened during the bake. When the timer sounded I turned off the oven and let the loaf coast, drying further and setting the crust. Now, this is the part where the story should say, "I removed my masterpiece at the forty-fifth minute and placed it on a rack to cool while crowds gathered outside the manger to celebrate the arrival of bread baby Jesus." In actuality, the birth was less spectacular. What emerged from the oven were misshapen forms—ripped where they should open gracefully, matte crusts that I had hoped would shine. Here was the product of my weeks of thinking and reading, growing my sourdough culture, and hoping like an expectant parent for my dream of dark French bakery loaves. When I look back at it, my work was leagues from being artisan. I was dejected. It may sound silly, but hope had been bound up in those loaves—I was searching for something and hoping I could find it there.

But then, as the oven cooled and the smell of my melting cabinets dissipated, something happened. As hot air moves from the center of a cooling loaf, traveling outward through crumb past crust and into the room, it picks up things along the way, releasing and exchanging, completing the transformation that began during baking as starches set and the loaf firms. As this happened an aroma perfumed the apartment, infusing everything. It was a dark, roasted smell; sniffing it, one could go on a sensory tour from bold coffee to toasting nuts, then over to malty sweetness and the flinty mineral hit of wheat and the lactic zip of aged cheese all in a noseful. A smile crept onto my face, my eyes widened, and I will admit to a kitchen dance . . . I had done it!

In all of the baking that I had done at home, I had never been able to achieve the flavor that I had tasted in loaves from great bakeries; there was always something lacking, some nuance missing. My bread had been good, and using a yeasted pre-ferment had moved me closer to but not into the realm of what I had hoped for. Until now. The culture was the key, the complexity, the fermentation, the bake. The loaves were ugly as hell but they were delicious *and* they were from my own damn hands. I was doing something. I was alive and *maybe* headed home, back to handwork, back to heritage. Let's make those loaves, but prettier.

Harpoon Miche
- Munich Dark Beer from Harpoon Brewery in Windsor, Vermont
- Rye Sour
- Liquid Levain
- Whole Wheat and Buckwheat

SOURDOUGH MICHE

Yield: **1 very large miche, or 2 medium boules**

TOTAL FORMULA
PREFERMENTED FLOUR: 25%

INGREDIENTS	METRIC (GRAMS)	VOLUMETRIC (APPROXIMATE)	BAKER'S %
All-purpose flour	536	4½ cups	65%
Whole wheat flour	288	2¼ cups + 2 tablespoons	35%
Water	619	2¾ cups	75%
Salt, fine	16	2¾ teaspoons	2%
Sourdough culture	41	heaping 2 tablespoons	5%
Total Weight	1,500	All	182%

STIFF LEVAIN

INGREDIENTS	METRIC (GRAMS)	VOLUMETRIC (APPROXIMATE)	BAKER'S %
All-purpose flour	103	¾ cup + 2 tablespoons	50%
Whole wheat flour	103	¾ cup + 2 tablespoons	50%
Water	136	½ cup + 2 tablespoons	66%
Sourdough culture	41	heaping 2 tablespoons	20%
Total weight	383	All	186%

FINAL DOUGH

INGREDIENTS	METRIC (GRAMS)	VOLUMETRIC (APPROXIMATE)
Water	483	2 cups + 2 tablespoons
Stiff levain	383	All
All-purpose flour	433	3½ cups + 2 tablespoons
Whole wheat flour	185	1½ cups
Salt, fine	16	2¾ teaspoons
Total Weight	1,500	All

RECICE CONTINUES

DAY ONE

STIFF LEVAIN

In a medium bowl, combine the tepid water (75°F to 80°F) and sourdough culture.

Mix with your hands and fingers until the culture is broken up and well distributed in the water, then add the flour.

Mix briefly, then knead until smooth.

Cover and set at room temperature for 12 to 16 hours.

DAY TWO

MIX

Calculate temperatures. See Setting Temperatures, page 320, for instructions. Desired dough temperature: 78°F

In a large mixing bowl, combine the final dough water and stiff levain. Mix with your hands until the levain is broken up in the water, then add the flours and salt. Stir with the handle end of a wooden spoon until the dough forms a shaggy mass. If you find it easier, after some stirring, scrape the dough out of the bowl with a plastic scraper onto your work surface and knead briefly with your hands just until the dough comes together. Resist the urge to add more flour. Scrape the dough off the work surface and return it to the bowl for bulk fermentation.

BULK FERMENTATION:

Scrape down the sides of the mixing bowl and allow the dough to rise, covered, for 3 hours at room temperature, folding as directed below.

FOLD

Fold after 30, 60, 90, and 120 minutes, then leave untouched for the third hour. See Folding, page 327, for instructions.

As you perform each series of folds, you'll begin to notice that the dough becomes smoother, stronger, and more cohesive.

DIVIDE AND PRESHAPE

For a single large miche, preshape as a round. See Preshaping, page 329, for instructions.

Cover and let rest for 15 minutes.

If making two loaves, divide the dough into 2 pieces weighing about 750 grams each. See Dividing, page 328, for instructions.

Preshape as rounds. See Preshaping, page 329 for instructions.

Cover and let rest for 10 to 15 minutes.

SHAPE

Shape as boules. See Shaping, page 331, for instructions.

Place the large miche, seam side up, in a floured banneton or floured, towel-lined bowl, approximately 12 inches wide and 5 inches deep.

Place the two medium boules, seam side up, in floured bannetons or floured, towel-lined bowls, approximately 9 inches wide and 3½ inches deep.

PROOF

Cover and proof for 60 to 75 minutes at room temperature.

During the proof, preheat the oven to 450°F with a baking stone and steaming system in place. See Baking, page 349, for instructions.

Transfer the loaf or loaves to parchment paper or a baker's peel, gently inverting the loaf so that the underside, which was against the dusted tea towel or banneton, becomes the top.

Score the bread prior to loading. See Scoring, page 339 for ideas and tips.

BAKE

Slide the loaf or loaves onto the preheated baking stone.

Bake with steam for 45 to 55 minutes. After 30 minutes, carefully remove any steaming devices, lids, parchment paper, or bowls. Rotate the loaf or loaves on the stone.

At 45 to 55 minutes the loaf or loaves should be well colored. If making a single large miche, bake 10 to 15 minutes longer than 2 medium loaves.

Turn off the oven, prop open the door a few inches, and allow to dry for an additional 10 minutes.

New York is a city of almost as many bakeries as ethnicities—the sheer scope and number are enough to send carb-haters into kicking meltdowns. From Mexican *conchas* to Moroccan *m'semen*, Italian *taralli* to the steamed buns of Asia, one can take a worldwide cross-borough walking tour stepping from polysaccharide chain to complex carbohydrate the entire way. And that is exactly what I tried to do. Each trip up, down, or across the island could be interrupted to bread-gawk at Balthazar, to grab a *stirato* and a slice at Sullivan Street, or to stop at Union Square and just walk around the market stalls for the sole purpose of proximity to bread. This was self-medication; bread taken via eyes, mouth, and nose could transport, improve, comfort, and soothe one and even support the walls of a dream in which these gorgeous things were the products of my own hands. Complementing the breads at the market were stalls selling vegetables from regional farms, endless wood crates of local apples, fresh cheese and meat from the Hudson Valley, and shining fish right off the boat from Long Island. As I walked by in pressed shirt and pants and looked across a stall at someone wearing muck boots and farm clothes I knew I was the one wearing a costume. These were my people.

Over time I developed favorites: a crispy baguette singing and cracking as pieces are twisted off with glassy crust and yellow crumb; a large pain de seigle dusted with rye flour, deep mahogany from the oven, sour but also carrying the flavor of chocolate and tobacco. Or brioche, light as air, leaving a trace of butter on fingers as it is pulled off a loaf in pieces and dissolves on your tongue like cotton candy. And in my case, loving led to making and making and making.

A couple of blocks south of where I worked in New York there was a Pain Quotidien, which, for the first few years I visited it, had a visible in-store bakery. I could lurk at the glass window and inhale the scene—a bakery still life with oven decks and doors as centerpiece. It was the first place I could stand and stare, studying the equipment used to make these loaves that I loved. I could devour details until the bakers looked uncomfortable, getting as close as I could to the professional face of my obsession. In front of the oven, the loader, a loaf-depositor, waiting, its canvas stretching open for the passage of large loaves to superheated masonry.

There were loaves rising in giant wicker baskets, sacks of flour stacked to the ceiling, and a man working in baker's whites, scoring loaves, almost dancing through the movements of his day at the mixer, bench, and oven.

One of my favorites was a rye. Poor rye, forever suffering from mistreatment at the hands of supermarkets, delis, marblers, and caraway. While the towering meat stack at Second Avenue Deli was as good as it was indulgent, the "rye bookends" to the pastrami sandwich differed significantly from the rye breads of Europe. *Pain de seigle*, literally "bread of rye" in French, describes a loaf that has a majority portion of whole rye flour. Rye berries have the most beautiful color, at once light gray, sea green, and silver. When milled, rye flour ferments extremely well, releasing a sweet grassy aroma with the freshness of a bitter green. During baking, flavors intensify and the crust happily progresses toward deep darkness and intensity.

This bread is not a ballerina, it is a hausfrau; it is peasant stock, sturdy, honest, and delicious, and will keep for days and days.

If you enjoy breads in this genre, you might also fall in love with them, yet again, through the addition of toasted nuts or dried fruit, or, what the heck, equal parts of each.

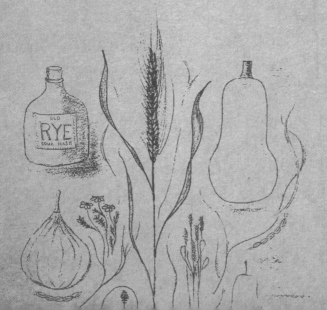

PAIN DE SEIGLE

Yield: **2 medium bâtards**

TOTAL FORMULA

PREFERMENTED FLOUR: 40%

INGREDIENTS	METRIC (GRAMS)	VOLUMETRIC (APPROXIMATE)	BAKER'S %
Whole rye flour	484	4½ cups	66%
All-purpose flour	250	2 cups + 1 tablespoon	34%
Water	587	2½ cups + 1 tablespoon	80%
Salt, fine	15	2½ teaspoons	2%
Yeast, dry instant	5	scant 2 teaspoons	0.70%
Sourdough culture	59	¼ cup	8%
Dried cherries or currants, toasted pecans, or walnuts (optional)	200	1¾ cups	
Total Weight	1,400	All	190.70%

RYE SOURDOUGH

INGREDIENTS	METRIC (GRAMS)	VOLUMETRIC (APPROXIMATE)	BAKER'S %
Whole rye flour	293	2¾ cups	100%
Water	235	1 cup	80%
Sourdough culture	59	¼ cup	20%
Total Weight	587	All	200%

FINAL DOUGH

INGREDIENTS	METRIC (GRAMS)	VOLUMETRIC (APPROXIMATE)
Water	352	1½ cups + 1 tablespoon
Rye sourdough	587	All
All-purpose flour	250	2 cups + 1 tablespoons
Whole rye flour	191	1¾ cups
Salt, fine	15	2½ teaspoons
Yeast, dry instant	5	scant 2 teaspoons
Dried cherries or currants, toasted pecans or walnuts, optional	200	1¾ cups
Total Weight	1,400	All

DAY ONE

RYE SOURDOUGH

In a medium bowl, combine the tepid water (75°F to 80°F) and the sourdough culture. Mix with your hands and fingers until the culture is broken up and well distributed in the water, then add the flour.

Mix briefly, then knead until smooth.

Cover and set at room temperature for 12 to 16 hours.

PREPARE

If adding toasted nuts to the pain de seigle, toast the nuts in a large frying pan over low heat, stirring occasionally until they take on some color and are fragrant. Different nuts and seeds toast at different rates, so keep an eye on them! Cool to room temperature. Chop them coarsely prior to use.

If adding dried fruit such as cherries or cranberries, chop them prior to use. Currants may be added whole.

DAY TWO

PREPARE

If adding toasted nuts or dried fruits, soak them in hot water for 5 minutes, then drain before using.

MIX

Calculate temperatures. See Setting Temperatures, page 320, for instructions. Desired dough temperature: 78°F to 80°F

In a large mixing bowl, combine the final dough water and rye sourdough. Mix with your hands until the rye sourdough is broken up in the water, then add the flours, salt, and yeast. Stir with the handle end of a wooden spoon until the dough forms a shaggy mass. If you find it easier, after some stirring, scrape the dough out of the bowl with a plastic scraper onto your work surface and knead briefly with your hands just until the dough comes together. Resist the urge to add more flour. Scrape the dough off the work surface and return it to the bowl for bulk fermentation.

If adding nuts or fruit, place them on top of the mixed dough and fold briefly to begin incorporation. It doesn't need to be homogeneous; these ingredients will fully incorporate during folding.

BULK FERMENTATION

Scrape down the sides of the mixing bowl and allow the dough to rise, covered, for 1 hour at room temperature, folding as directed below.

FOLD

Fold after 30 minutes, then leave untouched for the rest of the hour. See Folding, page 327, for instructions.

Note that doughs with a significant percentage of rye flour do not handle the same as wheat doughs. They will feel not stretchy or elastic, but rather more claylike.

DIVIDE AND PRESHAPE	Divide the dough into 2 pieces weighing about 700 grams each. Note that if you have opted to add fruit or nuts, the weight of the pieces of dough will increase. See Dividing, page 328, for instructions.
	Preshape as tubes. See Preshaping, page 329 for instructions.
	Cover and let rest for 15 minutes.
SHAPE	Shape as bâtards roughly 14 inches long. See Shaping, page 331, for instructions.
	Place, seam side up, on a baker's linen (couche) or tea towel generously floured with whole rye flour. Pleat the *couche* between the loaves to support their sides as they rise. See Shaping, page 331, for instructions.
PROOF	Cover and proof for 30 to 45 minutes at room temperature.
BAKE	During the proof, preheat the oven to 450°F with a baking stone and steaming system in place. See Baking, page 349, for instructions.
	Transfer the loaves to parchment paper or a baker's peel, gently inverting them so that the underside, which was against the dusted tea towel or linen, becomes the top.
	Score the bread prior to loading. See Scoring, page 339 for ideas and tips.
	Slide the loaves onto the preheated baking stone.
	Bake with steam for 35 to 40 minutes. After 25 minutes, carefully remove any steaming devices, lids, or parchment paper. Rotate the loaves on the stone.
	At 35 to 40 minutes the loaves should be well colored. Turn off the oven, prop open the door a few inches, and allow the loaves to dry for an additional 10 minutes.

In time our lives in the city took shape. I found steady work, we learned how to take a crosstown bus, and everyone in our apartment building became accustomed to loud singing. And amid all this living we decided we couldn't put off life any longer. No more compromise for a career, no more waiting for the perfect moment or the right amount of money in the bank; after years of avoiding it, we got pregnant. On a spring day with new growth everywhere, we shared the news with Julie's parents, showing an ultrasound picture of a blurry blob. We celebrated the excitement of a fresh chapter, our bond deepening at the prospect of a growing family and new roots. We watched, nervous and hopeful, as her belly grew. Held between her hips was so much promise, opportunity, excitement, and focus; something entirely spawned of our two lives and love. Well into the pregnancy she was away singing, and there were complications that were thought to have been resolved. But weeks later there was another round of complications, and with the knowledge that there was no hope for a positive outcome, she gave birth to our stillborn son, Huck Rainey. Some losses are anticipated; the order of events fits into the course of a life. In those times sadness is framed by expectation or circumstance, and one's inner voice offers comfort with "She lived a full life," or, in the case of Oma, even gratitude that she died at home in her rocking chair at the close of a day well into her eighth decade. If we could all be so lucky. The loss of a child is a slap wake-up, impossible to anticipate. Among the many sadnesses, the worst for me lay in the fact that I would never know who he would be, how he would grow and talk, run, or jump. He would not be my companion. I would never hold him longer than that single morning in a hospital room overlooking Manhattan and its bustle. All the potential was gone, with no opportunity or option to replace the loss or rise to the challenge of new experiences. And for all the tears I shed, Julie's were double. She had carried him for so long, feeling his fluttering movements, feeding him with her food and breath, the bond strengthening hour by hour, day by day. There is no recovering the subtraction of loss, a removal, a lessening.

The days and weeks following were a fog. What does one do with a layette knit by Mama and Oma for a child who won't be coming? Loss and grief alienate; internal dialogues chatter of pain or joy, yet remain unheard by the outside world. Six weeks after our loss, all of Manhattan, the boroughs, the state, and our country were brought to the same shattered place as planes hit the southern end of our island home and points beyond and all went upside down. Emergency vehicles streamed and screamed southbound for days, returning northward mute—there was no rescue, only recovery. The small Catholic church in our neighborhood lost dozens of members; our upstairs neighbor lost her son, a firefighter; and we had lost Huck. We were all brought together, living those difficult days on the same page, full of sad stories.

And yet the city never sleeps. Rhythms return and trains run, seasons arrive, then pass. Leaves of last year hold on like scars as fresh grass stretches out, in and among them. A week before the one-year anniversary of 9/11 we had a baby girl, Clementine. The pregnancy was pins and needles, extra checks, and fretful, but she came, healthy, in a shower of tears—there was never a more joyful arrival. In that moment much of my grief over Huck was forever buttoned; if we hadn't lost him we would never have had her. Somehow it felt like a trade, and because I was so grateful I could cry for him no more, never again.

It's OK to laugh at young parents; we are asking for it. As I think of the things we did for our first and juxtapose it with the treatment our third has received . . . it's appropriate to chuckle. With the first we set records for attentiveness, catering to every micro-need. Is that organic, is it natural, is it BPA-free? And what soap did you use to wash those bananas (before peeling them)? And on and on. But then, things slip with the second child. An exception here, an allowance for junk food there . . . and, if a third child arrives well, we're over the cliff now. "I'm hungry" can be fixed at a gas station. But before things relaxed we made quite a few delicious muffins for our baby girl—something to feed her amid spoon-fed meals of organic baby food.

CHOCOLATE-ORANGE MUFFINS

Yield: **12 muffins**

INGREDIENTS	METRIC (GRAMS)	VOLUMETRIC (APPROXIMATE)
Cocoa powder, dark, Dutch-process	51	½ cup + 1 tablespoon
Whole wheat flour	217	1¾ cups
Baking powder	5	1¼ teaspoons
Baking soda	2	scant ½ teaspoon
Salt, fine	4	heaping ½ teaspoon
Chocolate chips (dark or bittersweet)	153	scant 1 cup
Brown sugar	239	1 cup + 2 tablespoons
Orange zest, fresh	6	about 1 orange, zested
Eggs, large	100	2
Yogurt, plain (whole-fat is best, low-fat will do)	153	⅔ cup
Vanilla extract	10	1½ teaspoons
Oil	108	½ cup
Coarse sugar, for sprinkling on the muffins		

PREPARE   Preheat the oven to 400°F. Line a 12-well muffin pan with papers.

MIX   In a medium bowl, whisk together the cocoa powder, whole wheat flour, baking powder, baking soda, and salt.

Add the chocolate chips and stir to combine.

In a separate medium bowl, mix together the brown sugar, orange zest, eggs, yogurt, vanilla, and oil. Whisk until homogeneous.

Add the liquid to the dry ingredients, mixing with a spatula and folding gently to combine.

SCOOP   Portion the batter evenly into the prepared muffin pan. Garnish with coarse sugar.

BAKE   Bake for 18 to 20 minutes, rotating the pan after 12 minutes.

The top center of each muffin should be slightly firm to the touch when they are done.

BANANA-PECAN MUFFINS

Yield: **12 muffins**

INGREDIENTS	METRIC (GRAMS)	VOLUMETRIC (APPROXIMATE)
Whole wheat flour	263	2¼ cups
Baking powder	4	1 teaspoon
Baking soda	3	¾ teaspoon
Salt, fine	4	scant ¾ teaspoon
Pecans, chopped	160	1½ cups
Sugar	125	⅔ cup
Bananas, ripe (about 5 medium)	438	2 cups
Egg, large	50	1
Butter, unsalted	95	¼ cup + 2 tablespoons (6 tablespoons)

OAT STREUSEL

INGREDIENTS	METRIC (GRAMS)	VOLUMETRIC (APPROXIMATE)
Whole wheat flour	57	½ cup
Oats, thick rolled	25	¼ cup
Brown sugar	53	¼ cup
Cinnamon	3	1½ teaspoons
Salt, fine	Pinch	Pinch
Butter, unsalted, cold	56	¼ cup (4 tablespoons)

PREPARE

Preheat the oven to 400°F. Line a 12-well muffin pan with papers.

Peel and smash the bananas.

Melt the butter for the muffins.

STREUSEL

In a medium bowl, combine the streusel flour, oats, brown sugar, cinnamon, and salt. Stir to combine.

Grate the cold butter and add it to the dry ingredients, massaging it in with your hands to a cornmeal consistency.

Set aside and chill until use.

RECIPE CONTINUES

MIX

In a medium bowl, whisk together the muffin whole wheat flour, baking powder, baking soda, and salt; then add the pecans.

In a separate medium bowl, mix together the sugar, bananas, egg, and melted butter. Whisk until homogeneous.

Add the liquid to the dry ingredients and mix with a spatula, folding gently to combine.

SCOOP

Portion the batter evenly into the prepared pan. Garnish with the streusel, pressing it very gently to help it stick.

BAKE

Bake for 15 to 20 minutes, rotating the pan after 12 minutes.

The top center of each muffin should be slightly firm to the touch when they are done.

Riding downtown on the A train one day, I sat across from an ancient couple with weathered wrinkles creasing lines into loose skin of molasses hue. They were dressed like dust bowl apparitions; he held a beaten suitcase on the knees of pressed slacks, hugging it with threadbare jacket arms; she wore Sunday clothes and sagging knee-highs. As the train bounced and rocked he dozed and she watched the stops pass. I stared, mesmerized by the vision of ghost visitors from the twentieth century. As 125th Street approached, she readied herself, then rose as the doors opened, then turned and called to him, "Come on, Anthem" before they left, holding each other up. The image stuck with me; I held it like a pocket watch, turning it in my hand, wallowing in the mystery of antiques. Old things, trades, and remnants, like cellar holes, are grounding, they give context to current days. I came home and shared with Julie what I had seen, and a few weeks later our second girl arrived. We named her Anthem Rainey in honor of old things and Raineys.

In the blink of a sleepless eye, Clementine was soon able to crawl, stand, walk, and talk, and it wasn't long before she wanted in on what I was doing in the kitchen. She would toddle into the room, knowing that something in that bowl, hidden from little eyes, needed helping. Mixing sourdough cultures is perfect for little hands, eager with muck-lust for flour, batter, paste. She became a solid partner in the kitchen before she was even three. I would put a measured portion of culture in a large bowl with tepid water, allowing her to squeeze and agitate the mixture until it was frothy before following with the flour portion. We were a good team.

I was inspired by the wonderful breads at Balthazar Bakery in New York and, in particular, its signature loaf, which included dark beer in addition to water for hydration. Bread and beer have been in cahoots since the earliest days of bread making. Excavations at Egyptian sites clearly link beer, bread, and antiquity. You don't see many breweries and bakeries under the same roof anymore. I doubt either side got any work done with that arrangement, but I do think that beer—or "liquid bread," as some of us call it—is a wonderful thing in my mouth, my hand, or my bread. Here's one way to do it.

IRISH LEVAIN

Yield: 1 large miche, or 2 medium boules

TOTAL FORMULA

PREFERMENTED FLOUR: 20%

INGREDIENTS	METRIC (GRAMS)	VOLUMETRIC (APPROXIMATE)	BAKER'S %
All-purpose flour	521	4¼ cups + 1 tablespoon	80%
Whole rye flour	98	scant 1 cup	15%
Whole wheat flour	33	¼ cup	5%
Water	312	1¼ cups + 2 tablespoons	48%
Dark beer (stout or porter preferred)	195	¾ cup + 2 tablespoons	30%
Salt, fine	13	2⅛ teaspoons	2%
Yeast, dry instant	2	scant ¾ teaspoon	0.25%
Sourdough culture	26	scant 2 tablespoons	4%
Total Weight	1,200	All	184.25%

RYE SOURDOUGH

INGREDIENTS	METRIC (GRAMS)	VOLUMETRIC (APPROXIMATE)	BAKER'S %
Whole rye flour	65	½ cup + 2 tablespoons	100%
Water	52	¼ cup	80%
Sourdough culture	13	scant 1 tablespoon	20%
Total Weight	130	All	200%

LIQUID LEVAIN

INGREDIENTS	METRIC (GRAMS)	VOLUMETRIC (APPROXIMATE)	BAKER'S %
All-purpose flour	65	½ cup	100%
Water	65	¼ cup	100%
Sourdough culture	13	scant 1 tablespoon	20%
Total Weight	143	All	220%

FINAL DOUGH

INGREDIENTS	METRIC (GRAMS)	VOLUMETRIC (APPROXIMATE)
Water	195	¾ cup + 2 tablespoons
Rye sourdough	130	All
Liquid levain	143	All
All-purpose flour	456	3¾ cups + 1 tablespoon
Whole rye flour	33	¼ cup + 1 tablespoon
Whole wheat flour	33	¼ cup
Dark beer (stout or porter preferred)	195	¾ cup + 2 tablespoons
Salt, fine	13	2⅛ teaspoons
Yeast, dry instant	2	¾ teaspoon
Total Weight	1,200	All

DAY ONE

RYE SOURDOUGH

In a medium bowl, combine the tepid water (75°F to 80°F) and sourdough culture. Mix with your hands and fingers until the culture is broken up and well distributed in the water, then add the flour.

Mix briefly, then knead until smooth.

Cover and set at room temperature for 12 to 16 hours.

LIQUID LEVAIN

In a medium bowl, combine the tepid water (75°F to 80°F)-and-sourdough culture. Mix with your hands and fingers until the culture is broken up and well distributed in the water, then add the flour.

Mix until smooth.

Cover and set at room temperature for 12 to 16 hours.

DAY TWO

MIX

Calculate temperatures. See Setting Temperatures, page 320, for instructions. Desired dough temperature: 76°F

In a large mixing bowl, combine the final dough water, rye sourdough, and liquid levain. Mix with your hands until the cultures are broken up in the water, then add the flours, beer, salt, and yeast. Stir with the handle end of a wooden spoon until the dough forms a shaggy mass. If you find it easier, after some stirring, scrape

RECIPE CONTINUES

MIX CONT. the dough out of the bowl with a plastic scraper onto your work surface and knead briefly with your hands just until the dough comes together. Resist the urge to add more flour. Scrape the dough off the work surface and return it to the bowl for bulk fermentation.

BULK FERMENTATION Scrape down the sides of the mixing bowl and allow the dough to rise, covered, for 3 hours at room temperature, folding as directed below.

FOLD Fold after 20, 40, 60, 90, and 120 minutes, then leave untouched for the third hour. See Folding, page 327 for instructions.

As you perform each series of folds, you'll begin to notice that the dough becomes smoother, stronger, and more cohesive.

DIVIDE AND PRESHAPE For a single large miche, preshape as a round. See Preshaping, page 329 for instructions.

Cover and let rest for 15 minutes.

For two loaves, divide the dough into 2 pieces weighing about 600 grams each. See Dividing, page 328, for instructions.

Preshape as rounds. See Preshaping, page 329, for instructions.

Cover and let rest for 10 to 15 minutes.

SHAPE Shape as boules. See Shaping, page 331, for instructions.

Place the large miche, seam side up, in a banneton or towel-lined bowl, approximately 10 inches wide and 4 inches deep, and generously dusted with whole rye flour.

Place the two medium boules, seam side up, in bannetons or towel-lined bowls, approximately 9 inches wide and 3½ inches deep, and generously floured with whole rye flour.

PROOF Cover and proof for 50 to 60 minutes at room temperature.

BAKE During the proof, preheat the oven to 450°F with a baking stone and steaming system in place. See Baking, page 349, for instructions.

Transfer the loaves to parchment paper or a baker's peel, gently inverting them so that the underside, which was against the dusted tea towel or banneton, becomes the top.

Score the bread prior to loading. See Scoring, page 339, for ideas and tips.

Slide the loaves onto the preheated baking stone.

BAKE CONT.

Bake with steam for 40 to 45 minutes. After 30 minutes, carefully remove any steaming devices, lids, parchment paper, or bowls. Rotate the loaves on the stone.

At 40 to 45 minutes the loaves should be well colored. If making a single large miche, bake 10 minutes longer than the two medium loaves.

Turn off the oven, prop open the door a few inches, and allow the loaves to dry for an additional 10 minutes.

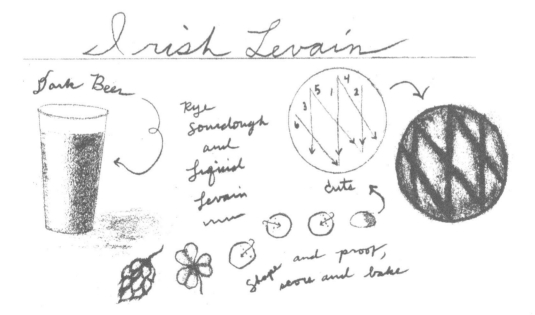

Irish Levain

Dark Beer

Rye Sourdough and Liquid Levain

cuts

shape and proof, score and bake

In the city I took classes at the Institute for Culinary Education and the Artisan Baking Center in Long Island City. Then I began to look further afield to study and found King Arthur Flour in Norwich, Vermont, and a treasure trove of year-round professional bread and pastry classes. I signed up for a multiday class, Survey of French Breads, which I could attend, and, with the guilt of a parent who knows full well the amount of work the other half is in for (and knowing that I might get an uninterrupted night of sleep!), I packed a few things and said my good-byes. When I drove north out of Manhattan, my shoulders dropped and my breath slowed as I crossed bridges. I saw the balance of color shift back to green trees; towering buildings turned to natural canyons; and traffic lights were swapped for the glimmer of the Hudson River. Vermont is my home state of sorts; my father grew up in Northfield, where they bathed on Saturday nights, and snow piles covered first-floor windows in winter. In spring, wood-fired sugaring was possible only with the help of farm horses. I arrived late in the day, blinded by the darkness of this rural place with no streetlights to shine over a city that actually sleeps.

Class began after I gorged on coffee and the best pastries I had ever eaten, and I could have levitated with the excitement of all that surrounded me after a decent night of sleep. We were quickly into our first day, mixing, folding, and dividing a French sourdough called *pain au levain*. There were two instructors. One was the chef and baker James McGuire, who translated and adapted one of the most important books on artisan baking ever written, *Taste of Bread*, by the French master Raymond Calvel. And co-teaching was a guy I had never heard of, Jeffrey Hamelman, the director of the King Arthur Flour Bakery. As we divided the first dough, the pace picked up, Jeffrey modeling the quick, efficient movement of a professional with three decades of experience at the bench, and the rest of us fumbling to keep up. After the divided and preshaped dough relaxed in its circular form, Jeffrey set about shaping the blobs into bâtards. Have you seen juggling before? Have you stood close while multiples fly skyward with flicking motions and fall back to Earth only to continue skyward again? In a juggler's movement are economy and beauty, the familiarity of ten thousand repetitions, the invisible adjustments that allow the motion to continue. Watching Jeffrey shape blew a fuse in me. Involuntarily, I stepped backward and leaned forward at the waist as my jaw dropped. . . . I cannot say others noticed, but I will never forget it. I saw the mastery. I saw passion, work, experience, and craft.

In this life that is all I hope to be: passionate, capable, and earnest. With practice and hopefully fewer than ten thousand repetitions you may make a beautiful pain au levain bâtard as well. Do not be discouraged if you throw skyward and hit the ceiling. Mastery takes time. This is how we learn.

Driving back to New York, I took country roads and meandering courses rather than interstates in order to prolong the trip in every way possible provided I still made it home to see my girls before bedtime. I returned to King Arthur for multiple classes, and in addition to the bags of baked goods I toted south at the end of each trip, I also took formulas and better skills, improving from poor to mediocre along the way. Baking was taking me somewhere, and I was a willing passenger.

Brioche is a miracle. How could mere flour support half its weight in both whole eggs *and* butter? How could it feel light as a feather and yet pack five million calories per serving? All right, maybe only a few hundred, but still, this shining chestnut-colored loaf with yolk-yellow crumb is a queen among baked goods. The brioche that Jeffrey taught became a steadfast favorite in our apartment building as neighbors learned my baking schedule. The basic dough is excellent when simply proofed, painted with egg wash, and baked—you will be amazed at the glorious sight as it is pulled from your oven. Or, as I did, you may take the brioche coffee cake, filled with pastry cream, topped with poached fruit and streusel, as a sign that you might have professional baking in your future. In either case, your mouth and neighbors will thank you.

BRIOCHE **PAGE 120**

BRIOCHE

For brioche and also the *pain de mie*, it can be helpful to have options for batch sizes. If you are headed to a potluck supper and need buns for a crowd, you may want the larger batch. It can even be doubled successfully, the only limitation being the capacity of your mixer. Consider what you would like to bake, and how many, and then refer to the section below to determine which batch size is appropriate.

HERE ARE
WEIGHTS
FOR VARIOUS
ITEMS

HAMBURGER BUNS: 75 grams, as many as desired. "Sliders" can be made with roughly half the weight.

NANTERRE (A FRENCH SANDWICH LOAF): 8 pieces at 60 grams or 75 grams, depending on pan size.

SAVORY TART: 200 grams

COFFEE CAKE: 300 grams

Divide the dough according to what you want to make, referencing the weights shown above. The batch size will accommodate a variety of options. See Dividing, page 322, for instructions.

INGREDIENTS	900 GRAMS	VOLUMETRIC (APPROXIMATE)	1,350 GRAMS	VOLUMETRIC (APPROXIMATE)	BAKER'S %
All-purpose flour	398	3¼ cups + 1 tablespoon	597	5 cups	100%
Water	36	2 tablespoons + 1½ teaspoons	53	scant ¼ cup	9%
Salt, fine	10	scant 1¾ teaspoons	15	2½ teaspoons	2.50%
Yeast, dry instant	10	1 tablespoon + ½ teaspoon	15	1 tablespoon + 2 teaspoons	2.50%
Eggs, large	199	4	299	6	50%
Butter, unsalted	199	¾ cup + 2 tablespoons (14 tablespoons)	299	1¼ cups + 1 tablespoon (21 tablespoons)	50%
Egg wash, if making hamburger buns or the Nanterre					
Sugar	48	¼ cup	72	¼ cup + 2 tablespoons	12%
Total Weight	900	All	1,350	All	226%

<table>
<tr><td>PREPARE</td><td>Scale and chill all ingredients.</td></tr>
</table>

DAY ONE

In the bowl of a stand mixer fitted with a dough hook, mix the flour, salt, and yeast until combined.

Add the water and whole eggs and mix on low speed until the dough is fully homogeneous, stopping to scrape the sides and bottom if necessary.

Cover the mixer bowl and allow the mixture to rest for 20 minutes.

While you wait, use a rolling pin to pound the chilled butter into flat pieces, roughly ¼ to ½ inch thick. Chill until use.

After the rest period, add all the sugar and mix for 4 to 5 minutes on medium speed, to achieve a smooth and elastic dough.

MIX

With the mixer on medium-low, add the butter in 5 to 6 stages. Allow each addition to incorporate before adding the next.

After all the butter is incorporated and the dough is smooth, place the dough on a floured sheet pan. Lightly flour the top surface and flatten the dough. Cover the dough to prevent a skin from forming.

Rest the dough for 1 hour at room temperature. At 30 minutes, fold it into thirds like a letter, then lightly dust the top and flatten it once again.

Cover the dough and place in the refrigerator for 4 to 24 hours. During this time the dough will firm and develop flavor. It will also be easier to shape when cold.

After the cooling stage you can use the dough in any of the following ways.

LATER ON DAY ONE; OR ON DAY TWO

SHAPING

Note that the final proof for brioche will be quite long. It may take 2 to 3 hours for the dough to warm and rise after being refrigerated. Put covered, shaped items in a warm, draft-free place to proof.

**HAMBURGER
BUNS (3-INCH)**

Lightly grease a 13 by 18-inch sheet pan, or line it with parchment paper.

Divide as many buns as desired at 75 grams. See Dividing, page 328, for instructions.

Round the pieces and place on the pan, leaving a few inches between them so that they don't touch while proofing. I space them 6 to a sheet pan.

Cover with plastic wrap, or place the pan inside a plastic bag to rise.

Proof until at least doubled.

RECIPE CONTINUES

HAMBURGER BUNS (3-INCH) CONT.

Toward the end of the proof, preheat the oven to 425°F.

Gently brush with egg wash. Bake for 14 to 16 minutes, until the buns are a deep golden brown.

NANTERRE (8½ BY 4½-INCH OR 9 BY 5-INCH PAN)

A *Nanterre* is brioche baked in a loaf pan.

Lightly grease an 8½ by 4½-inch or a 9 by 5-inch pan.

Divide 8 pieces of dough at about 60 grams each for the 8½ by 4½-inch pan, or about 75 grams each for the 9 by 5-inch pan. See Dividing, page 328, for instructions.

Round the pieces into balls and place in the prepared pan in two even rows. Cover with plastic wrap, or place inside a plastic bag to rise. See Shaping, page 331, for instructions.

When the rising dough feels very light to the touch (this often takes as long as 90 to 120 minutes to happen), gently brush with egg wash.

Toward the end of the proof, preheat the oven to 375°F.

Bake for 30 to 35 minutes, or until the loaf is a deep brown.

SAVORY TART (10-INCH)

A savory tart is similar to a quiche, but uses brioche dough for the crust instead of the standard *pâte brisée*.

Lightly grease a 10-inch tart pan.

Divide a dough piece at 200 grams. See Dividing, page 328, for instructions.

On a lightly floured surface, roll the dough into a rough 8-inch circle, then place in the tart pan.

Cover the pan and rest the dough for 20 minutes while preparing the toppings and filling.

TART FILLING

INGREDIENTS	METRIC (GRAMS)	VOLUMETRIC (APPROXIMATE)
Zucchini	150	1 medium
Onion	50	1 medium
Olive oil, extra virgin	11	1 tablespoon
Eggs, large, lightly beaten	150	3
Heavy cream	120	½ cup
Feta cheese, crumbled	40	⅓ cup
Salt, fine		
Black pepper, ground		

Cut the zucchini on the diagonal into ½-inch slices.

Peel the onion and cut in half. Place the flat side of the onion on the cutting board and cut the onion into ¼-inch-thick slices.

In a medium sauté pan, heat the oil until shimmering. Add the zucchini and the onion. Season to taste with salt and pepper and sauté until well colored. Cool and reserve until use.

In a small bowl, combine the beaten eggs and cream. Season with salt and pepper and reserve until use.

Preheat the oven to 425°F.

After 20 minutes, use your fingers to evenly flatten the relaxed dough into the pan and up the sides.

Arrange the cooled sautéed vegetables in the tart shell. Pour in the egg-and-cream mixture, stopping about ¼ inch from the top so that it won't overflow.

Garnish with the feta cheese.

Carefully slide the tart into the oven and bake for 30 to 35 minutes, or until the filling is set and the crust is a deep golden brown.

BRIOCHE COFFEE CAKE

Yield: **One 10-inch coffee cake**

After reading through this recipe you might think, "Wait, I have to make brioche dough, *and* pastry cream, *and* streusel, *and* poached pears? Booooo! This recipe sucks!"

It's true, there is no way around these chores if you want this delicacy. (And trust me, you do!) But there is *some* good news. While almost every task takes planning, this one can be spread out (as we do in the bakery) over the course of a few days. On one day, you may poach the pears and make the streusel; on another, you may make pastry cream and the dough; and so forth. If you become impatient while the days pass in slow motion, with time seeming to stall as the pears soak up red wine and the dough ferments, stop a moment and dream ahead. If you close your eyes, you can almost see it: toasting streusel above wine-infused pears floating on warm pastry cream over golden brioche. Patience; you will be there soon enough.

INGREDIENT AMOUNTS

Ginger-infused pastry cream	420 grams (1½ cups)
Poached pears	3
Streusel	1 batch

PREPARE

Prepare the Ginger-infused pastry cream (page 126), poached pears (page 128), and streusel (page 127).

Cut the poached pears into ½-inch slices.

Note: Other fruit fillings may be substituted for the poached pears. Try fresh blueberries, sliced apples (sautéed with butter and sugar), or poached plums.

METHOD

Lightly grease a 10-inch springform pan.

Divide a dough piece to about 300 grams. See Dividing, page 328, for instructions.

On a lightly floured surface, roll the dough into an 8-inch circle, then place it in the springform pan.

Cover the dough and let rest for 20 minutes.

FILL THE COFFEE CAKE

After 20 minutes, use your fingers to press the relaxed dough into the pan and about an inch up the sides.

Apply a ½-inch layer of pastry cream to the dough surface. Leave a ½-inch border of plain dough where it meets the sidewall of the springform.

Evenly distribute the pears on the pastry cream.

FILL THE COFFEE CAKE CONT.	Garnish with streusel, applying a generous, consistent layer that covers the entire coffee cake.
	Cover and proof for 30 to 45 minutes.
	Toward the end of the proof, preheat the oven to 400°F.
BAKE	Bake for 30 to 35 minutes, until the streusel is lightly golden. The cake will feel firm and set and pull away from the pan edges.
	Cool before removing from the springform mold and slicing.

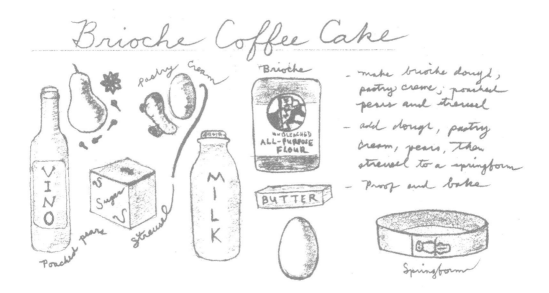

Brioche Coffee Cake

pastry cream · Brioche · UNBLEACHED ALL-PURPOSE FLOUR · VINO · Sugar · streusel · Poached pears · MILK · BUTTER · Springform

- make brioche dough, pastry creme, poached pears and streusel
- add dough, pastry cream, pears, then streusel to a springform
- Proof and bake

GINGER-INFUSED PASTRY CREAM

Yield: **560 grams (about 2 cups)**

INGREDIENTS	METRIC (GRAMS)	VOLUMETRIC (APPROXIMATE)
Ginger, fresh, 2½-inch piece	21	1½ tablespoons, packed grated
Lemon zest (optional)	4	Zest of 1 lemon
Sugar	99	½ cup
Cornstarch	28	¼ cup
Salt, fine	Pinch	Pinch
Egg yolks	72	4
Vanilla extract	13	1 tablespoon
Milk	460	2 cups + 2 tablespoons
Butter, unsalted	28	2 tablespoons

PREPARE

Grate the ginger. A box grater or Microplane works very well.

Zest the lemon.

MIX

Into a small bowl, sift together the sugar, cornstarch, and salt to combine.

In a medium bowl, stir the egg yolks with the vanilla. Add the cornstarch mixture, then whisk until smooth.

COOK

In a medium pot, add the ginger and lemon zest to the milk. Bring to a simmer over medium heat, then strain.

Return the infused milk to medium heat and bring back to a simmer.

Whisk 1 cup of the milk into the egg mixture to temper the eggs, stirring constantly. Whisk until fully combined. Continuing to whisk, return the egg mixture to the warm milk.

Cook, stirring constantly, over medium heat until the mixture boils and thickens, 1 to 2 minutes.

Remove the pot from the heat. Add the butter, stirring until it completely melts. Cover the pastry cream with plastic wrap and chill until use. Whisk briefly before using.

For the smoothest pastry cream you may strain it immediately after it sets. I rarely bother.

Pastry cream will keep for 3 to 4 days, chilled.

STREUSEL

Yield: **300 grams (about 2¼ cups)**

INGREDIENTS	METRIC (GRAMS)	VOLUMETRIC (APPROXIMATE)
Butter, unsalted, soft	75	⅓ cup (5 tablespoons + 1 teaspoon)
Sugar	75	⅓ cup
Salt, fine	Pinch	Pinch
All-purpose flour	150	1¼ cups
Total Weight	300	All

MIX

In a medium bowl, combine the butter, sugar, and salt, stirring until smooth.

Add the flour, mixing by hand or with a fork to a cornmeal consistency. A handful squeezed together will clump slightly. The ideal streusel is a mixture of two textures, the finer like cornmeal with some larger, marble-size lumps.

Chill until use. Any leftover streusel can be frozen in a plastic bag for up to 2 months and can be used on muffins, fruit crumbles, and a variety of other baked goods.

POACHED PEARS

Yield: **3 poached pears**

INGREDIENTS	METRIC (GRAMS)	VOLUMETRIC (APPROXIMATE)
Pears, fresh	540	3
Red wine	341	1½ cups
Sugar	149	¾ cup
Cloves, whole	0.20	5 cloves
Cinnamon stick	4	1
Peppercorns, black	0.20	5 peppercorns
Orange peel	6	1 large piece

PREPARE

Peel, core, stem, and halve the pears. I prefer the firm varieties because they hold their shape best.

PROCESS

Combine the wine, sugar, cloves, cinnamon, peppercorns, and orange peel.

Bring to a simmer.

When the sugar has dissolved, add the pears. A round cutout of parchment paper placed atop the pears in the pot will help them to cook evenly.

Reduce the heat and simmer for 30 to 45 minutes, gently turning the pears at the halfway point.

Different sizes of pears at different levels of ripeness will soften at varying rates. Check for tenderness by piercing the thickest portion with a knife; the knife should slip into the heart of the pears easily.

Pears can be cooled in the liquid and reserved for about a week. Strain them before use in the brioche coffee cake.

The poaching liquid can be retained for additional poaching, used as simple syrup, or reduced and used as a glaze or in vinaigrettes.

In 2005, I sat in a glass office high above Park Avenue looking south beyond the Flatiron Building toward a pit in lower Manhattan. The bent, twisted, buckled sections of the World Trade Center's windows and its girders, which had held so much high above the clouds, had been hauled away—110,000 truckloads to move a man-made mountain. Deep fires and hot spots had been extinguished, but Ground Zero remained—a scar, a dividing line between before and after, a silent encouragement to do something while there was time, for life was so short and precious.

I was working as a manager on the operational side of an investment bank—a stressful job with the expected perks, which allowed Julie to be at home with our children. Workweeks took me away to worry and concern, and weekends delivered me home to sweet family, baking, and giving "Martin bread" to the neighborhood. Baking consumed my time between diaper changes; I was in hot pursuit of this thing that connected my hands to my heart and my soul to my mouth.

One evening the fog of sleep deprivation broke for a moment and aligned with lightly sleeping children and we had a discussion at the end of which we said, "Let's do it." Let's jump, let's run. Let's leave this life as we know it and start over. Yes, there will be sacrifice and challenge, discomfort and change; but steps backward might enable steps forward toward country places, smaller challenges, and bigger spaces.

I applied for an opening for a baker at King Arthur Flour. It was more than a long shot—when I wasn't hired it made perfect sense. I had no professional experience in baking, no culinary school education; in *no way* did I belong on a team of professional bakers. But I am hardheaded, and a few months later I applied again. Still no luck. But did I mention hardheaded? Time passed, another opening came, and of course I applied yet again; this time Jeffrey invited me to come to Vermont and bring Julie and the kids for an interview. As the kids ran around his office, smiling and laughing, I knew I was in the right place, I knew that I could fit if given the chance. Please, oh, please, oh, please hire me. A few days later Jeffrey called and offered me the job. I accepted immediately and, in doing so, made what was on paper the most foolish choice of my life.

What idiot with a wife and two kids and a comfortable life in Manhattan would accept a job in food service in rural Vermont? I had no clue about the money, no idea whatsoever, and really didn't care. Money hadn't made me happy; maybe the lack of it would. I had a feeling that those things would sort themselves out, but, still, we were jumping with no clear landing, hoping that craft and a life in Vermont would answer, would provide, would nurture and sustain.

We packed our apartment, winnowing our possessions down to fit our smaller future home. I distinctly remember sitting in an empty room on a futon on the floor with the girls, playing my banjo as my heart lightened, in love with my essentials, my only true necessities, ready for whatever came next.

VERMONT

The Green Mountain State has a granite spine that rises, pushing hemlock and hop horn-beam forests high to blue sky. This backbone of rock snakes south to north, extending rib ridges east and west. In winter the mountains are snuggled in deep snow, which flattens and disappears in the spring melt. Then summer rains pour down and down, their waters pausing to pool or hurry and fall again before landing in Lake Champlain or the Connecti-cut River and running onward to the Atlantic Ocean. Water. Water to turn saw blades, spin bobbins, or move millstones; water to freeze and then run again; water for mud and trout, for hay and horses, for thirsty maples to drip back as sap; water to squeeze through aquifer sieves and bubble up again for drinking. I was raised near springs. In back of Watson's cabin in the Ozarks, covered with rusty corrugate, there was a dark, shaded corner, a bottomless pool, cool, a secret place where, using my hand as a ladle, I could scoop crisp sips of endless refreshment to my mouth. It is only right that I should return to a place with springs.

And coming here was more than a search to quench thirst; it was indeed travel to a source, a place closer to nourishment for soul *and* mouth. We found this home in the mountains not far from the bakery in Norwich, Vermont. If you live here and are not on a hill you are certainly near one, as this state is second only to Washington in a count of peaks per square mile. We unfurled easily, like a flag built to catch wind and whip. We spread out, stretching and marveling as the kids banged out the door to play in the dirt. Good, clean dirt. No needles, no trash, no broken glass or excrement. "Are the kids out-side?" "Yes." "Can you see them?" "Yes." "OK."

If my heart had been wounded, if worry was my steady companion, and if my chest ached not with passion but with stress, in the days between my work in the city and my new profession a lightness returned. Anxiety sloughed off and healing began underneath. I was starting over, newish and shinier, brighter, more present, a better father, a better spouse, a better human. It was also a time to prepare, to recharge and store energy for the task ahead, just around the corner.

As it turns out, baking is a nighttime trade. I like to pretend that work begins in the early morning but will acknowledge that we commute under stars well before the coldest hours of night arrive. I have my first coffee just after 3:00 a.m. while you snore; and I eat pizza for "lunch" while your breakfast scramble sizzles. The very first morning of my baking life, the alarm sounded, ending a sleepless night of twisting, fueled by fear of oversleeping. I shuffled through the house, trying not to wake anyone, dressed, grabbed my lunch, and ducked out the door with groggy eyes and a nervous stomach. New shirt, new shoes, new baker's pants, new life.

I arrived at the bakery and stepped into the bright, warm space, thick with the smell and steam of baking bread. Crews were already in motion, doing their daily work. This wasn't my ritual yet. Farmers know their seasons and the chores of each, as do ranchers and mechanics. Bakers know their days by the order of mixes and bakes. Me? I arrived knowing nothing.

At King Arthur Flour the bakery building is divided into separate clusters for bread and pastry work. The two disciplines have things in common but also individual needs, best served by grouping respective production areas into pods. For bread, the main tools include a steam-injected masonry oven, which can bake a few hundred baguettes at a time. Bakers fill these ovens using a large canvas loader, which looks like a hospital stretcher and deposits loaves directly onto the hearth of the oven. There are also mixers designed for artisan dough and wooden benches where hand shaping is done. And hands, experienced hands, the most flexible, versatile, and valuable tools in the world.

I was hired as a bread baker, so I gave a friendly wave to the pastry team as I passed by that first day, and headed to the bread area, where Sharon, the mixer, and Amber, the baker, were already hard at work. Sharon and Amber were working with an intern from the Culinary Institute of America, who was spending sixteen weeks at King Arthur in fulfillment of his academic requirement.

After advising me in her no-nonsense way that I needed to arrive earlier the following day, Sharon lifted me high above her head and threw me into the proverbial deep end of the pool, pointing to a board of dough blobs. "Shape some baguettes!" I gulped, stepped to the bench, grasped at my straws of knowledge for guidance, and nervously began.

The truth is, even if she had said, "Shape these boules" or "Shape those bâtards" or "Let's round rolls," she might as well have said, "Make a sugar sculpture!" Even with my best effort I was splashing within seconds, sucking water through my nose, coughing and flapping. Someone call a lifeguard! He's drowning! And I was. I was so bad that even the intern began throwing tips and bailing water as I waited for the call: Mayday! All hands on deck to help the career-changer suck less! I was so frustrated that I quickly soaked myself with the sweat of nerves, sadly watching as the secret got out. With shaping there is no hiding. Either one makes something beautiful, smooth, even, and symmetrical—or not. A piece of dough is a blank canvas that the hands transform. Skills are either apparent or not—there is no faking or copying. Yes, I had studied. I understood the science of baking—intellectually, I knew how to shape loaves—but craft and beauty lie in nuance. The micro-adjustments made by experienced hands that apply pressure here or delicacy there—such knowledge and skill come only with time and repetitions. It is here, in these details, that the novice is separated from the professional. With everything we did in the bakery I was in this beginner space . . . and this was the hardest part of the transition. I was at the bottom of the ladder, the lowest rung. If this team was a chain, then I was the link that would fail first. Welcome to humble pie bakery.

So, thank goodness for oatmeal bread. If shaping French bâtards was a dough-ripping nightmare, if my baguettes looked like snakes that had swallowed eggs, then I could take comfort here. Quickly shaping these pan loaves and rolling them across a moist towel, then through a pile of thick-cut rolled oats, was the first bakery dance I could do. My oatmeal loaf was "almost" indistinguishable from a professional's after I'd undergone only a few weeks of constant embarrassment. I will admit it is a low bar, but even tripping and falling, I could clear it.

OATMEAL BREAD

Yield: Two 9 by 5-inch pan loaves

TOTAL FORMULA

INGREDIENTS	METRIC (GRAMS)	VOLUMETRIC (APPROXIMATE)	BAKER'S %
All-purpose flour	648	5¼ cups + 3 tablespoons	75%
Whole wheat flour	216	1¾ cups	25%
Water	540	2¼ cups + 2 tablespoons	62.50%
Salt, fine	19	1 tablespoon + ¼ teaspoon	2.20%
Yeast, dry instant	9	1 tablespoon	1%
Oats, thick rolled or old-fashioned	143	scant 1½ cups	16.50%
Milk	95	¼ cup + 3 tablespoons	11%
Honey	65	3 tablespoons	7.50%
Vegetable oil	65	scant ⅓ cup	7.50%
Oats, thick rolled or old-fashioned, for the crust			
Total Weight	1,800	All	208.20%

OAT SOAKER

INGREDIENTS	METRIC (GRAMS)	VOLUMETRIC (APPROXIMATE)
Oats, thick rolled or old-fashioned	143	scant 1½ cups
Water	270	1¼ cups + 2 tablespoons
Milk	95	¼ cup + 3 tablespoons
Honey	65	3 tablespoons
Vegetable oil	65	scant ⅓ cup
Total Weight	638	All

FINAL DOUGH (CONT. ON FOLLOWING PAGE)

INGREDIENTS	METRIC (GRAMS)	VOLUMETRIC (APPROXIMATE)
All-purpose flour	648	5¼ cups + 3 tablespoons
Whole wheat flour	216	1¾ cups

RECIPE CONTINUES

FINAL DOUGH (CONT. FROM PREVIOUS PAGE)

INGREDIENTS	METRIC (GRAMS)	VOLUMETRIC (APPROXIMATE)
Salt, fine	19	1 tablespoon + ¼ teaspoon
Yeast, dry instant	9	1 tablespoon
Water	270	1 cup
Oat soaker	638	All
Total Weight	1,800	All

DAY ONE

SOAKER

In a medium bowl, combine the oats, water, milk, honey, and vegetable oil and allow to soak for 2 to 16 hours. The broad time range for the soaker is for convenience and texture. Even a few hours will be enough to soften the oats.

DAY TWO

MIX

Calculate temperatures. See Setting Temperatures, page 320, for instructions. Desired dough temperature: 76°F

In a large mixing bowl, whisk together the flours, salt, and yeast. Add the water and soaker. Mix with your hand or the handle end of a wooden spoon until the dough forms a shaggy mass. With some doughs you may have to knead for a few strokes in the bowl to incorporate everything. If you find it easier, after some stirring, scrape the dough out of the bowl with a plastic scraper onto your work surface and knead briefly with your hands just until the dough comes together. Resist the urge to add more flour. Scrape the dough off the work surface and return it to the bowl for bulk fermentation.

BULK FERMENTATION

Scrape down the sides of the mixing bowl and allow the dough to rise, covered, for 2 hours at room temperature, folding as directed below.

FOLD

Fold after 20, 40, and 60 minutes, then leave untouched for the second hour. See Folding, page 327, for instructions.

DIVIDE AND PRESHAPE

Divide the dough into 2 pieces weighing about 900 grams each. See Dividing, page 328, for instructions.

Preshape as rounds. See Preshaping, page 329 for instructions.

Cover and let rest for 15 minutes.

Grease or spray two 9 by 5-inch loaf pans.

To make the oat crust, place a ¼-inch layer of thick rolled oats on a sheet pan. On a second pan, place a well-moistened tea towel or dish towel.

SHAPE

Shape as a pan loaf. See Shaping, page 331, for instructions.

After shaping, roll the top of the loaves across the moist towel, and then roll the top through the oatmeal on the pan.

Place the loaves, oat side up, in the prepared pans.

PROOF

Cover and proof for 50 to 60 minutes at room temperature.

BAKE

Toward the end of the proof, preheat the oven to 425°F with your steaming system in place. See Baking, page 349, for instructions.

Bake with steam for 35 to 40 minutes. After 25 minutes, rotate the loaves.

The loaves are done when the top and sides are firm and the loaves are a deep golden brown.

Oh, the baguette. What could be so hard? In baking there is a triple-salchow, the bread equivalent of jumping from toe tip to land on one foot, on skates, on ice, no falling. The baguette is that jump. I say this not to discourage you, but only in order to frame its making, to acknowledge that the baguette is at the center of our craft; it is our basic benchmark of skills in the artisan bread world. It is the elusive bird that lands on your palm one day and drops something on your head the next. . . . I have made thousands and thousands and still hope, every single time I touch them, that they might be better, more consistent, and more beautiful. And, knowing the challenge, living daily in the place where what I want to be and what I actually am leave room for improvement, I can offer encouragement: Judge your success by the faces of your eaters. Are they happily crunching and munching? Did they ignore your uneven shaping or imperfect crumb structure? Of course they did. So take that as an endorsement and give it another shot, and another, and another.

For the baguette, a slightly less sticky dough we call "French dough" was a good place to start. French dough (which I use on page 143 for the Poolish Baguette) is an all-purpose recipe that can be used for a dozen unique products, from boules and baguettes to rolls, sandwich loaves, and even pizza or focaccia. It is a backbone, a daily catechism that forced me to practice the same three foundational shapes over and over: the *boule*, a round form meaning "ball" and the basis of the French word for baker and bakery (*boulanger* and *boulangerie*, respectively); the *baguette*, a stick shape from the word for "wand" or "baton," with tapered ends; and the *bâtard*, an elliptical form, which is neither baguette nor boule, thus the name, meaning "bastard." Learning these shapes is a fundamental skill; doing them well is a lifelong pursuit, like that of the artist forever sketching the perfect circle.

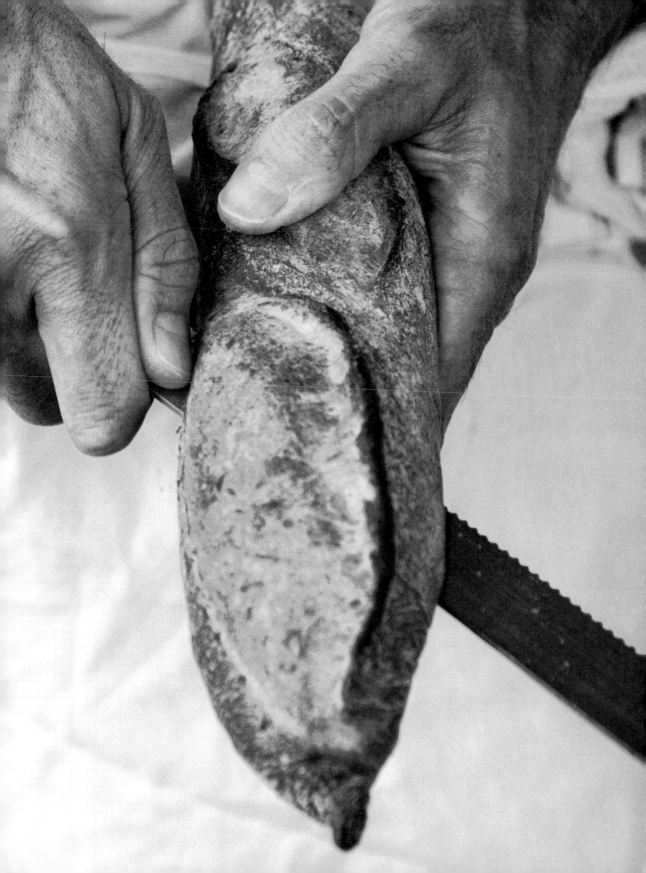

POOLISH BAGUETTE

Yield: 2 medium bâtards, or 4 baguettes, about 14 inches long

TOTAL FORMULA

PREFERMENTED FLOUR: 33%

INGREDIENTS	METRIC (GRAMS)	VOLUMETRIC (APPROXIMATE)	BAKER'S %
All-purpose flour	587	4¾ cups + 2 tablespoons	100%
Water	398	1¾ cups	68%
Salt, fine	12	2 teaspoons	2%
Yeast, dry instant	3	1 teaspoon	0.50%
Total Weight	1,000	All	170.50%

POOLISH

INGREDIENTS	METRIC (GRAMS)	VOLUMETRIC (APPROXIMATE)	BAKER'S %
All-purpose flour	194	1½ cups + 2 tablespoons	100%
Water	194	¾ cup	100%
Yeast, dry instant	Pinch	Pinch	0.10%
Total Weight	388	All	200.10%

FINAL DOUGH

INGREDIENTS	METRIC (GRAMS)	VOLUMETRIC (APPROXIMATE)
Water	204	1 cup
Poolish	388	All
All-purpose flour	393	3¼ cups
Salt, fine	12	2 teaspoons
Yeast, dry instant	3	1 teaspoon
Total Weight	1,000	All

RECIPE CONTINUES

DAY ONE

POOLISH

In a medium bowl, stir together the flour and yeast, then add the tepid water (75°F to 80°F).

Mix until smooth.

Cover and set at room temperature for 12 to 16 hours.

DAY TWO

MIX

Calculate temperatures. See Setting Temperatures, page 320, for instructions. Desired dough temperature: 76°F

In a large mixing bowl, combine the final dough water and poolish. Mix with your hands until the poolish is broken up in the water, then add the flour, salt, and yeast. Stir with the handle end of a wooden spoon until the dough forms a shaggy mass. If you find it easier, after some stirring, scrape the dough out of the bowl with a plastic scraper onto your work surface and knead briefly with your hands just until the dough comes together. Resist the urge to add more flour. Scrape the dough off the work surface and return it to the bowl for bulk fermentation.

BULK FERMENTATION

Scrape down the sides of the mixing bowl and allow the dough to rise, covered, for 2 hours at room temperature, folding as directed below.

FOLD

Fold after 15, 30, 45, and 60 minutes, then leave untouched for the second hour. See Folding, page 327, for instructions.

As you perform each series of folds, you'll begin to notice that the dough becomes smoother, stronger, and more cohesive.

DIVIDE AND PRESHAPE

For bâtards, divide the dough into 2 pieces weighing about 500 grams each. See Dividing, page 328, for instructions.

Preshape as rounds. See Preshaping, page 329, for instructions.

Cover and let rest for 10 to 15 minutes.

For baguettes, divide the dough into 4 pieces weighing about 250 grams each. See Dividing, page 328 for instructions.

Preshape as tubes. See Preshaping, page 329, for instructions.

Cover and let rest for 10 to 15 minutes.

SHAPE

Shape as bâtards or baguettes. See Shaping, page 331, for instructions.

Place, seam side up, on a floured couche, and pleat the couche between the loaves to support the sides as they rise.

PROOF | Cover and proof for 45 to 60 minutes at room temperature.

During the proof, preheat the oven to 475°F (for bâtards) or 500°F (for baguettes) with a baking stone and steaming system in place. See Baking, page 349, for instructions.

Transfer the loaves to parchment paper or a baker's peel, gently inverting them so that the underside, which was against the dusted tea towel or linen, becomes the top.

Score the bread prior to loading. See Scoring, page 339 for ideas and tips.

Slide the loaves onto the preheated baking stone.

BAKE | For bâtards, bake with steam for 35 to 40 minutes. After 20 minutes, carefully remove any steaming devices, lids, or parchment paper. Rotate the loaves on the stone.

At 35 to 40 minutes the bâtards should be well colored. Turn off the oven, prop open the door a few inches, and allow the loaves to dry for an additional 10 minutes.

For baguettes, bake with steam for 22 to 25 minutes. After 18 minutes, carefully remove any steaming devices, lids, parchment paper, or bowls. Rotate the loaves on the stone.

At 22 to 25 minutes the baguettes should be well colored and feel light when picked up. Turn off the oven, prop open the door a few inches, and allow the loaves to dry for an additional 5 minutes.

La Baguette

20% poolish, ~69% hydration, auto

1 k
- DOUGH, PULL AT DIVIDE, CHILL
- SHEET TO 4 MM, FREEZE

Decorative

SPRINKLE HALF WITH COCOA

CUT THROUGH OVERLAY w/ SCISSORS

THEN SCISSOR CUT, LAYING SECTIONS TO ONE SIDE

OIL

Overlay over the Baguette, trim ends with wheel

Chilling Shaped Loaves

There are times when the number of loaves proofing is greater than the amount of available oven space. It happens in bakeries of all sizes, and the home environment is no exception.

Refrigeration can be a great tool for slowing activity just enough to allow the oven to recover, or for holding shaped loaves for several hours or even overnight in some instances. As with each aspect of bread making, there is a learning curve. Different doughs rise and cool (and thus, slow their activity) at different rates, and tolerate cold (what bakers refer to as *retardation*) in differing degrees. With these baguettes, it may be that your oven can hold only a few at a time. If this is the case, cover and chill two of the four baguettes after shaping and leave the other two to rise at room temperature. To determine when to remove them from the cold, keep an eye on the chilled loaves, monitoring their proof.

After working the kinks out of your French dough baguettes you might try a slightly more challenging version, which uses a wetter, stickier dough. More water will make handling the dough a little tougher, but it will also open the interior structure more, leaving a lacy webbed landscape of fingertip-size air pockets. Grandma might say this loaf is "full of air!" and demand a refund. And it's the loaf that will send your baker friends into fits of envy. I present this as a "straight dough," meaning that there is no preferment. The straight dough baguette has a flavor that is simpler, a more straightforward presentation of natural sweetness (some say it tastes like the cornflakes cereal due to the malty sweetness) and a toasty quality from the bake.

STRAIGHT BAGUETTE

Yield: **Three 12- to 14-inch-long baguettes**

INGREDIENTS	METRIC (GRAMS)	VOLUMETRIC (APPROXIMATE)	BAKER'S %
All-purpose flour	380	3 cups + 2 tablespoons	100%
Water	285	1¼ cups	75%
Salt, fine	8	scant 1½ teaspoons	2%
Yeast, dry instant	2	¾ teaspoon	0.50%
Total Weight	675	All	177.50%

MIXING

Calculate temperatures. See Setting Temperatures, page 320, for instructions. Desired dough temperature: 75°F

In a large mixing bowl, whisk together the flour, salt, and yeast. Add the water and mix with your hand or the handle end of a wooden spoon until the dough forms a shaggy mass. With some doughs you may have to knead for a few strokes in the bowl to incorporate everything. If you find it easier, after some stirring, scrape the dough out of the bowl with a plastic scraper onto your work surface and knead briefly with your hands just until the dough comes together. Resist the urge to add more flour. Scrape the dough off the work surface and return it to the bowl for bulk fermentation.

BULK FERMENTATION

Scrape down the sides of the mixing bowl and allow the dough to rise, covered, for 3 hours at room temperature, folding as directed below.

FOLD

Fold after 20, 40, 60, and 120 minutes, then leave untouched for the last hour. See Folding, page 327, for instructions.

As you perform each series of folds, you'll begin to notice that the dough becomes smoother, stronger, and more cohesive.

DIVIDE AND PRESHAPE

Divide the dough into 3 pieces weighing about 225 grams each. See Dividing, page 328, for instructions.

Preshape as tubes. See Preshaping, page 329, for instructions.

Cover and let rest for 10 to 15 minutes.

SHAPE

Shape as baguettes roughly 12 to 14 inches long (or longer if your baking stone will allow). See Shaping, page 331, for instructions.

Place, seam side up, on a floured couche, and pleat the couche between the loaves to support the sides as they rise.

RECIPE CONTINUES

PROOF Cover and proof for 45 to 60 minutes at room temperature.

During the proof, preheat the oven to 500°F with a baking stone and steaming system in place. See Baking, page 349, for instructions.

Transfer the loaves to parchment paper or a baker's peel, gently inverting them so that the underside, which was against the dusted tea towel or linen, becomes the top.

Score the bread prior to loading. See Scoring, page 339, for ideas and tips.

BAKE Slide the loaves onto the preheated baking stone.

Bake with steam for 22 to 25 minutes. After 18 minutes, carefully remove any steaming devices, lids, or parchment paper. Rotate the loaves on the stone.

At 22 to 25 minutes the loaves should be well colored and feel light when picked up. Turn off the oven, prop open the door a few inches, and allow the loaves to dry for an additional 5 minutes.

If "French Baguette" grew up in the city, "country baguette," well . . . he lives outside town. His wine bottle never leaves the kitchen table; it stands sentry for cheese slab and home-cured meat—a centerpiece worthy of any season. Add a knife and a glass and an apple from the barrel, and one can live, unfussed and happy, at this table. As you would expect, "country" isn't the dresser; "French" is with his pressed pants, cane, and pince-nez—"country" likes his hands in the dirt, substance over form, age before beauty, and so forth. If delicious is on the menu but fuss seems a misfit, you should start here.

COUNTRY BAGUETTE

Yield: Three 12- to 14-inch-long baguettes

TOTAL FORMULA

PREFERMENTED FLOUR: 20%

INGREDIENTS	METRIC (GRAMS)	VOLUMETRIC (APPROXIMATE)	BAKER'S %
All-purpose flour	320	2⅔ cups	85%
Whole wheat flour	56	scant ½ cup	15%
Water	274	1 cup + 3 tablespoons	73%
Salt, fine	8	scant 1½ teaspoons	2%
Yeast, dry instant	2	¾ teaspoon	0.50%
Sourdough culture	15	1 tablespoon	4%
Total Weight	675	All	179.50%

LIQUID LEVAIN

INGREDIENTS	METRIC (GRAMS)	VOLUMETRIC (APPROXIMATE)	BAKER'S %
All-purpose flour	75	⅔ cup	100%
Water	94	½ cup	125%
Sourdough culture	15	1 tablespoon	20%
Total Weight	184	All	245%

FINAL DOUGH

INGREDIENTS	METRIC (GRAMS)	VOLUMETRIC (APPROXIMATE)
Water	180	½ cup + 3 tablespoons
Liquid levain	184	All
All-purpose flour	245	2 cups
Whole wheat flour	56	scant ½ cup
Salt, fine	8	scant 1½ teaspoons
Yeast, dry instant	2	¾ teaspoon
Total Weight	675	All

DAY ONE

LIQUID LEVAIN

In a medium bowl, combine the tepid water (75°F to 80°F) and the sourdough culture. Mix with your hands and fingers until the culture is broken up and well distributed in the water, then add the flour.

Mix until smooth.

Cover and set at room temperature for 12 to 16 hours.

MIX

Calculate temperatures. See Setting Temperatures, page 320, for instructions. Desired dough temperature: 76°F

In a large mixing bowl, combine the final dough water and liquid levain. Mix with your hands until the levain is broken up in the water, then add the flours, salt, and yeast. Stir with the handle end of a wooden spoon until the dough forms a shaggy mass. If you find it easier, after some stirring, scrape the dough out of the bowl with a plastic scraper onto your work surface and knead briefly with your hands just until the dough comes together. Resist the urge to add more flour. Scrape the dough off the work surface and return it to the bowl for bulk fermentation.

BULK FERMENTATION

Scrape down the sides of the mixing bowl and allow the dough to rise, covered, for 2 hours at room temperature, folding as directed below.

FOLD

Fold after 20, 40, and 60 minutes, then leave untouched for the second hour. See Folding, page 327, for instructions.

As you perform each series of folds, you'll begin to notice that the dough becomes smoother, stronger, and more cohesive.

DIVIDE AND PRESHAPE

Divide the dough into 3 pieces weighing about 225 grams each. See Dividing, page 332, for instructions.

Preshape as tubes. See Preshaping, page 329, for instructions.

Cover and let rest for 10 to 15 minutes.

SHAPE

Shape as baguettes roughly 12 to 14 inches long (or longer if your baking stone will allow) and place on a floured baker's linen (couche) or tea towel, seam side up. Pleat the couche between the loaves to support their sides as they rise. See Shaping, page 331 for instructions.

PROOF

Cover and proof for 45 to 60 minutes at room temperature.

RECIPE CONTINUES

During the proof, preheat the oven to 500°F with a baking stone and steaming system in place. See Baking, page 349, for instructions.

Transfer the loaves to parchment paper or a baker's peel, gently inverting them so that the underside, which was against the dusted tea towel or linen, becomes the top.

Score the bread prior to loading. See Scoring, page 339, for ideas and tips.

BAKE Slide the loaves onto the preheated baking stone.

Bake with steam for 22 to 25 minutes. After 18 minutes, carefully remove any steaming devices, lids, or parchment paper. Rotate the loaves on the stone.

At 22 to 25 minutes the loaves should be well colored and feel light when picked up. Turn off the oven, prop open the door a few inches, and allow the loaves to dry for an additional 5 minutes.

By 7:00 a.m. the bâtards, French loaves, and other early breads are out of the oven, cooled, and packaged in paper bags, and the baguettes are shaped. The dark breads have finished baking and the bread-packing station, right next to the oven, begins to overflow with racks and stacks upon stacks and baskets of bread, all queuing for a temporary home at a restaurant, market, or bakery counter before heading to your hand and mouth. In a matter of hours, bags of flour, goopy pre-ferments and soaking buckets of grains, tubs of eggs and cream, bricks of yeast, and bags of salt transform from inedible to incredible, a feast of crisp crunch and deliciousness. This daily miracle is anything but common. There is life here; within the folds of this doing, there is something to see, to appreciate, to love.

We push the oven temperature even higher in preparation for baguettes. Their open interior, toasty, cracker-crisp crust, and oven-kissed cuts must bake just long enough to color but not so long that they dry out. Their ratio of crust to crumb (the relationship between the area of the outside and the area of the interior) is very high, allowing them to bake in a relatively short time: 21 to 23 minutes. Getting two hundred or three hundred baguettes, each individually cut five to seven times with a razor, through the oven can take an hour or more. The motions we make, the use of the transfer peel that holds the unbaked loaf as it is moved from the linen cloth (couche) to the canvas of the loader, the cutting, the slide of the loader, the steaming—these things become natural with time, ingrained, embedded in physical memory, a tai chi sequence of baking judo.

Around 9:00 a.m. we break for lunch, sitting as a team when everyone reaches a stopping point. The mixer looks up, the baker steps back, those at the bench scrape boards or sweep and begin to transition to the second part of the day. "How are you looking?" "Ready to sit?" Consensus is reached; maybe we throw a lunch pizza into the oven and then pause for a few minutes before returning to spend the remaining portion of our day shaping our breads that will be cold-fermented and finish our setup and "prep" work for the next day.

Slowly these tasks became natural, my skills improved, and I began to recognize landmarks on our daily route. I was a crappy baker, no doubt. I could barely shape and hadn't even made my way to mixing or doing oven work, but I could tell good stories about my children, who provided daily opportunities for laughter and also tears over the challenges of parenting. There were bumps, to be sure. If I had known exactly where we were headed financially I might have been too scared to make the leap from our New York life. I lay awake one night in the throes of a panic attack, terrified that the decision to move was going to bankrupt us. But Julie began teaching voice and made enough to buy our food and we did everything we could to rid ourselves of extra expenses. At the bakery the word got out that although I was a novice baker I could run spreadsheets like a boss, and I became a fixture at financial and operational meetings. And I was willing to do any job; I drove the bakery delivery van one day a week, dropping bread off at wholesale accounts, restaurants, and groceries. Not my favorite task but I was willing to do anything possible to make myself valuable while waiting for some level of proficiency to show up.

As the day proceeds we look at what we have done, inspecting the quality of each bread, viewing it against our expectations, the previous day's work, the bar we hold in our mind's eye that separates mediocre from good or great. After a decade of doing this work I have yet to complete a bake day and take off my apron satisfied. I have come close, and to many, the things that I nitpick about may seem inconsequential. But this may also be the nature of craft; I can always improve, shape better, bake better, mix better. There is no arriving; perfection exists not for the maker but for the recipient. The perfect loaf and the misshapen one are celebrated in equal measure by my children as I come through the door holding everything in my arms.

HOME

Defining "home" is best done in retrospect—standing within four walls of our current existence doesn't allow the space or frame of time and place to provide the long view. As I watch my children grow I wonder what, of all this, will they long for or remember? What will be their "home" of memory? Will it be smells, a baking tradition, the music of voices and instruments, an overserious father? Memories are laid like bedrock, deep, under our very feet, invisible in the forming but ever active. There are things that I hope will remain as family memories—small weekly rituals, meals, seasonal recurrences, and holiday events. I may be wrong, but some of these might be keepers, and if strung together may fill their scrapbooks of home. Only time will tell.

Arlo Rennie Philip arrived in May 2008. I wasn't sure what to do with a boy; at first I was worried, concerned for silly reasons that I would feel awkward kissing and loving him as much as I did my girls. Those fears were immediately thrown out—he kisses me relentlessly and as I return his love, we are bound together, savoring the inescapable rope of family bonds.

There is an intersection in my house. Footpaths converge, and patterns of traffic are marked by crumb trails leading to and fro. At the center of this crossroads is a board as deep as a counter and wide as a baguette. It is constantly littered with a chronology of stale remnants and new hunks of loaves, a bread knife, and butter. It is here that little hands have learned to saw and smear, biting and tugging as they move along their merry way, back to Legoland or the woodstove to enjoy the snack. *Miche* is the word that the French use to describe a large round loaf. Many miches are over a foot in diameter with a round nest-shape that is similar to the form made when arms are wrapped to hold or embrace. These large loaves are our abundance, our sustenance, and our comfort; sitting on the cutting board, cut side down, ever diminishing and sustaining in fulfilling their purpose and ensuring our enjoyment. Our bread, our soul food.

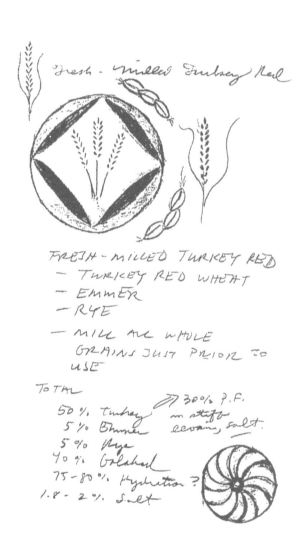

FRESH - MILLED TURKEY RED
— TURKEY RED WHEAT
— EMMER
— RYE

— MILL ALL WHOLE
   GRAINS JUST PRIOR TO
   USE

TOTAL   30% P.F.
   50% Turkey   in stiff
   5% Emmer   eevains, salt.
   5% Rye
   40% Galahad
   75-80% Hydration ?
   1.8 - 2% Salt

FRESH-MILLED MICHE

Yield: **1 large miche, or 2 medium boules**

TOTAL FORMULA

PREFERMENTED FLOUR: 30%

INGREDIENTS	METRIC (GRAMS)	VOLUMETRIC (APPROXIMATE)	BAKER'S %
Wheat, freshly milled	323	2½ cups + 3 tablespoons	50%
All-purpose flour	259	2 cups + 2 tablespoons	40%
Emmer, freshly milled (can substitute rye, spelt, Khorasan, or einkorn)	32	¼ cup	5%
Rye, freshly milled	32	¼ cup + 1 tablespoon	5%
Water	505	2¼ cups	78%
Salt, fine	13	2¼ teaspoons	2%
Yeast, dry instant	1	heaping ¼ teaspoon	0.20%
Sourdough culture	35	heaping 2 tablespoons	5.40%
Total Weight	1,200	All	185.60%

STIFF LEVAIN

INGREDIENTS	METRIC (GRAMS)	VOLUMETRIC (APPROXIMATE)	BAKER'S %
Wheat, freshly milled	194	1½ cups + 2 tablespoons	100%
Water	113	½ cup	65%
Salt, fine	4	½ teaspoon	2%
Sourdough culture	35	heaping 2 tablespoons	20%
Total Weight	346	All	187%

FINAL DOUGH (CONT. ON FOLLOWING PAGE)

INGREDIENTS	METRIC (GRAMS)	VOLUMETRIC (APPROXIMATE)
Water	392	1¾ cups
Stiff levain	346	All
All-purpose flour	259	2 cups + 2 tablespoons
Wheat, freshly milled	129	1 cup + 1 tablespoon
Emmer, freshly milled (optionally substitute rye, spelt, Khorasan, or einkorn)	32	¼ cup
Rye, freshly milled	32	¼ cup + 1 tablespoon

FINAL DOUGH (CONT. FROM PREVIOUS PAGE)

INGREDIENTS	METRIC (GRAMS)	VOLUMETRIC (APPROXIMATE)
Salt, fine	9	1¾ teaspoons
Yeast, dry instant	1	heaping ¼ teaspoon
Total Weight	1,200	All

DAY ONE

PREPARE

Mill the grain for the stiff levain, according to the mill manufacturer's directions, making the finest flour possible.

STIFF LEVAIN

In a medium bowl, combine the tepid water (75°F to 80°F) and the sourdough culture. Mix with your hands and fingers until the culture is broken up and well distributed in the water, then add the flour and salt.

Mix briefly, then knead until smooth.

Cover and set at room temperature for 12 to 16 hours.

DAY TWO

PREPARE

Mill the grains for the final dough.

MIX

Calculate temperatures. See Setting Temperatures, page 320, for instructions. Desired dough temperature: 76°F

In a large mixing bowl, combine the final dough water and stiff levain. Mix with your hands until the levain is broken up in the water, then add the flours, salt, and yeast. Stir with the handle end of a wooden spoon until the dough forms a shaggy mass. If you find it easier, after some stirring, scrape the dough out of the bowl with a plastic scraper onto your work surface and knead briefly with your hands just until the dough comes together. Resist the urge to add more flour. Scrape the dough off the work surface and return it to the bowl for bulk fermentation.

BULK FERMENTATION

Scrape down the sides of the mixing bowl and allow the dough to rise, covered, for 3 hours at room temperature, folding as directed below.

FOLD

Fold after 15, 30, 45, 60, and 120 minutes, then leave untouched for the last hour. See Folding, page 327, for instructions.

As you perform each series of folds, you'll begin to notice that the dough becomes smoother, stronger, and more cohesive.

RECIPE CONTINUES

DIVIDE AND PRESHAPE

For a single large miche, preshape as a round. See Preshaping, page 329, for instructions.

Cover and let rest for 15 minutes.

For 2 loaves, divide the dough into 2 pieces weighing about 600 grams each. See Dividing, page 328 for instructions.

Preshape as rounds. See Preshaping, page 329, for instructions.

Cover and let rest for 10 to 15 minutes.

SHAPE

Shape as boules. See Shaping, page 331, for instructions.

Place the large miche, seam side up, in a floured banneton or floured, towel-lined bowl, approximately 10 inches wide and 4 inches deep.

Place the two medium boules, seam side up, in floured bannetons or floured, towel-lined bowls, approximately 9 inches wide and 3½ inches deep.

PROOF

Cover and proof for 50 to 60 minutes at room temperature.

BAKE

During the proof, preheat the oven to 450°F with a baking stone and steaming system in place. See Baking, page 349, for instructions.

Transfer the loaves to parchment paper or a baker's peel, gently inverting them so that the underside, which was against the dusted tea towel or banneton, becomes the top.

Score the bread prior to loading. See Scoring, page 339, for ideas and tips.

Slide the loaves onto the preheated baking stone.

Bake with steam for 35 to 40 minutes. After 30 minutes, carefully remove any steaming devices, lids, parchment paper, or bowls. Rotate the loaves on the stone. If making a single large loaf, bake 10 minutes longer than the two medium loaves.

At 35 to 40 minutes the loaves should be well colored. Turn off the oven, prop open the door a few inches, and allow the loaves to dry for an additional 10 minutes.

Thanksgiving is the best holiday. It holds its moorings against the tide of year-round commercial tsunamis, where drugstore Halloween sales debark in the wake of Labor Day specials and stale candy corn stares at Santa Claus from the bargain bin. Thanksgiving is a time to gather and celebrate seasonal bounty with food as the centerpiece and spokes of family and friends—none excluded by race, religion, or sports affiliation—equally able to pause and be thankful.

As the holiday winds its way across the United States, the course changes regionally and traditions vary, rightfully reflecting who we are, *where* we are, and what we come from. Tofurky (soy mock turkey) has yet to eclipse the feathered bird, but almost everything else is up for grabs. In the South we show our colors with cornbread dressing and rice stuffing; in California, a spinach salad with olives, blood orange, caramelized almonds, and avocado complements the meal. In Vermont, we may deglaze with fresh cider, make apple stuffing, or serve a salad of roasted beets, blue cheese, and maple syrup. At the heart of tradition is the use of what is at hand, for memories are strongest when tied to places.

Oma's house was our place. We'd race from the car to her door, entering the aroma envelope of roasting turkey, dressing with herbs and celery, and steaming boiled potatoes. Her large clawfoot table was always expanded to accommodate all auxiliary leaves, then covered with a pressed linen tablecloth and set with silver cutlery, wedding china, and crystal glassware.

Moving deeper into the house, we glimpsed her pies. Our traditional favorites—pumpkin, pecan, mincemeat, and molasses—and the newcomer, a mile-high strawberry pie sitting in the icebox until service. I hope that if I cannot take my children to Thanksgiving at Oma's, then perhaps I am, in my own way, giving them some experience worthy of nostalgia, some winged wedge of memory to which they may return someday in the same way I do when seated and ready to bite the point of a pie slice or enjoy a soft roll.

PAIN DE MIE **PAGE 166**

PAIN DE MIE

Yield: **One 9 by 5-inch loaf, 25 to 30 small rolls, or 15 cinnamon rolls**

As with the brioche formula, two batch sizes are offered below. I can't imagine an instance when a single loaf of bread, a single pan of cinnamon rolls, or just a few dozen rolls will do—but I am a bread hog, and will always make two and freeze the backup if I don't give it away! Consider what you would like to bake, and how many, and then refer to the section below to determine which batch size is appropriate.

INGREDIENTS	750 GRAMS		1,500 GRAMS		
	METRIC (GRAMS)	VOLUMETRIC (APPROXIMATE)	METRIC (GRAMS)	VOLUMETRIC (APPROXIMATE)	BAKER'S %
All-purpose flour	426	3½ cups	852	7 cups + 1 tablespoon	100%
Milk	85	¼ cup + 2 tablespoons	170	¾ cup	20%
Water	136	½ cup + 2 tablespoons	273	1¼ cups	32%
Salt, fine	9	1½ teaspoons	17	scant 1 tablespoon	2%
Yeast, dry instant	9	1 tablespoon	17	scant 2 tablespoons	2%
Butter, unsalted, soft	64	¼ cup + 1½ teaspoons (4½ table-spoons)	128	½ cup + 1 tablespoon (9 tablespoons)	15%
Honey	21	1 tablespoon	43	2 tablespoons	5%
Total Weight	750	All	1,500	All	176%

PREPARE   Warm the milk to room temperature (70°F to 75°F).

Calculate temperatures. See Setting Temperatures, page 320, for instructions. Desired dough temperature: 78°F

MIX   In a large mixing bowl, stir together the flour, salt, and yeast. Add the water, milk, butter, and honey. Mix with a hand or the handle end of a wooden spoon until the dough forms a shaggy mass. With some doughs you may have to knead for a few strokes in the bowl to incorporate everything. If you find it easier, after some stirring, scrape the dough out of the bowl with a plastic scraper onto your work surface and knead

RECIPE CONTINUES

MIX CONT. briefly with your hands just until the dough comes together. Resist the urge to add more flour. Scrape the dough off the work surface and return it to the bowl for bulk fermentation.

BULK FERMENTATION Scrape down the sides of the mixing bowl and allow the dough to rise, covered, for 1½ hours at room temperature, folding as directed below.

FOLD Fold after 15, 30, and 60 minutes, then leave untouched until the divide. See Folding, page 327, for instructions.

As you perform each series of folds, you'll begin to notice that the dough becomes smoother, stronger, and more cohesive.

DIVIDE This versatile dough can be used to make many basic baked goods, including pull-apart rolls, a soft white pan loaf, or cinnamon rolls.

HERE ARE WEIGHTS **SANDWICH LOAF**, 9 by 5-inch pan: 750 grams

PULL-APART ROLLS (each): 28 grams

CINNAMON ROLLS (TOTAL): 750 grams

Divide the dough according to what you want to make, referencing the weights shown above. The batch size will accommodate a variety of options. See Dividing, page 328, for instructions.

SANDWICH LOAF Spray or grease a 9 by 5-inch loaf pan.

Preshape as a tube. See Preshaping, page 329, for instructions.

Cover and let rest for 15 minutes.

Shape as a pan loaf. See Shaping, page 331, for instructions. The final tube should be the same length as the intended pan.

After shaping, place the tube in the prepared pan.

Cover and proof until the dough is about 1½ inches above the edge of the pan, about 60 to 75 minutes.

BAKE Toward the end of the proof, preheat the oven to 425°F.

Bake the loaf for 30 to 35 minutes. Rotate the loaf after 20 minutes. Bake until the top is deeply colored and the sides are golden.

Immediately after baking, remove from the pan and place on a rack to cool. Cooling in the pan will cause the crust to be soggy.

Lightly grease a 13 by 18-inch sheet pan, or line it with parchment paper, or lightly grease a cast-iron pan.

PULL-APART ROLLS

Divide as many rolls as you need. See Dividing, page 328 for instructions.

Shape into rolls and place on your pan, distributing them evenly with roughly ½-inch spaces between them. See Shaping, page 331 for instructions.

Cover and proof until they are touching, 50 to 60 minutes.

BAKE

Toward the end of the proof, preheat the oven to 425°F.

Bake the rolls for 18 to 22 minutes. Bake until the sides are golden and the top is well colored. For more shine, brush with melted butter after baking.

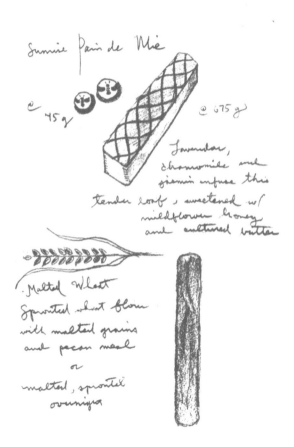

Sunrise Pain de Mie

@ 45 g   @ 675 g

Lavender, chamomile and jasmin infuse this tender loaf, sweetened w/ wildflower honey and cultured butter

· Malted Wheat Sprouted wheat flour with malted grains and pecan meal

or

malted, sprouted ovemigra

Before she could speak, we pushed birthday cakes on Anthem. But as soon as she could talk, the homemade tiered cake with pink icing and rock sugar bling, pretty as it was, was voted down for something simpler. Something warm, sugar-iced, and cinnamon-infused. I am sure there are others who have found the cinnamon roll worthy of birthdays. For me, I see no reason to celebrate only annually, and will eat them daily with black coffee.

CINNAMON ROLLS

Place a 750-gram piece of Pain de Mie dough (page 166) on a lightly floured surface. Gently pat and stretch into a rough 9 by 6-inch rectangle. Cover and allow it to relax for 15 to 30 minutes. While the dough rests, prepare the filling.

CINNAMON ROLL FILLING

INGREDIENTS	METRIC (GRAMS)	VOLUMETRIC (APPROXIMATE)
Brown sugar	250	1¼ cups
Cinnamon	20	1 tablespoon
Milk, cream, or egg wash, for brushing the dough		

Stir together the brown sugar and cinnamon. Set aside.

Generously grease or spray a 9 by 13-inch baking dish.

After the rest, lift the dough with a bench scraper to be sure it is not sticking. Lightly flour the surface underneath. Roll and pat the dough into a 14 by 20-inch rectangle with the long side running horizontally on your work surface. If the dough resists being stretched or rolled, let it relax for another 15 minutes, covered.

Using a pastry brush, paint the entire surface of the dough with milk, cream, or egg wash.

Evenly spread the brown sugar and cinnamon mixture over the surface of the dough. Leave an inch margin of dough along the long side, closest to you, with no sugar or cinnamon filling. This will allow the rolls to be sealed closed.

Begin at the long edge of dough farthest from you. Roll the dough toward you, tensioning it slightly as you go, stretching it gently away from yourself, then rolling forward to take up the slack.

Repeat this process until you reach the edge closest to you.

Brush the final edge again with egg wash. Press to seal the tube closed.

With a chef's knife or sharp bench knife cut 1 to 1¼-inch segments (about 15 pieces) and place in your baking dish. Distribute the pieces evenly, leaving ¼-inch spaces between them.

Cover and proof until the rolls are light and puffy, 60 to 75 minutes.

BAKE Toward the end of the proof, preheat the oven to 425°F. Bake for 22 to 26 minutes. Rotate after 15 minutes. The rolls are done when they are golden brown.

While the rolls bake, prepare the glaze.

RECIPE CONTINUES

CINNAMON ROLL GLAZE

INGREDIENTS	METRIC (GRAMS)	VOLUMETRIC (APPROXIMATE)
Confectioners' sugar	227	2 cups
Butter, unsalted, softened	56	2 tablespoons
Vanilla extract or whiskey	5	1 teaspoon
Milk	17	1 tablespoon

Sift the confectioners' sugar and mix with the butter and vanilla or whiskey.

Whisk to combine, then add the milk all at once. Whisk again.

After baking, the rolls can be left in the baking dish and glazed after they have cooled for 5 minutes.

Alternatively, immediately after baking invert the baking dish onto a large platter or sheet pan. To do this, place the platter or pan over the rolls and hold it and the baking dish together. Invert the two, letting the rolls slowly fall. Lift off the baking dish. Glaze after they have cooled for 5 minutes.

The lights are finally out. Teeth have been brushed, books are read, the remnants of a day are processed in reflected light from the hall. This is when I lean in to tuck them in, wedging covers under small bodies—a barrier against cold and dark—and then embrace, smother, kiss, and field final questions. "Will you be here in the morning, Daddy?" Most days the answer is "No," it's a baker's life, and so forth, but occasionally I get to say, "Yes." And I ask, "You want pancakes?" "Yes!" They never lose enthusiasm for the morning space occupied by hot tea, hot pancakes, butter, syrup, and family.

These are 100 percent whole wheat not because our health will soar from extra fiber, minerals, and wheat germ, but because they taste better and are as light and fluffy as any made with white flour. Endless options exist for substitutions— whole rye, whole spelt, whole buckwheat, or many other grains may replace or be blended, gram for gram, with the whole wheat. Some grains will require more moisture; look for batter consistency and adjust as necessary with buttermilk or milk.

Pancakes

A few tips for fluffier pancakes.

Room-temperature ingredients combine more easily, more smoothly, and with less mixing. Eggs may be left out overnight or warmed briefly in a bowl of warm water. Buttermilk may be warmed briefly in a microwave or in a metal bowl set on the griddle or frying pan for a couple of minutes as it preheats.

Stir the batter gently, until barely homogeneous, with a rubber spatula, using a folding motion, as you would for making mousse or a tender cake batter.

Rest the batter before cooking. Even a couple of minutes will be enough for the baking soda and baking powder to do their work, lightening the batter before it hits the griddle. Modern baking powder is double-acting, meaning that it works two times—once when hydrated and then again when heated.

WHEAT PANCAKES

Yield: **Ten to twelve 4- to 5-inch pancakes**

INGREDIENT	METRIC (GRAMS)	VOLUMETRIC (APPROXIMATE)
Butter, unsalted	28	2 tablespoons
Whole wheat flour	200	1⅔ cups
Baking powder	4	1 teaspoon
Baking soda	3	½ teaspoon
Salt, fine	1.5	¼ teaspoon
Sugar (or substitute 1 tablespoon of honey or maple syrup)	24	2 tablespoons
Eggs, large	100	2
Buttermilk	350	1½ cups
Butter, for greasing the pan or griddle		

PREPARE

Have all ingredients at room temperature.

Melt the 2 tablespoons of butter and allow it to cool slightly.

MIX

In a medium bowl, whisk together the flour, baking powder, baking soda, salt, and (if using) sugar.

In a small bowl, whisk together the cooled melted butter, eggs, buttermilk, and (if using) honey or maple syrup.

Pour the wet ingredients into the dry ingredients, stirring gently until mostly combined; a few small lumps are OK.

Set aside the batter to rest while you preheat an electric griddle to 350°F, or heat a frying pan over medium heat.

COOK

With a small amount of butter, grease your griddle or pan. Use a paper towel to fully distribute the fat and remove any excess.

Using a ¼-cup measure, drop the batter onto the griddle or pan, spreading it into 4- to 5-inch circles with the bottom of the cup if necessary.

Cook on the first side until bubbles cover the surface and the edges are set. Flip the pancakes, and cook an additional 1 to 2 minutes on the second side. Repeat with the remaining batter.

Enjoy with maple syrup, honey, molasses, or jam!

I've never dreamed of sugarplums like the children in Moore's "A Visit from St. Nicholas," but I have certainly felt my heart quicken at the thought of a batter rising, waiting for stirred eggs and melted butter, the sputter of pancakes on a griddle, coffee brewing, warm sleepy faces coming down the stairs, delighting in risen pancakes. The evening before (or the morning, if you would like pancakes for dinner) buttermilk, yeast, and flour are mixed and allowed to sit. The resulting pancakes rise over the course of time, infusing the breakfast plate with the flavor of fresh bread. They may also be prepared using sourdough culture for yet another level of flavor complexity.

RISEN PANCAKES

Yield: **Ten to twelve 4- to 5-inch pancakes**

INGREDIENT	METRIC (GRAMS)	VOLUMETRIC (APPROXIMATE)
Whole wheat flour	200	1⅔ cups
Yeast, dry instant, or 1 tablespoon (15 grams) of sourdough culture	Pinch	Pinch
Buttermilk	350	1½ cups
Butter, unsalted	28	2 tablespoons
Sugar (or substitute 1 tablespoon of honey or maple syrup)	24	2 tablespoons
Salt, fine	1.5	¼ teaspoon
Baking powder	2	½ teaspoon
Baking soda	3	½ teaspoon
Eggs, large	100	2
Butter, for greasing the pan or griddle		

DAY ONE

PREPARE

In a medium bowl, combine the flour and yeast.*

Add the buttermilk and stir until combined.

Cover and allow to rise at room temperature overnight, or for 8 to 10 hours.

DAY TWO

MIX

Melt the 2 tablespoons of butter and allow it to cool slightly.

In a small bowl whisk together the sugar (if using), salt, baking powder, and baking soda.

In a separate small bowl, whisk the eggs, then add the honey or maple syrup (if using), the cooled melted butter, and the dry ingredients. Stir to combine.

Pour the egg mixture into the flour mixture, which has risen overnight. Stir to combine.

Set the bowl to rest while you preheat an electric griddle to 350°F, or heat a frying pan over medium heat.

* If using sourdough culture, add it to the buttermilk and whisk to distribute, then add the flour.

COOK

With a small amount of butter, grease your griddle or pan. Use a paper towel to fully distribute the fat and remove any excess.

Using a ¼-cup measure, drop the batter onto the griddle or pan, spreading it into 4- to 5-inch circles with the bottom of the cup.

Cook on the first side until bubbles cover the surface and the edges are set. Flip the pancakes and cook an additional 1 to 2 minutes on the second side. Repeat with the remaining batter.

Enjoy with maple syrup, honey, molasses, or jam!

A scone is a crisp combination of butter, tenderness, and crunch. Like pasta, pizza, vanilla cake, and white walls, scones take color well—they're the perfect place to use your culinary imagination. This scone was inspired by spiced tea, or chai, which I learned about from an Indian friend. Hot milk, black tea, grated ginger, and a spoonful of sugar are combined and steeped, then strained, and served. The tea is invigorating, perfect in cold months. The scones are best if made with freshly ground whole spices.

Spices

The difference between freshly ground spices and the dusty jars of ground cloves you inherited from grandma is similar to the gap between ramen flavor packets and bone broth made with aromatics. I don't use freshly ground spices for everything, but in recipes such as Ginger Scones (page 182) or Spiced Honey Bread (page 209), the difference is worth the effort.

If you don't have a dedicated spice mill, keep an eye out for one at your thrift store. I see them all the time. I also have a small mortar and pestle, which I use with surprising regularity and excellent results, even if just for bruising things such as cumin seeds before adding them to a dish.

If you need to go with packaged ground spices, check to see that what you have is still vibrant and aromatic, or, mention the name of a well-reviewed spice house to a loved one a few weeks before your birthday. You, your mouth, and those you bake for will thank you!

Scones are versatile and can be bent toward sweet or savory. If you'd like, we can spend time debating whether these are simply biscuits with extra ingredients or true scones. While you give your opening remarks, considering the ingredients and lack of eggs and citing "traditional" accompaniments to afternoon tea, I will stuff my face. I will enjoy the hit of pepper on the top crust, the color of fresh chives, the chew of roasted corn, the pockets of melted cheese, and the crunch of grits. So keep talking; my mouth is full, anyway.

You may imagine these with a zesty bowl of tomato soup or even rich vegetable stew. . . . Honestly, I have never saved any for dinner.

Egg Wash

Brushing or glazing is quite common before baking. It adds to the color and the shine of the finished product, and helps toppings stick. One whole egg, whisked together with a few grains of salt to help break up the proteins, is sufficient for a few batches of bread or scones. Once made, the egg wash may be stored, covered in the fridge for up to 3 days.

You can also add another egg to any leftover wash and scramble up some breakfast.

GINGER SCONES

Yield: **8 medium scones**

INGREDIENTS	METRIC (GRAMS)	VOLUMETRIC (APPROXIMATE)
All-purpose flour	240	2 cups
Baking powder	8	2 teaspoons
Baking soda	3	½ teaspoon
Salt, fine	3	½ teaspoon
Black pepper, freshly ground	1	½ teaspoon
Cinnamon, freshly ground	2	1 teaspoon
Coriander, freshly ground	1	½ teaspoon
Cardamom, freshly ground	1	½ teaspoon
Cloves, freshly ground	0.5	¼ teaspoon
Ginger, crystallized	92	½ cup
Butter, unsalted	60	¼ cup (4 tablespoons)
Heavy cream	177	¾ cup
Brown sugar, light or dark	53	¼ cup
Egg wash		
Coarse sugar, for garnish (optional)		

PREPARE

Position an oven rack in the top third of the oven.

Preheat the oven to 425°F.

Lightly grease a 13 by 18-inch sheet pan, or line it with parchment paper.

Weigh and chill the dry ingredients.

Chop the crystallized ginger into pea-size pieces.

Cut the butter into ⅛-inch-thick slices. Chill until use.

MIX

In a medium bowl, whisk together the flour, baking powder, baking soda, and salt. Add the ground dry spices.

Add the cold butter and toss to coat with the dry ingredients. Then press the butter slices between your thumb and forefinger into small flat pieces or "leaves."

Add the chopped crystallized ginger and toss to combine.

RECIPE CONTINUES

In a small bowl, whisk together the cream and brown sugar.

MIX CONT. Add the wet ingredients to the dry ingredients and mix gently until the mixture is just combined. The dough should be firm and barely cohesive (some dry bits are OK).

Transfer the dough to a lightly floured work surface, and fold a few times to incorporate any dry bits if necessary.

SHAPE Pat the dough into a circle about 1 inch thick and 7 inches across. At this point you may chill the dough until set for easier cutting.

Cut the dough into 8 pieces with a chef's knife, cutting directly down; don't saw, as this will interfere with the rising. Arrange the scones evenly on the sheet pan, or freeze, well wrapped, for up to a month.

Brush the scones with egg wash and garnish with coarse sugar, if desired.

BAKE Bake for 18 to 22 minutes on the top rack, rotating after 14 minutes, until they are lightly golden and firm to the touch.

If you are baking them after freezing, keep them covered and allow them to thaw overnight in the refrigerator before baking them as directed above.

ROASTED CORN-CHIVE SCONES

Yield: **8 medium scones**

INGREDIENTS	METRIC (GRAMS)	VOLUMETRIC (APPROXIMATE)
Corn kernels, fresh or frozen	125	¾ cup
Water, boiling	100	scant ½ cup
Corn grits, instant or regular	75	½ cup
All-purpose flour	230	scant 2 cups
Baking powder	8	2 teaspoons
Salt, fine	6	1 teaspoon
Black pepper, freshly ground	1	1 teaspoon
Butter, unsalted	56	¼ cup (4 tablespoons)
Cheese, cheddar, grated	56	½ cup
Chives, fresh, snipped into ¼-inch pieces	14	¼ cup
Heavy cream	170	¾ cup
Egg wash		
Black pepper, freshly cracked, for garnish		

PREPARE

Position an oven rack in the top third of the oven.

Preheat the oven to 425°F.

Lightly grease a 13 by 18-inch sheet pan, or line it with parchment paper.

Char the corn kernels in a dry cast-iron skillet over high heat until colored—some charring and smoky spots are good. Chill until use.

Pour the boiling water over the corn grits. Chill until use.

Measure the dry ingredients. Chill until use.

Cut the butter into ⅛-inch-thick slices. Chill until use.

MIX

In a medium bowl, whisk together the flour, baking powder, salt, and pepper.

Add the butter, and toss to coat with the flour mixture. Then press the butter slices between your thumb and forefinger into small flat pieces or "leaves."

Stir in the cheese, chives, and corn until evenly distributed.

In a small bowl, combine the cream and the reserved chilled soaked grits.

RECIPE CONTINUES ⚜

MIX CONT. Add the wet ingredients to the dry ingredients and mix gently until the mixture is just combined. The dough should be firm and barely cohesive (some dry bits are OK).

SHAPE

Transfer the dough to a lightly floured work surface, and fold a few times to incorporate any dry bits.

Pat the dough into a circle about 1 inch thick and 8 inches across. Chill until set for easier cutting.

Cut the dough into 8 pieces with a chef's knife, cutting directly down; don't saw, as this interferes with the rising. Arrange evenly on the sheet pan, or freeze, well wrapped, for up to a month.

BAKE

Brush the scones with egg wash and garnish with freshly cracked pepper.

Bake for 22 to 24 minutes on the top rack, rotating after 15 minutes, until they are golden and crisp with bits of lightly browned cheese.

If you are baking them after freezing, keep them covered and allow them to thaw overnight in the refrigerator before baking them as directed above.

FIG-ANISE SCONES

Yield: **8 to 10 medium scones**

INGREDIENTS	METRIC (GRAMS)	VOLUMETRIC (APPROXIMATE)
Whole wheat flour	200	1½ cups + 2 tablespoons
Sugar	35	3 tablespoons
Baking powder	6	1½ teaspoons
Baking soda	3	½ teaspoon
Salt, fine	6	1 teaspoon
Figs, dried, stemmed	104	⅔ cup
Water, boiling	120	½ cup
Earl Grey tea bag or loose tea	2	1 bag or 1 teaspoon
Anise seeds	2	1 teaspoon
Butter, unsalted	71	4½ tablespoons
Eggs, large	100	2
Orange zest	6	1 tablespoon
Buttermilk	74	¼ cup + 1 tablespoon
Egg wash		
Coarse sugar, for garnish		

PREPARE

Position an oven rack in the top third of the oven.

Preheat the oven to 425°F.

Lightly grease a 13 by 18-inch sheet pan, or line it with parchment paper.

Weigh and chill the dry ingredients.

Chop the figs into marble-size pieces.

Pour the boiling water over the tea and set aside to steep for 5 to 10 minutes. Strain before use.

Put the chopped figs in a bowl and pour the tea over them. Allow the figs to soak for 10 to 15 minutes. Strain and reserve until use.

Toast the anise seeds in a dry pan over low heat. Cool and then crush before use.

Cut the butter into ⅛-inch-thick slices. Chill until use.

MIX

In a medium bowl. whisk together the flour, sugar, baking powder, baking soda, salt, and crushed anise seeds.

MIX CONT. Add the cold butter and toss to coat with the dry ingredients. Then press the butter slices between your thumb and forefinger into small flat slices, or "leaves."

In a small bowl, whisk together the strained figs, eggs, orange zest, and buttermilk.

Add the wet ingredients to the dry ingredients and mix gently until the mixture is just combined. The dough should be firm and barely cohesive (some dry bits are OK).

SHAPE The scones may be scooped from a large spoon or patted an inch thick on a floured surface, the tops lightly dusted with flour, and cut with a biscuit cutter or chef's knife. Arrange evenly on the sheet pan, or freeze, well wrapped, for up to a month.

BAKE Apply an egg wash and sprinkle with coarse sugar.

Bake for 18 to 22 minutes on the top rack, rotating after 14 minutes, until the scones are lightly golden and firm to the touch.

If you are baking them after freezing, keep them covered and allow them to thaw overnight in the refrigerator before baking them as directed above.

In my job at King Arthur Flour I've been lucky to travel and use an allotted forty hours of paid volunteer time per year to share what I know of baking. This has taken me to the Dominican Republic to work with rural communities using wood-fired ovens, to Hot Bread Kitchen in New York City, and also to Homeboy Industries in Los Angeles. In each instance, without fail, I receive more than I could ever give. Each experience has been an enrichment that deepens my understanding of and love for humanity.

Homeboy Industries, founded by Father Greg Boyle, "provides hope, training, and support to formerly gang-involved and previously incarcerated men and women." I worked in the bakery for a few days and came home searching to re-create a bread that Jesse, Vidal, and "Caballo" made, and were extremely proud of—easily the best grilled cheese sandwich bread the world will ever know. I've made some small changes but it's almost as good—with a tender crumb, fresh-cured jalapeños, and local cheddar.

JALAPEÑO-CHEDDAR BREAD

Yield: **Two 9 by 5-inch pan loaves or one 9 by 5-inch loaf and 10 rolls**

INGREDIENTS	METRIC (GRAMS)	VOLUMETRIC (APPROXIMATE)	BAKER'S %
All-purpose flour	318	2½ cups + 2 tablespoons	47%
Durum flour	318	2½ cups + 1 tablespoon	47%
Cornmeal, yellow	40	¼ cup + 1 tablespoon	6%
Water	406	1¾ cups	60%
Salt, fine	14	2½ teaspoons	2.10%
Yeast, dry instant	7	2½ teaspoons	1%
Butter, unsalted, soft	101	¼ cup + 3 tablespoons (7 tablespoons)	15%
Cheddar cheese, block	95	generous ¾ cup	14%
Jalapeños, pickled, drained	67	½ cup	10%
Sugar	34	scant 3 tablespoons	5%
Jalapeños, pickled, for garnish if making rolls			
Cheddar cheese, grated, for garnish if making rolls			
Cornmeal, for the crust			
Total Weight	1,400	All	207.10%

DAY ONE

Make the pickled jalapeños (see below).

DAY TWO

PREPARE   Grate half the cheese and cut the other half into ½-inch cubes.

Dice the ½ cup jalapeños. Slice the garnish jalapeños.

MIX   Calculate temperatures. See Setting Temperatures, page 320, for instructions. Desired dough temperature: 80°F

RECIPE CONTINUES

MIX

In a large mixing bowl, whisk together the flours, cornmeal, sugar, salt, and yeast. Add the water and butter and mix with your hand, or the handle end of a wooden spoon, until the dough forms a shaggy mass. With some doughs you may have to knead for a few strokes in the bowl to incorporate everything. If you find it easier, after some stirring, scrape the dough out of the bowl with a plastic scraper onto your work surface and knead briefly with your hands just until the dough comes together. Resist the urge to add more flour. Scrape the dough off the work surface and return it to the bowl for bulk fermentation.

Place the diced pickled jalapeños and grated and cubed cheese on top of the mixed dough and fold briefly to begin incorporation. It doesn't need to be homogeneous; these ingredients will fully incorporate during folding.

BULK FERMENTATION

Scrape down the sides of the mixing bowl and allow the dough to rise, covered, for 90 minutes at room temperature, folding as directed below.

FOLD

Fold after 15, 30, 45, and 60 minutes, then leave untouched until the divide. See Folding, page 327, for instructions.

As this is a stiffer dough, it will be easiest to fold by hand in the bowl rather than with a plastic scraper.

DIVIDE AND PRESHAPE

For 2 loaves, divide the dough into 2 pieces, each weighing about 700 grams. See Dividing, page 328, for instructions.

For 1 loaf and 10 rolls, divide one of the 700-gram pieces into 10 pieces (about 70 grams each). See Dividing, page 328, for instructions.

Preshape the loaves as tubes and the rolls as rounds. See Preshaping, page 329, for instructions.

Cover and let rest for 5 to 10 minutes.

SHAPE

Spray or grease two 9 by 5-inch loaf pans. If you're making both a loaf and rolls, grease a 9 by 5-inch loaf pan and lightly grease a 13 by 18-inch sheet pan, or line it with parchment paper.

To make the cornmeal crust, sprinkle some cornmeal on a sheet pan. On a second pan, place a well-moistened tea towel or dish towel.

Shape the bread as a pan loaf. See Shaping, page 331, for instructions.

For the loaves: After shaping, roll the loaves across the moist towel and then through the cornmeal. Place in the loaf pans.

For the rolls: Round and then dip in cornmeal, following the same process as for the loaves, but place the rolls on the sheet pan instead.

RECIPE CONTINUES ⚜

SHAPE CONT.	This loaf is beautiful if scored before proofing, but you may skip that step if you like. To score, cut the loaves at a 45-degree angle and place in the prepared loaf pans.
PROOF	Cover the loaves and proof until the dough is an inch above the top of the pan, 50 to 60 minutes.
	If making rolls, cover them and proof until soft and puffy. They should yield easily when gently pressed.
BAKE	Toward the end of the proof, preheat the oven to 425°F with your steaming system in place. See Baking, page 349, for instructions.
	Just before baking the rolls, cut deeply with scissors (1 to ½ inches) into the top. To garnish, insert a single slice of pickled jalapeño and top with a large pinch of grated cheddar cheese.
	Bake the loaves with steam for 30 to 35 minutes. After 25 minutes, rotate the loaves.
	The loaves are done when the top and sides are firm and a deep golden brown.
	Immediately after baking, remove from the pans and place on a rack to cool. Cooling in the pan will cause the crust to be soggy.
	Bake the rolls with steam for 18 to 22 minutes, or until they are a rich golden brown and the cheese is melted and crisp.

PICKLED JALAPEÑOS

INGREDIENTS	METRIC (GRAMS)	VOLUMETRIC (APPROXIMATE)
Jalapeños, fresh, sliced ¼ inch thick	150	1¼ cups
Water	150	⅔ cup
Vinegar, white or cider	150	⅔ cup
Salt, fine	16	1 tablespoon
Sugar	16	1 tablespoon
Garlic, fresh, coarsely chopped	3	1 teaspoon

PREPARE	In a small saucepan, combine the water, vinegar, salt, and sugar. Bring to a boil.
	Combine the jalapeños and garlic in a nonreactive bowl, jar, or plastic container.
	Pour the vinegar mixture over the jalapeños and garlic. Let the mixture steep 12 hours or overnight.

NOTE: I love these, and always make extra. Using these proportions you should have enough left to eat on just about everything for a few days.

I've not met Willis or Tina Wood, but I'm due to meet both. It seems everyone around me has found the way down to Springfield, Vermont, either to see them press apples for cider or to hang out on a cool fall day around the wood-fired evaporator while they make boiled cider or cider jelly. Perhaps I'm saving the meeting like an after-dinner treat, knowing how moving it will be to see the press, which was purchased in 1882 and is still running.

This bread is a hat tip to two continents. In Eastern Europe some rye breads are made with beet syrup for a slight sweetness that pairs perfectly with the flavors of fermented whole rye flour.

Searching for a closer option, I chose boiled cider. It imparts just the right amount of sweetness and tartness. And if you don't find your way to southeastern Vermont, I would encourage you to try making your own boiled cider. The recipe is included with the bread instructions.

WOOD'S BOILED CIDER BREAD

Yield: **2 medium boules**

TOTAL FORMULA

PREFERMENTED FLOUR: 45%

INGREDIENTS	METRIC (GRAMS)	VOLUMETRIC (APPROXIMATE)	BAKER'S %
Whole rye flour	837	7¾ cups + 2 tablespoons	100%
Water	669	2¾ cups + 3 tablespoons	80%
Salt, fine	17	scant tablespoon	2%
Yeast, dry instant	6	2 teaspoons	0.75%
Sourdough culture	29	scant 2 tablespoons	3.50%
Boiled cider	42	2 tablespoons	5%
Total Weight	1,600	All	191.25%

RYE SOURDOUGH

INGREDIENTS	METRIC (GRAMS)	VOLUMETRIC (APPROXIMATE)	BAKER'S %
Whole rye flour	293	2¾ cups	100%
Water	293	1¼ cups	100%
Sourdough culture	29	scant 2 tablespoons	10%
Total Weight	615	All	210%

FINAL DOUGH

INGREDIENTS	METRIC (GRAMS)	VOLUMETRIC (APPROXIMATE)
Water	376	1½ cups + 3 tablespoons
Rye sourdough	615	All
Whole rye flour	544	5 cups + 2 tablespoons
Boiled cider	42	2 tablespoons
Salt, fine	17	scant 1 tablespoon
Yeast, dry instant	6	2 teaspoons
Total Weight	1,600	All

RECIPE CONTINUES

DAY ONE

PREPARE

First, make the boiled cider by reducing apple cider to one-eighth of its volume. Over low heat, reduce 2 cups of cider (454 grams) to ¼ cup (about 56 grams, of which 42 grams will be used in the bread). Set aside to cool. Boiled cider syrup will keep for several months in the refrigerator.

RYE SOURDOUGH

In a medium bowl, combine the tepid water (75°F to 80°F) and sourdough culture. Mix with your hands and fingers until the culture is broken up and well distributed in the water, then add the flour.

Mix briefly, then knead until smooth.

Cover and set at room temperature for 12 to 16 hours.

DAY TWO

MIX

Calculate temperatures. See Setting Temperatures, page 320, for instructions. Desired dough temperature: 78°F

In a large mixing bowl, combine the final dough water and rye sourdough. Mix with your hands until the rye sourdough is broken up in the water, then add the flour, boiled cider, salt, and yeast. Stir with a wooden spoon or plastic spatula until the dough forms a shaggy, homogeneous mass. You may find it helpful to use a plastic scraper to ensure that all ingredients are incorporated from the bottom and sides of the bowl.

Note: The rye dough will mix together more like a thick batter bread. Don't expect an elastic mass that expands and contracts.

BULK FERMENTATION

Scrape down the sides of the mixing bowl and allow the dough to rise, covered, for an hour at room temperature.

DIVIDE

Divide the dough into 2 pieces weighing about 800 grams each. See Dividing, page 328 for instructions.

Proceed directly to shaping.

SHAPE

Shape as boules and place in bannetons or towel-lined bowls, approximately 8 inches wide by 3 inches deep and generously dusted with whole rye flour. See Shaping, page 331, for instructions.

PROOF

During the proof, preheat the oven to 450°F with a baking stone and steaming system in place. See Baking, page 349, for instructions.

After 30 minutes of proofing, invert the loaves onto a piece of parchment paper cut to the size of your baking stone, arranging them with as much space between them as possible.

PROOF CONT.   Allow the loaves to proof for another 10 to 15 minutes, or until small cracks begin to appear in the surface.

Slide the loaves onto the preheated baking stone.

BAKE   Bake with steam for 45 to 50 minutes. After 25 minutes, carefully remove any steaming devices, lids, parchment paper, or bowls. Rotate the loaves on the stone.

At 45 to 50 minutes the loaves should be well colored. Turn off the oven, prop open the door a few inches, and allow the loaves to dry for an additional 10 minutes.

Fall in the Northeast is the end cap of abundance, which we enjoy before daylight takes a break and candles come to our table to buoy us through the season of light. Apples enter as tomatoes wane; kale, carrots, and broccoli sweeten as the first frosts arrive; and tender lettuces make way for spinach and hardy greens. This apple bread took much trial and error to sort out. I give full credit to Carrie Brisson, a baker at King Arthur, for her tireless work and excellence in all things. She stuck with this as we tried dried apples, cooked apples, mixtures of both, applesauce, and every other permutation of apples in search of the perfect apple bread. In the end the best option was found to be fresh apples that we cubed and half dried in a low oven. They are somewhere between fresh apples and the more leathery dried apples, which may be purchased. They offer the benefits of both with plenty of tart sweetness.

Carrie Apple Bread

DRIED APPLE, WHOLE AND BUCKWHEAT WHEAT

- CORE, CHOP AND DRY APPLES
- SET A STIFF LEVAIN
  └ FLAVOR! →
- MIX, FERMENT, FOLD
- DIVIDE + PRESHAPE ROUND
  3 BALLS / BASKET @ 180g
- SCORE WITH SCISSORS IN AN "X" PATTERN

SIDE VIEW

INVERT, SCORE AND LOAD

CARRIE'S APPLE BREAD

Yield: **2 medium round loaves**

TOTAL FORMULA

PREFERMENTED FLOUR: 15%

INGREDIENTS	METRIC (GRAMS)	VOLUMETRIC (APPROXIMATE)	BAKER'S %
All-purpose flour	409	3¼ cups + 2 tablespoons	80%
Whole wheat flour	77	½ cup + 2 tablespoons	15%
Whole buckwheat flour	26	3 tablespoons	5%
Water	348	1½ cups + 1½ teaspoons	68%
Salt, fine	11	scant 2 teaspoons	2.20%
Yeast, dry instant	4	scant 1½ teaspoons	0.75%
Sourdough culture	15	1 tablespoon	3%
Apples (about 2 pounds raw, unpeeled, cubed, cored, and dried, will yield the required amount)	230	2 cups	45%
Total Weight	1,120	All	218.95%

STIFF LEVAIN

INGREDIENTS	METRIC (GRAMS)	VOLUMETRIC (APPROXIMATE)	BAKER'S %
Whole wheat flour	77	½ cup + 2 tablespoons	100%
Water	54	¼ cup	70%
Salt, fine	2	scant ½ teaspoon	2%
Sourdough culture	15	1 tablespoon	20%
Total Weight	148	All	192%

FINAL DOUGH (CONT. ON FOLLOWING PAGE)

INGREDIENTS	METRIC (GRAMS)	VOLUMETRIC (APPROXIMATE)
Water	294	1¼ cups + 1½ teaspoons
Stiff levain	148	All
All-purpose flour	409	3¼ cups + 2 tablespoons

RECIPE CONTINUES

INGREDIENTS	METRIC (GRAMS)	VOLUMETRIC (APPROXIMATE)
Whole buckwheat flour	26	3 tablespoons
Salt, fine	9	1½ teaspoons
Yeast, dry instant	4	scant 1½ teaspoons
Apple, fresh, cubed, dried	230	2 cups
Total Weight	1,120	All

DAY ONE

STIFF LEVAIN

In a medium bowl, combine the tepid water (75°F to 80°F) and sourdough culture. Mix with your hands and fingers until the culture is broken up and well distributed in the water, then add the flour and salt.

Mix briefly, then knead until smooth.

Cover and set at room temperature for 12 to 16 hours.

PREPARE

Preheat the oven to 350°F. Line a sheet pan with parchment paper.

To make the apple dried weight of 232 grams, begin with 900 grams (about 2 pounds) of unpeeled apples.

Core the apples and chop into ¾-inch pieces; some smaller pieces are fine. Place on the sheet pan and dry in the oven for 45 to 60 minutes, or until the pieces feel leathery on the outside but remain tender when pressed. A convection oven with a fan setting will do this more quickly than a standard home oven.

DAY TWO

MIX

Calculate temperatures. See Setting Temperatures, page 320, for instructions. Desired dough temperature: 76°F

In a large mixing bowl, combine the final dough water and stiff levain. Mix with your hands until the levain is broken up in the water, then add the flours, salt, and yeast. Stir with the handle end of a wooden spoon until the dough forms a shaggy mass. If you find it easier, after some stirring, scrape the dough out of the bowl with a plastic scraper onto your work surface and knead briefly with your hands just until the dough comes together. Resist the urge to add more flour. Scrape the dough off the work surface and return it to the bowl for bulk fermentation.

Place the dried apples on top of the mixed dough and fold briefly to begin incorporation. It doesn't need to be homogeneous; the apples will fully incorporate during folding.

BULK FERMENTATION	Scrape down the sides of the mixing bowl and allow the dough to rise, covered, for 2 hours at room temperature, folding as directed below.
FOLD	Fold after 15, 30, 45, and 60 minutes, then leave untouched for the second hour. See Folding, page 327 for instructions. As you perform each series of folds, you'll begin to notice that the dough becomes smoother, stronger, and more cohesive.
DIVIDE AND PRESHAPE	Divide the dough into 6 pieces weighing about 180 grams each. Each loaf will consist of 3 balls that grow together slightly as they proof. See Dividing, page 328, for instructions. Preshape as rounds. See Preshaping, page 329, for instructions. Cover and let rest for 15 minutes.
SHAPE	Shape each piece as a small boule. See Shaping, page 331, for instructions. Then place 3 pieces together, seam side up, on the bottom of a generously floured banneton or towel-lined bowl, approximately 8 inches wide and 3 inches deep. The balls should not be stacked; place them side by side forming a two-dimensional triangular shape. They will grow together some as they proof. Repeat for the second loaf.
PROOF	Cover and proof for 45 to 60 minutes at room temperature.
BAKE	During the proof, preheat the oven to 450°F with a baking stone and steaming system in place. See Baking, page 349, for instructions. Transfer the loaves to parchment paper or a baker's peel, gently inverting them so that the underside, which was against the dusted tea towel or banneton, becomes the top. Score the bread prior to loading. See Scoring, page 339 for ideas and tips. I like to use scissors or a razor blade to cut a small "x" on each ball. Slide the loaves onto the preheated baking stone. Bake with steam for 30 to 35 minutes. After 20 minutes, carefully remove any steaming devices, lids, parchment paper, or bowls. Rotate the loaves on the stone. At 30 to 35 minutes the loaves should be well colored. Turn off the oven, open the door a few inches, and allow the loaf to dry for an additional 10 minutes.

Dessert. I do *like* dessert. I will eat it. Do I swoon, though? Not usually. Unless . . . unless it has pastry cream, buttery shortcakes, strawberry-rhubarb compote, fresh whipped cream, and berries. These I will anticipate. Although the shortcakes are very similar to biscuits, they are made slightly more decadent with fresh cream and just a little sugar. They are the vehicle that, when combined with the compote, pastry cream, whipped cream, and berries, moves to the place where roads from unctuousness, piquancy, and creaminess meet.

SHORTCAKE BISCUITS

Yield: **8 biscuits**

INGREDIENTS	METRIC (GRAMS)	VOLUMETRIC (APPROXIMATE)
All-purpose flour	355	scant 3 cups
Sugar	36	3 tablespoons
Salt	6	1 teaspoon
Baking powder	6	1½ teaspoons
Butter, unsalted	113	½ cup (8 tablespoons)
Cream	240	1 cup + 2 teaspoons
Milk, egg wash, or cream, for brushing (optional)		

PREPARE

Position an oven rack in the top third of the oven.

Preheat the oven to 425°F.

Lightly grease a 13 by 18-inch sheet pan, or line it with parchment paper.

Measure the dry ingredients, and chill until use.

Cut the butter into ⅛-inch-thick slices. Chill until use.

MIX

In a medium bowl, whisk together the flour, sugar, salt, and baking powder.

Add the cold butter and toss to coat with the flour mixture. Then press the butter slices between your thumb and forefinger into small flat pieces or "leaves."

Add the cream all at once and mix gently until the mixture is just combined. The dough should be firm and barely cohesive; some dry bits are OK.

SHAPE

Transfer the dough onto a lightly floured surface and pat into a rectangle about ¾ inch thick. There may be a few dry bits; they will incorporate in the following steps.

Fold the dough in thirds as you would a letter and gently roll or pat into a rectangle. Repeat this folding and rolling process once more if the dough isn't cohesive.

Lightly flour the top of the dough and cut into circles with a sharp 2-inch biscuit cutter, or square the sides and edges and cut into 8 even squares with a chef's knife.

BAKE

Place the biscuits on the sheet pan.

Brush the tops of the biscuits with milk, cream, or egg wash, if desired.

Bake for 16 to 18 minutes, rotating the pan after 14 minutes, until the biscuits are golden.

STRAWBERRY-RHUBARB COMPOTE

Yield: 900 grams (about 3 cups)

INGREDIENTS	METRIC (GRAMS)	VOLUMETRIC (APPROXIMATE)
Strawberries, fresh	454	2¾ cups
Rhubarb, fresh	228	scant 2 cups
Butter, unsalted	5	1 teaspoon
Brown sugar	106	½ cup
Lemon juice, fresh	28	2 tablespoons
Cornstarch	10	1 tablespoon + 1½ teaspoons
Water	199	¾ cup + 2 tablespoons

PREPARE

Cut the strawberries into quarters, or into eighths if they are very large.

Chop the rhubarb on the diagonal into ½-inch pieces.

In a medium pot over medium heat, stir together the rhubarb, butter, sugar, and lemon juice.

Bring the mixture to a boil, stirring occasionally, and let it cook for 3 to 5 minutes, or until the rhubarb softens.

In a small bowl or measuring cup, stir together the cornstarch and 29 grams (2 tablespoons) water, then add to the boiling liquid.

When the mixture boils, add the strawberries and 170 grams (¾ cup) of water, then return to a boil, stirring gently. Reduce for 3 to 5 minutes, stirring so it doesn't stick to the bottom of the pot. Then remove from the heat.

Cool and refrigerate until use.

The compote will last for at least a week, chilled.

Pain d'épices, meaning literally "bread of spices" is a dark, moist French quick bread traditionally made of rye flour, honey, and spices. It is so darn good that in Alsace there is a museum, the Musée du Pain d'Epices et de l'Art Populaire Alsacien, dedicated to this delicious combination of ingredients. And the bread, viewed in the context of history, can be attributed to cultures in nearly every part of the globe. We all love these flavors!

Within the community of bakers, upholding our values is something we treasure as highly as our baked goods. We are a friendly bunch, open to sharing recipes, techniques, and tips, with little proprietary concern. We know that recipes are a good starting point, as they provide the syntax and words for our work, but the poetry—our unique combination and contribution—comes from beyond the written lines.

The inspiration for this bread could have come from the Chinese more than a thousand years ago, or from the French in Alsace, or from the modern version of German *Lebkuchen*, but I found it at a closer source, my good friend Richard Miscovich. Richard is a great baker, whose book *From the Wood-Fired Oven* is a deep, well-written reference for bakers, cooks, and lovers of fire.

SPICED HONEY BREAD

Yield: **Four 3½ by 5½-inch loaves**

INGREDIENTS	METRIC (GRAMS)	VOLUMETRIC (APPROXIMATE)	BAKER'S %
Whole rye flour	408	3¾ cups + 2 tablespoons	100%
Baking soda	10	2½ teaspoons	2.50%
Salt, fine	6	1 teaspoon	1.50%
Milk	245	1 cup + 1 tablespoon	60%
Honey	327	1 cup	80%
Honeycomb (if available, otherwise, use honey)	163	½ cup	40%
Molasses	163	½ cup	40%
Anise, freshly ground	1	½ teaspoon	0.25%
Nutmeg, freshly ground	1	½ teaspoon	0.25%
Coriander, freshly ground	1	½ teaspoon	0.25%
Cinnamon, freshly ground	1	½ teaspoon	0.25%
Cloves, freshly ground	1	½ teaspoon	0.25%
Orange zest	16	2 tablespoons + 2 teaspoons	4%
Egg yolks, large	49	scant 3 yolks	12%
Rum	41	3 tablespoons	10%
Apple, dried	82	1 cup	20%
Total Weight	1,515	All	

PREPARE

Preheat oven to 350°F. Grease four 3½ by 5½-inch pans.

Chop the dried apple into ½-inch pieces. Place in a bowl and combine with the rum. Set aside.

MIX

In a large mixing bowl, whisk together the rye flour, baking soda, and salt.

In a medium pot, combine the honey, honeycomb, molasses, spices, orange zest, milk, and soaked apple pieces (including any unabsorbed liquid) and bring to a simmer over medium heat, stirring to combine.

In a small bowl, whisk together the egg yolks, then add 1 cup of the simmering liquid in a slow stream, whisking continually as you pour.

RECIPE CONTINUES

MIX CONT.

Add the egg yolk mixture back to the simmering liquid, stirring constantly while pouring in a steady stream. This process tempers the eggs, preventing them from scrambling.

Add the liquid ingredients to the dry, stirring until combined.

PAN

Pour the batter into the prepared pans, filling each about three-quarters of the way to the top. The contents of each pan will weigh about 350 grams. Evenly distribute any remaining batter among the pans.

BAKE

Bake for 15 minutes at 350°F, then reduce the oven temperature and bake for an additional 20 to 25 minutes at 325°F. The loaves are done when the crust is set and bounces back when pressed. Let the loaves cool for a few minutes in the pan before removing.

These small loaves keep well for a week or so at room temperature, or for up to a month frozen.

Sunrise Farm sits on a grassy bench bordered by hardwood forests on the eastern side of a mountain. In the morning, fields receive the sun as it arcs overhead, shining on meat birds, laying hens, pigs, sheep, bees, and vegetables . . . endless vegetables. Things grow, things die, some enter the food chain through our mouths, others feed animals, and the remainder returns to dirt in compost piles—it's an old cycle. And while much of this scene is idyllic, nothing is hidden. Food choices are out in the open, sprouting in lines or strutting and wallowing.

Rows of vegetables near the farmhouse and barn are nestled in thick beds of lavender and chamomile, their flowers abuzz with bees from nearby hives. Honey, aromatic flowers, an old barn, which had once been a dairy—the clues are here, a whispered suggestion to bake with these ingredients. The lavender and chamomile are steeped in sweetened milk overnight, then the liquid is added to the final dough, along with some good butter.

Durum flour with lavender and chamomile milk tea, sweet with honey and softened with butter. A biga for preferment with fifty percent of total flour

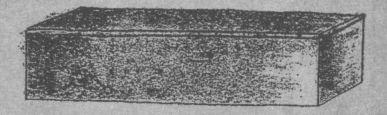

BEEKEEPER'S PAIN DE MIE

Yield: **Two 9 by 5-inch pan loaves, or two 8½ by 4½-inch pan loaves**

TOTAL FORMULA

PREFERMENTED FLOUR: 50%

INGREDIENTS	METRIC (GRAMS)	VOLUMETRIC (APPROXIMATE)	BAKER'S %
Durum flour	410	3¼ cups + 1 tablespoon	50%
All-purpose flour	410	3¼ cups + 3 tablespoons	50%
Water	352	1½ cups + 1 tablespoon	43%
Wildflower tea (see below)	172	¾ cup + 1 teaspoon	21.05%
Salt, fine	17	scant 1 tablespoon	2.10%
Yeast, dry instant	16	1 tablespoon + 2¼ teaspoons	2%
Butter, unsalted, soft	123	½ cup + 1 tablespoon (9 tablespoons)	15%
Total Weight	1,500		183.15%

BIGA

INGREDIENTS	METRIC (GRAMS)	VOLUMETRIC (APPROXIMATE)	BAKER'S %
All-purpose flour	410	3¼ cups + 3 tablespoons	100%
Water	246	1 cup + 2 tablespoons	60%
Yeast, dry instant	Pinch	Pinch	0.20%
Total Weight	656	All	160.20%

TEA

INGREDIENTS	METRIC (GRAMS)	VOLUMETRIC (APPROXIMATE)
Milk	170	¾ cup
Wildflower honey	21	1 tablespoon
Sugar	57	¼ cup + 1 tablespoon
Chamomile flowers	2	heaping 1 tablespoon
Lavender flowers	4	heaping 2 tablespoons
Total Weight	254	

FINAL DOUGH

INGREDIENTS	METRIC (GRAMS)	VOLUMETRIC (APPROXIMATE)
Wildflower tea	172	¾ cup + 1 teaspoon
Biga	656	All
Water	106	¼ cup + 3 tablespoons
Durum flour	410	3¼ cups + 1 tablespoon
Butter, unsalted, soft	123	½ cup + 1 tablespoons (9 tablespoons)
Salt, fine	17	scant 1 tablespoon
Yeast, dry instant	16	1 tablespoon + 2¼ teaspoons
Total Weight	1,500	All

DAY ONE

BIGA

In a medium bowl, stir together the room-temperature flour and yeast, then add the tepid water (75°F to 80°F).

Mix briefly, then knead until smooth.

Cover and set at room temperature for 12 to 16 hours.

TEA

Combine the milk, honey, and sugar in a small pot.

Over low heat, slowly warm the mixture until the honey and sugar dissolve. Stir constantly.

When the mixture reaches a very low simmer with small bubbles around the edge of the pot, add the chamomile and lavender and turn off the heat.

Cover and set at room temperature for 12 to 16 hours. Strain through a fine-mesh sieve before using. The tea needs to be 80°F for use in the dough.

DAY TWO

Calculate temperatures. See Setting Temperatures, page 320, for instructions. Desired dough temperature: 80°F

MIX

In a large mixing bowl, combine the strained tea, biga, and water. Mix with your hands until the biga is broken up, then add the flour, butter, salt, and yeast. Stir with the handle end of a wooden spoon or with your hands until the dough forms a shaggy mass. If you find it easier, after some stirring, scrape the dough out of the bowl with a plastic scraper onto your work surface and knead briefly with your hands just until the dough comes together. Resist the urge to add more flour. Scrape the dough off the work surface and return it to the bowl for bulk fermentation.

RECIPE CONTINUES

BULK FERMENTATION	Scrape down the sides of the mixing bowl and allow the dough to rise, covered, for 1½ hours at room temperature, folding as directed below.
FOLD	Fold after 30 and 60 minutes, then leave untouched until the divide. See Folding, page 327, for instructions.
DIVIDE AND PRESHAPE	Divide the dough into 2 pieces weighing about 750 grams each. See Dividing, page 328 for instructions. Preshape as tubes. See Preshaping, page 329, for instructions. Cover and let rest for 15 minutes.
SHAPE	Spray or grease two 9 by 5-inch loaf pans. Shape as pan loaves. See Shaping, page 331, for instructions. Place the dough in the prepared loaf pans, seam down, pressing with your knuckles to evenly fill the pan.
PROOF	Cover and proof until the dough is about 1 to 1½ inches above the top of the pan, 1 to 1½ hours.
BAKE	Toward the end of the proof, preheat the oven to 425°F. Bake the loaves for 30 to 35 minutes. Rotate the loaves after 20 minutes. Bake until the top is deeply colored and the sides are golden. Immediately after baking, remove the loaves from the pans and place on a rack to cool. Cooling in the pan will cause the crust to be soggy.

Beekeepers Pain de Mie

- Enriched loaf with a lavender and chamomile milk tea.

- Durum flour to favor yellow visual tones

- 50% of flour prefermented in a biga to balance the sweet and aromatic notes

Rolls @ 40 grams

shill and sheet 1K of dough for lattice and roll caps —

String Pullman pan = 675g

Lavandula Lavender Lavender

Vermont is many things, but let's agree that our population doesn't usually conjure up adjectives like "exotic," "ethnic," or "diverse." Our population is slowly diversifying to reflect the rich fabric of this country; but with our current nonwhite proportion of less than 5 percent, we are better known for another basic palette: a black-and-white cow, a red barn, green mountains. Coming here from New York City, my family gorged on these primary colors, eating pecks of apples; bushels of winter squash, and wheels of cheese, and drinking growlers of beer. We also yearned for the full spectrum: the yellow-orange of turmeric and brown-red of smoked paprika; the purple of Japanese eggplant and tan of roasted tahini; the colors, fabrics, and smells of spice routes far from our mountain passes and gaps. So I began my own patchwork quilt in pots, making curries and other spiced delicacies.

When we make butternut curry with coconut milk, spicy garlic hummus, smoked paprika baba ganoush, or zesty poached egg and tomato shakshuka, we want fresh flatbreads, too. They are ridiculously easy—so easy, in fact, that our children, with a gram scale, rolling pin, hot griddle, and open flame, can have them buttered and on the table in less than an hour. And this process does more than bring the children to the table for sustenance; it brings them the nourishment of handcraft. It fills them with confidence and empowers them to transform the inedible to the edible. Not unlike knitting, when yarn becomes a scarf, this sleight of hand lets them see flour become flatbread. Get rid of the handhelds and set children to making something.

This recipe is more than an exact list of ingredients in measured quantities. It is a daily bread in many cultures and, as such, should be adaptable. Can it be made with all whole wheat or with the addition of rye or even lentil flour? Absolutely. This is subsistence baking—take what you get, make what you can.

ROTI

Yield: **Twelve 6- to 7-inch flatbreads**

INGREDIENTS	METRIC (GRAMS)	VOLUMETRIC (APPROXIMATE)	BAKER'S %
Whole wheat flour	347	scant 3 cups	100%
Water	122	½ cup + 1 tablespoon	35%
Salt, fine	7	1⅛ teaspoons	2%
Baking powder	2	½ teaspoon	0.50%
Yogurt, whole-milk	122	heaping ½ cup	35%
Total Weight	600		172.50%

MIX

In a medium mixing bowl, whisk together the flour, salt, and baking powder.

Add the water and yogurt and mix with a hand or the handle end of a wooden spoon until the dough forms a shaggy mass. You may have to knead for a few strokes in the bowl to incorporate everything. If you find it easier, after some stirring, scrape the dough out of the bowl with a plastic scraper onto your work surface and knead briefly with your hands just until the dough comes together. Resist the urge to add more flour. Proceed directly to dividing.

DIVIDE

Divide the dough into 12 pieces weighing about 50 grams each. See Dividing, page 328, for instructions.

Preshape as rounds. See Preshaping, page 329, for instructions.

Cover and let rest on a well-floured surface for 15 to 45 minutes.

COOKING

Preheat a 10-inch cast-iron skillet over medium heat.

On a floured surface, roll the roti balls out very thinly, to about the thickness of a penny. They should be round and roughly 7 inches in diameter.

Put the roti in the preheated dry pan. Flip with tongs after small bubbles appear, approximately 1 minute. After 30 seconds on the second side, transfer to an adjacent burner set to medium.

Set the roti directly on the open flame, and flip after 5 to 10 seconds. They will puff up some and char in spots. If working with an electric stovetop, you may finish them on a grill or simply cook them longer on each side.

Butter and serve with Hummus (page 227), Romesco (page 225), Lentils (page 219), and Raita (page 221).

A piece of the warm flatbread ripped and bent to fashion a scoop for gathering warm lentils accented with crunchy pickled onion and cooled with creamy raita . . .

LENTILS

Yield: 990 grams (about 5½ cups cooked lentils)

INGREDIENTS	METRIC (GRAMS)	VOLUMETRIC (APPROXIMATE)
Lentils, dried (brown, green, or French)	454	2¼ cups
Water	1,500	6½ cups
Olive oil, extra virgin	25	2 tablespoons
Garlic, minced	27	3 large cloves
Cumin seeds	5	2 teaspoons
Paprika, smoked	5	2 teaspoons
Salt, fine	9	1½ teaspoons
Black pepper, ground	3	1 teaspoon
Onion, minced	142	1 medium
Turmeric, ground	3	1 teaspoon
Tahini	71	½ cup
Lemon juice, fresh	9	1 teaspoon
Cooking liquid, reserved; or stock	454	2 cups
Raita, for serving (page 221)		
Cilantro, fresh, minced, for garnish		
Pickled onion, for garnish (recipe below)		

PREPARE

Rinse the lentils and pick them over to remove stones or shriveled lentils.

Put the lentils in a medium pot and cover them with 2 inches of water.

Bring to a boil, then reduce the heat to a simmer. Cook until the lentils are tender but not mushy, 20 to 25 minutes, depending on the age of the lentils.

Drain, reserving 2 cups of the cooking liquid.

PROCESS

In a large sauté pan over medium heat, warm the oil. Add the garlic, cumin seeds, paprika, salt, pepper, onion, and turmeric and sauté until the mixture is fragrant and the onion is translucent, 3 to 4 minutes.

Add the lentils and tahini and stir to combine. Add the reserved cooking liquid or stock.

Bring the mixture to a simmer and reduce the liquid for 5 to 10 minutes. Add the lemon juice, then check the seasoning and adjust to taste.

RECIPE CONTINUES

Just before eating, smooth the mixture slightly by pressing the lentils against the bottom of the pan with a fork or potato masher.

Garnish with fresh cilantro.

Serve with pickled onion, raita, and a side of roti bread.

PICKLED ONION

Yield: **about 1 cup of onion, drained**

INGREDIENTS	METRIC (GRAMS)	VOLUMETRIC (APPROXIMATE)
Red onion	340	1 large
Water	150	⅔ cup
Sugar	16	1 tablespoon
Salt	16	1 tablespoon
Garlic, fresh, coarsely chopped	9	1 large clove
Vinegar, white or cider	150	⅔ cup

PROCESS

Peel the onion, then slice it in half, cutting from the root end to the flowering end.

Place the onion, cut side down, on a cutting board and cut into ¼-inch slices.

Put the onion in a medium bowl.

In a small pot, mix the water, sugar, salt, garlic, and vinegar and bring to a simmer. Stir briefly to combine.

Pour the heated liquid over the onion slices. Stir to combine.

Chill for 2 hours before use.

The onion will keep for a month, chilled.

RAITA

INGREDIENTS	METRIC (GRAMS)	VOLUMETRIC (APPROXIMATE)
Yogurt, whole-milk	224	1 cup
Salt, fine	3	½ teaspoon
Sugar	4	1 teaspoon
Lemon juice, fresh	18	2 teaspoons
Cucumber, peeled, seeds removed, cut into ½-inch dice	118	1 cup

PROCESS Stir together the yogurt, salt, sugar, and lemon juice, then fold in the cucumber. Chill until use.

I thought crackers were hard. From the outside they seem fussy—requiring a full dose of attention to detail, improved with a side of precision. As it turns out, they are damn easy and foolproof and can be made in the cracks of a day. Once prepared, they will hold for longer than it will take you to eat them.

SEEDED CRACKERS

Yield: **Two sheet pans of crackers**

INGREDIENTS	METRIC (GRAMS)	VOLUMETRIC (APPROXIMATE)	BAKER'S %
Whole wheat flour	93	¾ cup	40%
All-purpose flour	70	½ cup + 1 tablespoon	30%
Any combination of rye, buckwheat, millet, or lentil flours, or cornmeal	70	½ cup	30%
Water	113	½ cup	49%
Salt, fine	5	scant 1 teaspoon	2%
Yeast, dry instant	1	heaping ¼ teaspoon	0.50%
Sugar	7	1¾ teaspoons	3%
Seed blend, for the crust (flaxseeds, sesame, cumin, black pepper, and coarse salt)			
Cayenne pepper	Pinch	Pinch	0.30%
Butter, unsalted	41	1½ tablespoons	17.50%
Total Weight	400	All	172.30%

PREPARE

Melt the butter.

Calculate temperatures. See Setting Temperatures, page 320, for instructions. Desired dough temperature: 76°F

MIX

In a large mixing bowl, whisk together the flours, sugar, salt, yeast, and cayenne. Add the water and the melted butter. Mix with your hand or the handle end of a wooden spoon until the dough forms a shaggy mass. With some doughs you may have to knead for a few strokes in the bowl to incorporate everything. If you find it easier, after some stirring, scrape the dough out of the bowl with a plastic scraper onto a counter or bench and knead briefly with your hands just until the dough comes together. Resist the urge to add more flour.

DIVIDE

Divide the dough into 2 pieces weighing about 200 grams each. See Dividing, page 328, for instructions.

Stretch and preform into rectangles; this will make it easier to make a rectangle shape after chilling.

RECIPE CONTINUES

Cover and chill for 1 to 2 hours.

Preheat the oven to 425°F. Line two 13 by 18-inch sheet pans with parchment paper. If you'd like to bake these crackers on a baking stone, you'll still want parchment paper to make an easier transfer into the oven.

Place a generous blend of salt, pepper, and seeds on your work surface. Flaxseeds, sesame, and cumin seeds along with black pepper and a little salt are a flavorful combination. Fennel is a wonderful addition. Look in ethnic food stores for interesting blends you may not have thought of. No rules here!

Place a chilled dough piece on top of the seeds, turning once to coat.

SHAPE Roll the dough, turning it over periodically to fully coat both sides with seeds, to a rough 10 by 15-inch rectangle, or to dimensions that match your sheet pan. Try to keep the dough at an even thickness so it will bake evenly. The seed blend will keep the dough from sticking. If the dough begins to stick, add more seeds.

Gently transfer the rolled dough to the prepared pan or paper. You may find it helpful to roll up the cracker dough on the rolling pin, and then unroll it on the sheet pan.

Score with a pizza wheel, cutting diamonds, rectangles, or squares. Scoring makes for evenly shaped crackers that can be snapped apart after baking. You may also prick the dough with the tines of a fork.

BAKE Bake for 10 to 12 minutes, or until nicely browned.

ROMESCO

Yield: **496 grams (3 cups)**

INGREDIENTS	METRIC (GRAMS)	VOLUMETRIC (APPROXIMATE)
Garlic, roasted, 1 bulb, purchased or homemade (directions below)	20	3 to 4 tablespoons
Red bell peppers, blackened (3 or 4 large peppers)	340	2½ cups
Cream cheese	139	½ cup
Almonds, whole, toasted	46	⅓ cup
Raisins, golden	93	1 cup
Paprika, smoked	5	2½ teaspoons
Cayenne pepper	1	½ teaspoon
Salt, fine	3	½ teaspoon
Lemon juice, fresh	5	1 teaspoon
Black pepper, ground	3	1¼ teaspoons

PREPARE

If you already have roasted garlic and blackened bell peppers on hand, skip down to the process. Bottled varieties of roasted bell peppers are a suitable option here.

To cook the garlic: Put a bulb's worth of peeled garlic cloves and ½ cup of olive oil in a medium saucepan over low heat. Cook until the cloves are tender, 10 to 15 minutes. Remove from the heat and cool in a bowl to prevent overcooking.

Alternatively, if the oven is on for something else, cut the stalk end off a bulb of garlic, exposing the cloves. Drizzle with olive oil and wrap in aluminum foil. Roast for 30 to 40 minutes or until the garlic cloves are tender.

To roast or blacken the peppers: Place the bell peppers over an open flame, turning occasionally until well blackened. Place in a paper bag or bowl. Close the bag or cover the bowl, and let the peppers cool. Scrape off most of the blackened skin, then seed and stem the peppers, and reserve until use.

PROCESS

Place the cream cheese in a food processor fitted with a cutting blade. Pulse to soften.

Add the almonds, raisins, and garlic. Pulse briefly, 5 to 10 seconds.

Add the bell peppers, paprika, cayenne, salt, lemon juice, and black pepper and pulse briefly to combine. Again, pulse just a few seconds; the texture should be coarse, not pureed.

Chill for an hour before serving, to allow it to set up.

The romesco will hold for up to a week, chilled.

Years before our children were part of the mix, the search for hummus began. Julie returned from a summer of singing in Tel Aviv, praising the regional food and describing a hummus to me. This hummus was not the gritty paste that is a staple of vegetarian cookbooks, but light, almost whipped, and silky smooth. It was slightly bitter from roasted tahini; spiced with ample garlic, lemon, and salt; and enriched with olive oil. In time I was able to make something close to the delicacy she described. Dragging fresh, buttered roti through hummus drizzled with green olive oil and sprinkled with spicy paprika is perfection for me and for her, and transports to a hot day in Haifa.

HUMMUS

Yield: **623 to 651 grams (3 cups)**

INGREDIENTS	METRIC (GRAMS)	VOLUMETRIC (APPROXIMATE)
Chickpeas (garbanzo beans), cooked	425	two 15-ounce cans
Garlic	9	2 cloves
Salt, fine	9	1½ teaspoons
Lemon juice, fresh	35	2 tablespoons and 1 teaspoon
Tahini	35	¼ cup
Olive oil, extra virgin	99	½ cup
Cayenne pepper, smoked paprika, toasted sesame or cumin seeds, for garnish		

PREPARE Drain the chickpeas, reserving ¼ cup of liquid.

PROCESS

Place the chickpeas, garlic, salt, lemon juice, and tahini in a food processor fitted with a cutting blade. Puree until smooth.

While the machine is running, add the olive oil in a thin stream. Puree until the mixture is silky smooth and light, almost the consistency of pastry cream or pudding. If it feels pasty at all (like prepackaged hummus in stores), drizzle in 1 or 2 tablespoons or more of the drained liquid from the beans and process to incorporate. Check the seasoning. Adjust as necessary.

Serve the hummus with a drizzle of olive oil and a sprinkle of cayenne or smoked paprika and toasted sesame or cumin seeds.

The hummus can be stored in the refrigerator for up to a week. Allow it to come to room temperature before use. If it thickens in the refrigerator, whisk in some olive oil or water to return it to a creamy consistency.

In our small house the woodstove is enough to heat us. Fires begin in late September and burn without breaks until sometime in May or even June. In warm months, when the stove is cool and the hearth is dark, things are not the same. I miss the heat that penetrates and restores—a nap on the hearth rug in front of a woodstove is the best medicine. In January, when temperatures don't break freezing all month, the stove is kept at a searing level, with its soapstone sides and top burning to the slightest touch. This is perfect for making stews, roasting squash, baking potatoes, or simply boiling beans in a pan on top. And if the options for cooking on top are many, there are additional opportunities inside with the live fire. Here is one of my favorite sides to go with grilled kebabs, turmeric-and-cumin-spiced rice, and cooling yogurt raita.

Double-wrap a large eggplant in aluminum foil and place inside the stove on ashen coals. Turn occasionally until the fruit softens and is fully baked—it should be very soft, especially at the ends, which generally take longer to cook. If there is no woodstove, fireplace, or firepit handy, place the eggplant, cut side down, on a baking sheet lined with foil and place under the broiler until the skin blackens. When eaten from a nice bowl, scooped up with warm roti, or used as a garnish for a roti wrap of falafel or kebab with rice and raita, this provides it all—flavor, nutrition, and sustenance.

BABA GANOUSH

Yield: **524 grams (about 2 cups)**

INGREDIENTS	METRIC (GRAMS)	VOLUMETRIC (APPROXIMATE)
Eggplant, roasted, charred (1,360 grams or 3 pounds raw will yield the required amount)	446	scant 2 cups
Garlic, roasted	16	3 or 4 large cloves
Tahini	9	1 tablespoon
Honey	12	1 teaspoon
Lemon juice, fresh	14	1 tablespoon
Salt, fine	9	1½ teaspoon
Cayenne pepper	1	¼ teaspoon
Cilantro leaves	17	½ cup
Cilantro, fresh, minced, for garnish		
Smoked paprika or cayenne pepper, for garnish		
Olive oil, for garnish		
Honey, for garnish		

PREPARE

Begin with 2 large eggplants, about 1½ pounds (680 grams) each.

Deeply pierce the skin of the eggplants a few times with a knife.

Char in a fireplace, on a woodstove, under the broiler in the oven (cut in half; place cut side down on a lined sheet pan), or on a hot grill.

Cook until the skin is well charred and blistered and the flesh is fully tender.

Let cool until you can handle them, then scrape out the insides and discard the skin.

PROCESS

Put the garlic, tahini, honey, lemon juice, salt, and cayenne in a food processor fitted with a cutting blade. Puree until smooth.

Add the roasted eggplant and cilantro leaves and pulse briefly to combine. Check the seasoning and adjust to taste.

Serve with a garnish of fresh minced cilantro, cayenne or smoked paprika, olive oil, and a generous drizzle of honey.

"Socca," "Farinata!" "GARBANZOOOOOOOOO!" Even if you have no intention of eating something made with chickpea flour, you must try this for the sole purpose of hollering these words that feel so good in the mouth. Let your inner Roman loose and gesticulate wildly about the house. "What's for dinner, Daddy?" Farinaaaaaaaaaaaaaaaaataaaaaaahhhhhh! And I promise that the dancing will continue long after your charade, for socca is addictive.

Socca, sometimes called "farinata," is essentially a thin pancake that is pan-fried in olive oil and served plain or sparsely topped. During cooking, the oil infuses the pancake, crisping the edges, and begging for salt and pepper or caramelized onions and a drizzle of maple syrup.

SOCCA

Yield: **Two 9-inch socca, topped**

INGREDIENTS	METRIC (GRAMS)	VOLUMETRIC (APPROXIMATE)	BAKER'S %
Chickpea or garbanzo bean flour	192	2¼ cups	100%
Water	385	1½ cups + 3 tablespoons	200%
Olive oil, extra virgin	19	1 tablespoon + 1½ teaspoons	10%
Salt, fine	4	¾ teaspoon	2%
Olive oil, for the socca pan	56	4 tablespoons	
Parmesan cheese, for garnish (optional)	28	¼ cup (4 tablespoons)	
Prepared toppings, as desired			

PREPARE

Whisk together the flour, water, olive oil, and salt until smooth.

Cover the batter and let it rest for 30 minutes or up to a few hours.

Prepare the toppings. Alternatively, socca served plain and simple is delicious; it will be crisp and flavorful with good oil and a little extra salt.

BAKE

Preheat the oven to broil with an oven rack on the top set of rungs, or as close as possible to the broiler element; 4 to 5 inches is usually about right.

Over medium-high heat on the stovetop, heat 2 tablespoons of olive oil in a 10-inch cast-iron skillet. When the oil is very hot and shimmering, add half the batter (roughly 300 grams or 1½ cups) and tilt the pan to swirl and distribute it evenly. It should sputter, so be careful.

As the edges sizzle, but before the pancake is fully set, add prepared toppings of your choice, or simply garnish with salt, pepper, and a handful of grated Parmesan.

Place the socca in the pan under the broiler to finish. Watch closely! It's done when the toppings have a nice color, 2 to 3 minutes.

The pan will be extremely hot, so remove the socca carefully using a metal spatula.

To cook the second socca, begin again with the olive oil and repeat the process.

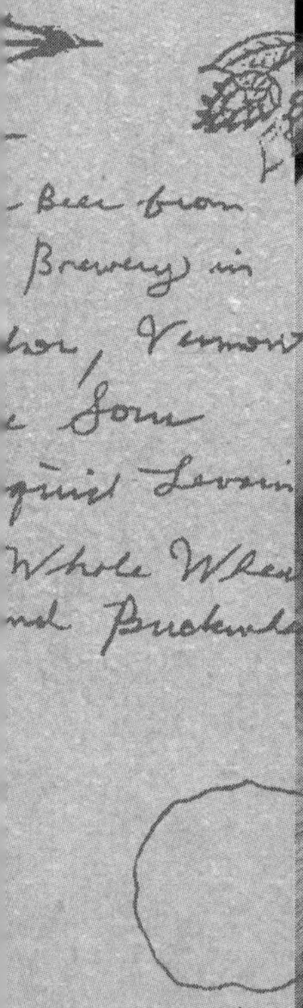
Beer from
Brewery in
Vermont
Whole
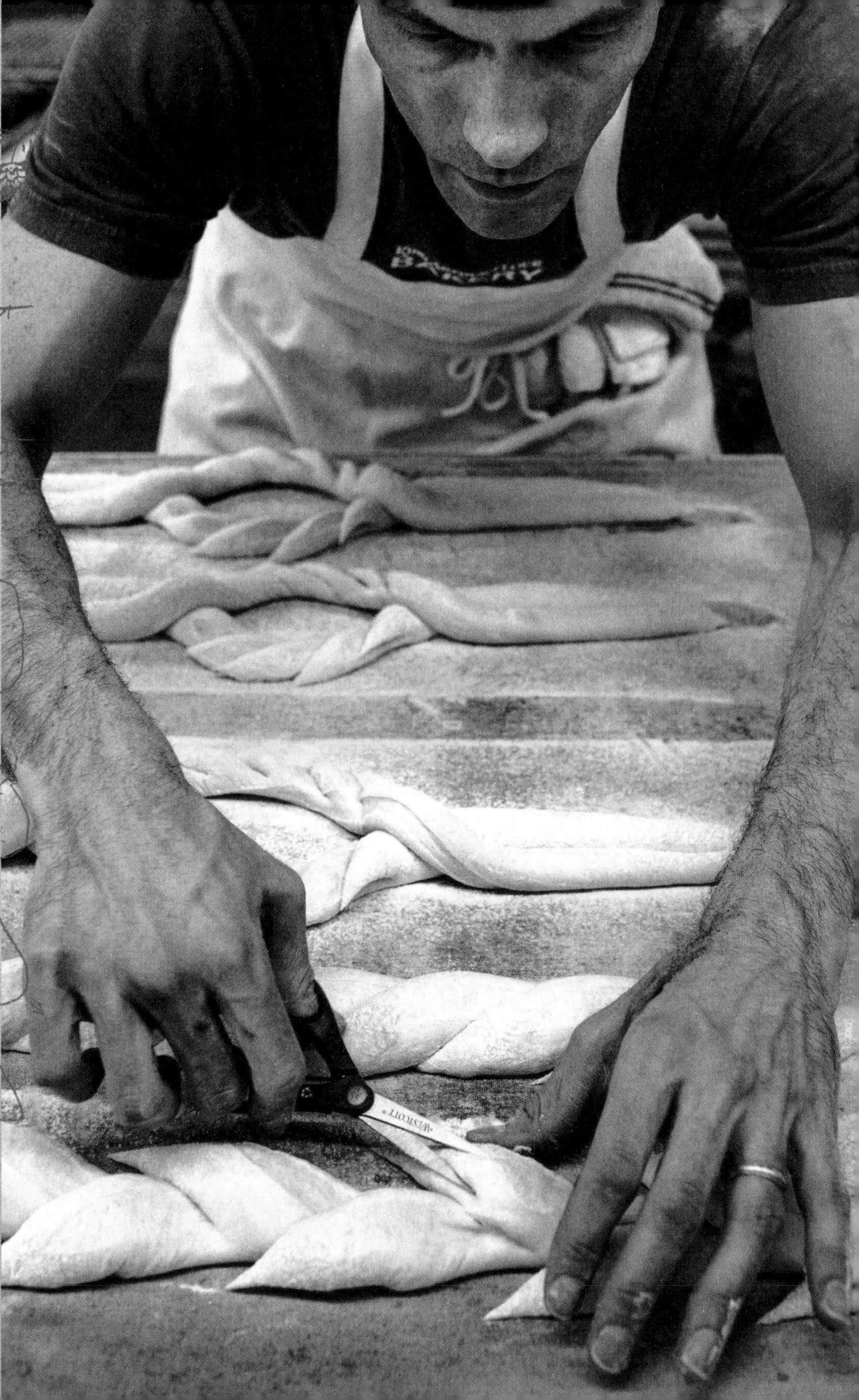

GROWTH AND COMPETITION

Years of daily work in the bakery grew my tiny trees of skill and competence into forests, forming regions, continents, and connected plates in my small universe of bread. When a woodworker gains proficiency with the plane and band saw, the tools recede to the background and a door opens to let in creativity and expression. After many, many repetitions I grew to where I could feel doughs and sense what they needed, and my hands began to adjust in gentle increments while shaping. I wrote formulas in my head, foreseeing outcomes and making adjustments to improve results before even trying them in the bakery. Through the syntax, structure, and language of baking, I slowly gained the ability to speak through bread and shifted my focus to expression. I didn't know where this path would lead, I had heard of the "world cup of bread baking," but I was busy enough and content to follow my heart, exploring the delicious world of bread, finding my own way and words.

In the beginning of this exploration I wanted the greatest hits. I played my way from French baguette and pain de seigle north into Germany for Vollkornbrot and down to the Mediterranean for Italian schiacciata, and to points beyond, all in an attempt to learn a corner of the landscape before working in my own backyard. When I did begin to do my own design work, I found it helped to think of bread in the abstract; a loaf was like a house to be built or a theater production to be mounted. I considered the elements, balancing them as if on a design board with the requisite cohesion and contrast. When we bite, we sense in waves that roll in, forming the totality of the eating experience. As bakers we can guide this, making choices at each intersection of crust and crumb, fermentation and grain choice. We can push sweet against salt and find shapes that affect the interior structure of bread; or we can choose visual options from stenciling to decorative scoring with a razor blade before baking, all of which tease the eyes with beauty—for visual richness is the first bite we take. There are endless opportunities to play and grow and express.

Durum wheat—appropriately named, meaning "hard" in Latin (think "durable")—is primarily grown in North Dakota and is used in making pasta. It is so hard that it resists pressure to become flour, and when crushed during milling, initially only shatters into small sandy pieces that many know as *semolina*, literally, "half-milled." But if pressed further with stones, rollers, or hammers it will eventually yield, producing a flour with the yellow hue of butter and wildflowers. I wanted to make a bread that celebrated this color—a loaf whose slices could shine across a room, sending the sunlight of last summer from the Dakota plains to our table. And wouldn't the loaf be even better with yellow raisins dotting the field here and there, glistening jewels of bright sweetness? To contrast with the raisins I wanted a clean tone, a refreshing push, so I added a small amount of fresh rosemary, so small as to raise only a question mark of taste, not an exclamation point. I mixed the base dough, and while it rested in the bowl I sprinkled the raisins and rosemary on top. The soft yellow, pooling mass of durum flour forming a background, with yellow raisins and green rosemary flecks for garnish, was enough. If bread making stopped at this point, I would still be doing it. It is enough to simply look and touch, with the supple glistening stretch of dough and rich colors of nature transforming in the mixing bowl. But it doesn't end there; it gets even better. Before baking, I rolled the loaf in semolina to add an exterior texture to the crust that browns and toasts beautifully in the oven. When baked, the loaf gives a sweet aroma with the faintest whiff of rosemary.

DURUM-ROSEMARY BREAD

Yield: **2 medium bâtards**

TOTAL FORMULA

PREFERMENTED FLOUR: 20%

INGREDIENTS	METRIC (GRAMS)	VOLUMETRIC (APPROXIMATE)	BAKER'S %
All-purpose flour	379	3 cups + 2 tablespoons	60%
Durum flour	253	2 cups	40%
Water	455	2 cups	72%
Salt, fine	13	2⅛ teaspoons	2%
Yeast, dry instant	5	1¾ teaspoons	0.75%
Raisins, golden	82	¾ cup	13%
Rosemary, fresh	13	1 tablespoon	2%
Semolina or cornmeal, for the crust			
Total Weight	1,200	All	189.75%

POOLISH

INGREDIENTS	METRIC (GRAMS)	VOLUMETRIC (APPROXIMATE)	BAKER'S %
All-purpose flour	126	1 cup	100%
Water	126	½ cup	100%
Yeast	Pinch	Pinch	0.10%
Total Weight	252		200.10%

FINAL DOUGH

INGREDIENTS	METRIC (GRAMS)	VOLUMETRIC (APPROXIMATE)
Water	329	1½ cups
Poolish	252	All
All-purpose flour	253	2 cups + 2 tablespoons
Durum flour	253	2 cups
Salt, fine	13	2⅛ teaspoons
Yeast, dry instant	5	scant 1¾ teaspoons
Raisins, golden	82	¾ cup
Rosemary, fresh	13	1 tablespoon
Semolina or cornmeal, for the crust		All
Total Weight	1,200	All

DAY ONE

POOLISH

In a medium bowl, stir together the flour and yeast, then add the tepid water (75°F to 80°F).

Mix until smooth.

Cover and set at room temperature for 12 to 16 hours.

DAY TWO

PREPARE

Pour warm water over the raisins and allow them to soak while you gather ingredients, 5 to 10 minutes. Drain and reserve until use.

Finely mince the fresh rosemary.

MIX

Calculate temperatures. See Setting Temperatures, page 320, for instructions. Desired dough temperature: 76°F

In a large mixing bowl, combine the final dough water and poolish. Mix with your hands until the poolish is broken up in the water, then add the flours, salt, and yeast. Stir with the handle end of a wooden spoon until the dough forms a shaggy mass. If you find it easier, after some stirring, scrape the dough out of the bowl with a plastic scraper onto your work surface and knead briefly with your hands just until the dough comes together. Resist the urge to add more flour. Scrape the dough off the work surface and return it to the bowl for bulk fermentation.

Place the raisins and rosemary on top of the mixed dough and fold briefly to begin incorporation. It doesn't need to be homogeneous; these ingredients will fully incorporate during folding.

BULK FERMENTATION

Scrape down the sides of the mixing bowl and allow the dough to rise, covered, for 2 hours at room temperature, folding as directed below.

FOLD

Fold after 15, 30, 45, and 60 minutes, then leave untouched for the second hour. See Folding, page 327, for instructions.

As you perform each series of folds, you'll begin to notice that the dough becomes smoother, stronger, and more cohesive.

DIVIDE AND PRESHAPE

Divide the dough into 2 pieces weighing about 600 grams each. See Dividing, page 328, for instructions.

Preshape as rounds. See Preshaping, page 329, for instructions.

Cover and let rest for 10 to 15 minutes.

To make the semolina or cornmeal crust, fill a sheet pan with ¼ inch of semolina or cornmeal. On a second pan, place a well-moistened tea towel or dish towel.

SHAPE

Shape the dough as bâtards roughly 10 inches long. See Shaping, page 331, for instructions. Press the top side into the moistened towel, then roll in the semolina or cornmeal. Place the loaves on a floured baker's linen (couche) or tea towel, top side down. Pleat the couche between the loaves to support their sides as they rise.

PROOF

Cover and proof for 45 to 60 minutes at room temperature.

During the proof, preheat the oven to 450°F with a baking stone and steaming system in place. See Baking, page 349, for instructions.

Transfer the loaves to parchment paper or a baker's peel, gently inverting them so that the underside, which was against the dusted tea towel or linen, becomes the top.

BAKE

Score the bread prior to loading. See Scoring, page 339, for ideas and tips.

Slide the loaves onto the preheated baking stone.

Bake with steam for 35 to 40 minutes. After 30 minutes, carefully remove any steaming devices, lids, or parchment paper. Rotate the loaves on the stone.

At 35 to 40 minutes the loaves should be well colored. Turn off the oven, prop open the door a few inches, and allow the loaves to dry for an additional 10 minutes.

SEEDED SOURDOUGH

Yield: 1 large miche, or 2 medium boules

TOTAL FORMULA

PREFERMENTED FLOUR: 25%

INGREDIENTS	METRIC (GRAMS)	VOLUMETRIC (APPROXIMATE)	BAKER'S %
All-purpose flour	270	2¼ cups	50%
Whole wheat flour	270	2¼ cups	50%
Water	485	2 cups + 2 tablespoons	90%
Salt, fine	12	2 teaspoons	2.20%
Yeast, dry instant	1	scant ½ teaspoon	0.25%
Sourdough culture	27	scant 2 tablespoons	5%
Oats, thick rolled or old-fashioned	81	¾ cup	15%
Sunflower seeds, raw (alternatively, chopped pumpkin seeds, walnuts, or pecans)	27	scant ¼ cup	5%
Millet (alternatively, flaxseeds or cracked wheat)	27	2 tablespoons	5%
Seed blend of flaxseeds, thick rolled oats, and sunflower seeds for the crust (optional)			
Total Weight	1,200		222.45%

STIFF LEVAIN

INGREDIENTS	METRIC (GRAMS)	VOLUMETRIC (APPROXIMATE)	BAKER'S %
All-purpose flour	108	1 cup	80%
Whole wheat flour	27	¼ cup	20%
Water	89	¼ cup + 2 tablespoons	66%
Salt, fine	3	½ teaspoon	2%
Sourdough culture	27	scant 2 tablespoons	20%
Total Weight	254	All	188%

TOASTED GRAIN SOAKER

INGREDIENTS	METRIC (GRAMS)	VOLUMETRIC (APPROXIMATE)	BAKER'S %
Oats, thick rolled or old-fashioned	81	¾ cup	60%
Sunflower seeds, raw (optionally, chopped pumpkin seeds, walnuts, or pecans)	27	scant ¼ cup	20%
Millet (alternatively, flaxseeds or cracked wheat)	27	2 tablespoons	20%
Water	148	½ cup + 2 tablespoons	110%
Total Weight	283	All	210%

FINAL DOUGH

INGREDIENTS	METRIC (GRAMS)	VOLUMETRIC (APPROXIMATE)
Water	248	1 cup + 2 tablespoons
Stiff levain	254	All
All-purpose flour	162	1¼ cups
Whole wheat flour	243	2 cups
Salt, fine	9	1½ teaspoons
Yeast, dry instant	1	scant ½ teaspoon
Soaker	283	All
Total Weight	1,200	All

DAY ONE

STIFF LEVAIN

In a medium bowl, combine the tepid water (75°F to 80°F) and the sourdough culture. Mix with your hands and fingers until the culture is broken up and well distributed in the water, then add the flours and salt.

Mix briefly, then knead until smooth.

Cover and set at room temperature for 12 to 16 hours.

TOASTED GRAIN SOAKER

Put the grains and any seeds for the soaker in a large heavy pan and set over low to medium heat. Toast the soaker mixture, stirring it and moving it around, until golden. This toasting may also be done on a sheet pan in a 400°F oven.

Add the toasted blend to the soaker water. Cover and set at room temperature for 12 to 16 hours.

RECIPE CONTINUES

DAY TWO

MIX

Calculate temperatures. See Setting Temperatures, page 320, for instructions. Desired dough temperature: 78 F

In a large mixing bowl, combine the final dough water and stiff levain. Mix with your hands until the levain is broken up in the water, then add the flours, salt, and yeast. Stir with the handle end of a wooden spoon until the dough forms a shaggy mass. If you find it easier, after some stirring, scrape the dough out of the bowl with a plastic scraper onto your work surface and knead briefly with your hands just until the dough comes together. Resist the urge to add more flour. Scrape the dough off the work surface and return it to the bowl for bulk fermentation.

Place the toasted soaker on top of the mixed dough and fold briefly to begin incorporation. It doesn't need to be homogeneous; these ingredients will fully incorporate during folding.

BULK FERMENTATION

Scrape down the sides of the mixing bowl and allow the dough to rise, covered, for 3 hours at room temperature, folding as directed below.

FOLD

Fold after 30, 60, 90, and 120 minutes, then leave untouched for the last hour. See Folding, page 327, for instructions.

As you perform each series of folds, you'll begin to notice that the dough becomes smoother, stronger, and more cohesive.

DIVIDE AND PRESHAPE

For a single large miche, preshape as a round. See Preshaping, page 329, for instructions.

Cover and let rest for 15 minutes.

For two loaves, divide the dough into two pieces weighing about 600 grams each. See Dividing, page 328, for instructions.

Preshape as rounds. See Preshaping, page 329, for instructions.

Cover and let rest for 10 to 15 minutes.

SHAPE

To make the seeded crust, place a ¼-inch layer of mixed seeds on a sheet pan. On a second pan, place a well-moistened tea towel or dish towel.

Shape as boules. See Shaping, page 331, for instructions.

Press the top side of the boules into the moistened towel and roll the moist top through the seed blend, thoroughly and heavily coating the top of each loaf.

Place the large miche, seam side up, in a banneton or towel-lined bowl, approximately 10 inches wide and 4 inches deep.

Place the two medium boules, seam side up, in bannetons or towel-lined bowls, approximately 9 inches wide and 3½ inches deep.

PROOF Cover and proof for 60 to 75 minutes at room temperature.

During the proof, preheat the oven to 450°F with a baking stone and steaming system in place. See Baking, page 349, for instructions.

Transfer the loaves to parchment paper or a baker's peel, gently inverting them so that the underside, which was against the dusted tea towel or banneton, becomes the top.

Score the bread prior to loading. See Scoring, page 339, for ideas and tips.

BAKE Slide the loaves onto the preheated baking stone.

Bake with steam for 35 to 40 minutes. After 30 minutes, carefully remove any steaming devices, lids, parchment paper, or bowls. Rotate the loaves on the stone.

At 35 to 40 minutes the loaves should be well colored. If making a single large loaf, bake 10 minutes longer than the two medium loaves.

Turn off the oven, prop open the door a few inches, and allow the loaves to dry for an additional 10 minutes.

In baking we've long relied upon the big hitters of the grain world to meet the bulk of our flour needs. This situation hasn't improved much in the past hundred years; in fact, it may have worsened as farms have grown in size and wheats have been bred for protein content, yield, and other commercial factors. But we can help, you and I. First, we can become bakers. And second, we can look for farmers and growers in our own backyard, seeking niche grains or legume flours that can add flavor and nutrition and do good things for the soil when grown in rotation with wheat.

"Cranbuck" was a one of a kind. When developing new breads, I usually begin with a design board. I think of color, shape, flavor, and texture and appropriate percentages of flour, water, and other ingredients before putting things into a spreadsheet, and eventually, an oven. This is rarely a straight line, always more of a meander, a long process of tests, each of which takes a minimum of two days. But Cranbuck was different. Straight out of the gate, it worked. When nonglutenous legume flours or nut flours are used in artisan bread, I have found that making a swelling (adding boiling water to the flour and allowing it to cool before the mix) is a good way to improve handling. The eating quality is also improved. I use the swelling technique with this bread and, after making the swelling and letting it cool, I inoculate the buckwheat mixture with sourdough culture, fermenting it for increased flavor.

CRANBUCK

Yield: **2 medium bâtards or boules**

TOTAL FORMULA

PREFERMENTED FLOUR: 13%

INGREDIENTS	METRIC (GRAMS)	VOLUMETRIC (APPROXIMATE)	BAKER'S %
All-purpose flour	432	3½ cups	87%
Whole buckwheat flour	65	½ cup	13%
Water	388	1¾ cups	78%
Salt, fine	10	1¾ teaspoons	2%
Yeast, dry instant	3	1 teaspoon	0.60%
Sourdough culture	13	scant 1 tablespoon	2.65%
Cranberries, dried, coarsely chopped	89	¾ cup	18%
Total Weight	1,000	All	201.25%

BUCKWHEAT PREFERMENT

INGREDIENTS	METRIC (GRAMS)	VOLUMETRIC (APPROXIMATE)	BAKER'S %
Whole buckwheat flour	65	½ cup	100%
Water, boiling	52	¼ cup	80%
Sourdough culture	13	scant 1 tablespoon	20%
Total Weight	130	All	200%

FINAL DOUGH

INGREDIENTS	METRIC (GRAMS)	VOLUMETRIC (APPROXIMATE)
Water	336	1½ cups
Buckwheat preferment	130	All
All-purpose flour	432	3½ cups
Salt, fine	10	1¾ teaspoons
Yeast, dry instant	3	1 teaspoon
Cranberries, dried, coarsely chopped	89	¾ cup
Total Weight	1,000	All

RECIPE CONTINUES

DAY ONE

BUCKWHEAT PREFERMENT

In a medium bowl, combine the boiling water and the buckwheat flour.

Stir with the handle end of a wooden spoon to combine. Once the mixture has cooled slightly, knead to fully combine.

Cool at room temperature for 10 to 15 minutes, then knead in the sourdough culture.

Cover and set at room temperature for 12 to 16 hours.

DAY TWO

MIX

Calculate temperatures. See Setting Temperatures, page 320, for instructions. Desired dough temperature: 76°F

In a large mixing bowl, combine the final dough water and buckwheat preferment. Mix with your hands until the preferment is broken up in the water, then add the flour, salt, and yeast. Stir with the handle end of a wooden spoon until the dough forms a shaggy mass. If you find it easier, after some stirring, scrape the dough out of the bowl with a plastic scraper onto your work surface and knead briefly with your hands just until the dough comes together. Resist the urge to add more flour. Scrape the dough off the work surface and return it to the bowl for bulk fermentation.

Place the cranberries on top of the mixed dough and fold briefly to begin incorporation. It doesn't need to be homogeneous; the cranberries will fully incorporate during folding.

BULK FERMENTATION

Scrape down the sides of the mixing bowl and allow the dough to rise, covered, for 2½ hours at room temperature, folding as directed below.

FOLD

Fold after 20, 40, 60, and 80 minutes, then leave untouched until the divide. See Folding, page 327, for instructions.

As you perform each series of folds, you'll begin to notice that the dough becomes smoother, stronger, and more cohesive.

DIVIDE AND PRESHAPE

Divide the dough into 2 pieces weighing about 500 grams each. See Dividing, page 328, for instructions.

Preshape as rounds. See Preshaping, page 329, for instructions.

Cover and let rest for 15 minutes.

SHAPE

Shape as bâtards. See Shaping, page 331, for instructions.

Place, seam side up, on a floured baker's linen (couche), and pleat the couche between the loaves to support the sides as they rise.

PROOF Cover and proof for 50 to 60 minutes at room temperature.

During the proof, preheat the oven to 475°F with a baking stone and steaming system in place. See Baking, page 349, for instructions.

Transfer the loaves to parchment paper or a baker's peel, gently inverting them so that the underside, which was against the dusted tea towel or linen, becomes the top.

BAKE Score the bread prior to loading. See Scoring, page 339, for ideas and tips.

Slide the loaves onto the preheated baking stone.

Bake with steam for 22 to 25 minutes. After 15 minutes, carefully remove any steaming devices, lids, or parchment paper. Rotate the loaves on the stone.

At 22 to 25 minutes the loaves should be well colored. Turn off the oven, prop open the door a few inches, and allow the loaves to dry for an additional 10 minutes.

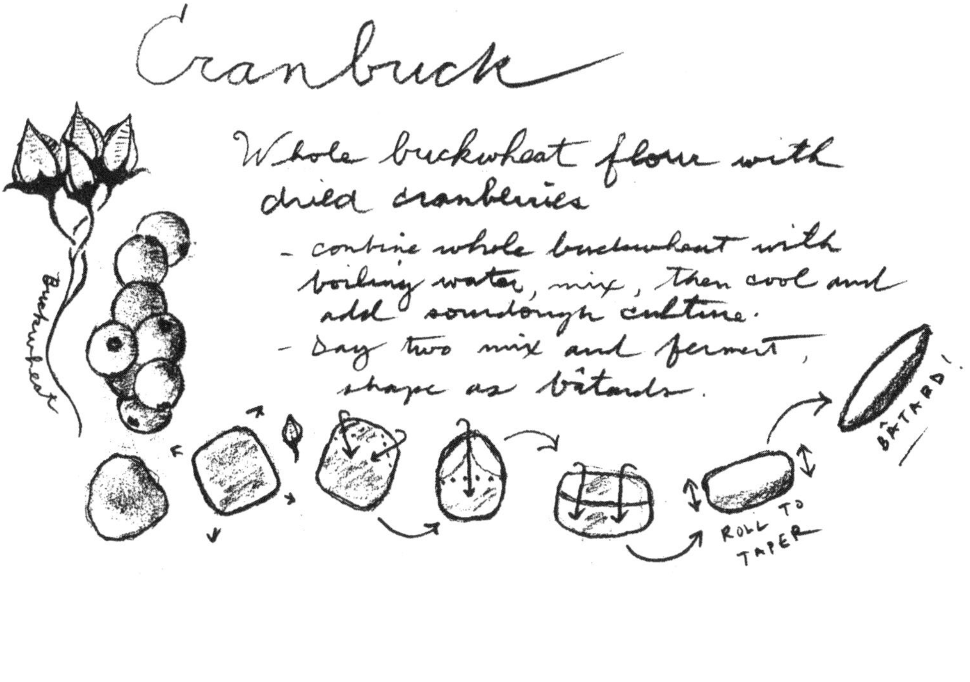

Cranbuck

Whole buckwheat flour with dried cranberries

- combine whole buckwheat with boiling water, mix, then cool and add sourdough culture.
- Day two mix and ferment, shape as bâtards.

ROLL TO TAPER

BÂTARD!

Buckwheat

The Appalachian Trail runs from Georgia to Maine and passes within a quarter mile of the bakery—you can see it from the parking lot. Hikers with large packs pass daily, traveling north or south, followed by a cloud of scent, as evidence of the difficulty (and infrequent showers!) of the 2,100-mile route. Shortly after we arrived in Vermont, I began running our many miles of wooded trails, following ribbons of dirt or snow down the endless tree tunnel, foraging in cellar holes and old rock walls that had been retaken by forest. In time I found that if short runs were good, then longer ones were even better. I spent hours in the woods sweating and covering long distances, and I worked my way up to six- or seven-hour trail runs and then races, competing at distances greater than the length of a marathon, sometimes up to fifty miles in a day. The racing wasn't about competing—I certainly wasn't winning anything—it was about journeying, beginning something tremendous, a challenge that dwarfed fitness and confidence and, in the end, surviving. We don't have to run super-distances to find challenges; even parenting will work, and it certainly requires more than what we possess as we leave the hospital with a swaddled bundle—we grow into *and* within the challenge. I grew as a runner and found my craft by signing up for races that I doubted I could complete. Failure is OK. The improvement, the training, the practice of the craft . . . *that* is winning.

I found my way to this same place with bread. A friend of mine, Michael Rhodes, was the team captain for a small group of bakers chosen to represent the United States in the SIGEP Cup competition in Italy. Michael called the bakery one day and asked if I would be a late addition to the team. Competitive bread baking takes bread design, shaping, and baking to a level far above what is normally expected. Every aspect, from texture to flavor, color, shape, innovation, and finishing techniques, is scrutinized and examined.

After we developed and practiced our individual items at our respective bakeries, the small four-person team gathered for intensive sessions in the snowy dead of January at New England Culinary Institute in Montpelier, Vermont, where Michael was chair of the baking and pastry department. The SIGEP competition requires teams to prepare multiple breads, *viennoiserie* (pastry products using laminated brioche or croissant doughs), and a decorative sculptural piece made entirely of dough. In some competitions the components must all be completed, start to finish, during the eight-hour competition day and usually include an additional one to two timed hours of setup the evening before. The year that we competed, SIGEP allowed teams to arrive with pieces of a decorative bread sculpture already made and finish the sculpture on-site. Decorative works are large dioramas made entirely of doughs that handle like Play-Doh; these sculptures are often colored with spices, textured with seeds and grains, and even silk-screened before being assembled with glue made from molten sugar. Michael built, among the many other preparations for the trip, a large multicolored rooster that he had designed to perch on a log (also made of dough). After days of practice we packed his sculpture; loaded our many ingredients, tools, aprons, and passports; and headed south to fly out of JFK. Arriving in Heathrow, we found that all outbound flights were canceled due to snow.

Traveling with sourdough culture is not unlike traveling with a baby. It must be fed on a schedule, held, wooed, and even burped occasionally; and it presents the additional challenge of airport security tending to dislike it. After finding flour in a mini-mart near the hotel (our bags weren't accessible) and spending a night on British soil, we headed back to the airport to try to make our way to Italy. While we were waiting among the delayed, cranky masses, our needy babies eventually hollered for another feeding of flour and water. We debated our options for the feeding; clandestine option A, which was to hide behind a construction barrier and conceal this strange activity; or option B, "nothing to see here . . . just mixing strange pastes and pouring them into sealed stainless-steel vials to put in our carry-on luggage." We chose B and proceeded, tasting the culture even more than was necessary, trying to project the edible nature of our science experiment goop to those huddled around us, gawking and confused.

Eventually we were able to board and move on, but because of our delayed arrival, we made it to Rimini very late and lost our entire preparation day. We frantically set about making doughs and final preparations in our hotel rooms, working well into the night and finishing only a few hours before our competition day would begin. Somewhere in the middle of that dark night, Michael opened the suitcase with the rooster and I heard a significant amount of cursing. I ran next door to find him with pieces of the shattered rooster in his hands. We eventually advanced beyond the crying stage, ready to give our best effort in spite of our broken bird, and I began the rituals I had rehearsed, making the three breads that were to be my contribution.

The first bread was a walnut ciabatta with a dark, barklike crust and an open interior, accented with toasted black walnuts and English walnuts and infused with walnut oil. I rolled the dough in coarse bran for texture and made a stencil by photographing the bark of a walnut tree, then cut out the dark lines between the bark pieces. I applied the stencil and dusted over it with white flour just before baking. While the stencil is fun, this loaf will disappear quickly with or without the stunning visual.

RUSTIC WALNUT CIABATTA

Yield: **2 large loaves**

TOTAL FORMULA
PREFERMENTED FLOUR: 33%

INGREDIENTS	METRIC (GRAMS)	VOLUMETRIC (APPROXIMATE)	BAKER'S %
All-purpose flour	517	4¼ cups + 1 tablespoon	100%
Water	414	1¾ cups + 1 tablespoon	80%
Salt, fine	12	2 teaspoons	2.30%
Yeast, dry instant	2	heaping ½ teaspoon	0.50%
Walnuts, halves	155	1½ cups	30%
Walnut oil (optional)	10	2 teaspoons	2%
Coarse wheat bran	10	3 tablespoons	2%
Coarse wheat bran, for the crust			
Total Weight	1,120	All	216.80%

BIGA

INGREDIENTS	METRIC (GRAMS)	VOLUMETRIC (APPROXIMATE)	BAKER'S %
All-purpose flour	170	1½ cups	100%
Water	102	½ cup	60%
Yeast, dry instant	Pinch	Pinch	0.10%
Total Weight	272	All	160.10%

SOAKER

INGREDIENTS	METRIC (GRAMS)	VOLUMETRIC (APPROXIMATE)
Walnuts, halves	155	1½ cups
Water	85	½ cup
Walnut oil	10	2 teaspoons
Coarse wheat bran	10	3 tablespoons
Total Weight	260	All

RECIPE CONTINUES

RUSTIC WALNUT CIABATTA
PAGE 249

FINAL DOUGH

INGREDIENTS	METRIC (GRAMS)	VOLUMETRIC (APPROXIMATE)
Water	227	¾ cup + 1 tablespoon
Biga	272	All
All-purpose flour	347	2¾ cups + 1 tablespoon
Salt, fine	12	2 teaspoons
Yeast, dry instant	2	scant 1 teaspoon
Soaker	260	All
Total Weight	1,120	All

DAY ONE

BIGA

In a medium bowl, stir together the flour and yeast, then add the tepid water (75°F to 80°F).

Mix briefly, then knead until smooth.

Cover and set at room temperature for 12 to 16 hours.

DAY TWO

PREPARE

Put the walnuts in a large heavy pan set over low to medium heat.

Toast them, stirring and moving them around, until they darken some and are fragrant. Toasting may also be done on a sheet pan in a 400°F oven for approximately 10 minutes.

After they cool, break them up some by rolling over them with a rolling pin.

SOAKER

Combine the walnuts, soaker water, walnut oil, and wheat bran. Allow the soaker to sit for 5 to 10 minutes while you gather and measure ingredients for the final mix.

MIX

Calculate temperatures. See Setting Temperatures, page 320, for instructions. Desired dough temperature: 76°F

In a large mixing bowl, combine the final dough water and biga. Mix with your hands until the biga is broken up in the water, then add the flour, salt, and yeast. Stir with the handle end of a wooden spoon until the dough forms a shaggy mass. If you find it easier, after some stirring, scrape the dough out of the bowl with a plastic scraper onto your work surface and knead briefly with your hands just until the dough comes together. Resist the urge to add more flour. Scrape the dough off the work surface and return it to the bowl for bulk fermentation.

Place the walnut soaker on top of the mixed dough and fold briefly to begin incorporating the nuts. It doesn't need to be homogeneous; these ingredients will fully incorporate during folding.

BULK FERMENTATION	Scrape down the sides of the mixing bowl and allow the dough to rise, covered, for 2½ hours at room temperature, folding as directed below.
FOLD	Fold after 15, 30, 45, 60, 75, and 90 minutes, then leave untouched for the last hour. See Folding, page 327, for instructions.
DIVIDE AND SHAPE	To make the bran crust, layer ¼ inch of bran on a sheet pan. On a second pan, place a well-moistened tea towel or dish towel.
	Transfer the dough onto a generously floured surface and gently stretch to an 8 by 10-inch rectangle.
	Using a bench knife or chef's knife, cut exactly in half along the long axis. Set the top side on the moistened towel, then roll in coarse bran and place on a lightly floured baker's linen (couche) or tea towel, top side down. Repeat with the second loaf. Pleat the couche between the loaves to support their sides as they rise.
PROOF	Cover and proof for 30 to 45 minutes at room temperature.
BAKE	During the proof, preheat the oven to 475°F with a baking stone and steaming system in place. See Baking, page 349, for instructions.
	Transfer the loaves to parchment paper or a baker's peel, gently inverting them so that the underside, which was against the dusted tea towel or linen, becomes the top.
	Slide the loaves onto the preheated baking stone.
	Bake with steam for 32 to 35 minutes. After 20 minutes, carefully remove any steaming devices, lids, or parchment paper. Rotate the loaves on the stone.
	At 32 to 35 minutes the loaves should be well colored. Turn off the oven, prop open the door a few inches, and allow the loaves to dry for an additional 10 minutes.

As a counterpoint to the open-textured walnut ciabatta, I settled on a German rye bread baked in a slender loaf pan and made with whole rye flour, candied orange peel, and freshly ground coriander. These flavors were inspired by Belgian beers, which blend the sweetness of malt with citrus and aromatics. For visual appeal I made a tiny crate out of small dough pieces that I dried and painted with a coffee reduction stain to look like wood, then assembled and filled with miniature oranges made from a dense white dough, dyed orange, and pressed with the tines of a grater. The tiny crate was to be placed on the loaf after baking. I took the pieces of the crate with me to Italy, assembled it in the middle of the night before the competition, and filled it with the oranges.

Citrus Vollkornbrot

Candied orange peel
Honey
Rye
Coriander

- Rye sourdough w/ a rye chop soaker and candied peel, coriander and honey

- Day one, set rye preferment and the soaker.

- Day two, mix, shape and bake.

CITRUS VOLLKORNBROT

Yield: **Two 3½ by 5½-inch tea loaves**

TOTAL FORMULA
PREFERMENTED FLOUR: 35%

INGREDIENTS	METRIC (GRAMS)	VOLUMETRIC (APPROXIMATE)	BAKER'S %
Whole rye flour	365	3½ cups	100%
Water	391	1¾ cups	107%
Salt, fine	9	1½ teaspoons	2.50%
Yeast, dry instant	4	heaping 1¼ teaspoons	1%
Sourdough culture	26	scant 2 tablespoons	7%
Rye chops	91	1 cup	25%
Candied orange peel	84	½ cup	23%
Honey, wildflower	27	heaping 1 tablespoon	7.50%
Coriander, freshly ground	3	1½ teaspoons	0.90%
Total Weight	1,000	All	273.90%

RYE SOURDOUGH

INGREDIENTS	METRIC (GRAMS)	VOLUMETRIC (APPROXIMATE)	BAKER'S %
Whole rye flour	128	1¼ cups	100%
Water	102	½ cup	80%
Sourdough culture	26	scant 2 tablespoons	20%
Total Weight	256	All	200%

SOAKER

INGREDIENTS	METRIC (GRAMS)	VOLUMETRIC (APPROXIMATE)	BAKER'S %
Rye chops	91	1 cup	100%
Water	100	½ cup	110%
Total Weight	191	All	210%

RECIPE CONTINUES

FINAL DOUGH

INGREDIENTS	METRIC (GRAMS)	VOLUMETRIC (APPROXIMATE)
Water	189	¾ cup
Honey, wildflower	27	heaping 1 tablespoon
Rye preferment	256	All
Whole rye flour	237	2¼ cups
Salt, fine	9	1½ teaspoons
Yeast, dry instant	4	scant 1¼ teaspoons
Candied orange peel	84	½ cup
Coriander, freshly ground	3	1½ teaspoons
Soaker	191	All
Whole rye flour, for rolling the loaves		
Total Weight	1,000	All

DAY ONE

RYE SOURDOUGH

In a medium bowl, combine the tepid water (75°F to 80°F) and sourdough culture. Mix with your hands and fingers until the culture is broken up and well distributed in the water, then add the flour.

Mix briefly, then knead until smooth.

Cover and set at room temperature for 12 to 16 hours.

RYE CHOP SOAKER

Combine the rye chops and water in a medium bowl.

Cover and set at room temperature for 12 to 16 hours.

DAY TWO

MIX

Calculate temperatures. See Setting Temperatures, page 320, for instructions. Desired dough temperature: 78°F

In a large mixing bowl, combine the final dough water, honey, and rye preferment. Mix with your hands until the sourdough is broken up in the water, then add the flour, salt, orange peel, coriander, yeast, and soaker. Stir with the handle end of a wooden spoon until the dough forms a cohesive mass. This wet, sticky dough is easier to handle if kept in the mixing bowl.

BULK FERMENTATION

Due to the large amount of prefermented flour, this dough goes directly to divide and shape.

DIVIDE AND PRESHAPE

Spray or grease two 3½ by 5½-inch tea loaf pans.

Divide the dough into 2 pieces weighing about 500 grams each. See Dividing, page 328, for instructions.

SHAPE

Shape on a surface well dusted with rye flour. Roll the pieces into a tube slightly shorter than the length of the pan. See Shaping, page 331, for instructions.

Roll further in whole rye to entirely coat each loaf, then place in the pans. Press gently with your knuckles to evenly flatten the dough into the form. Sprinkle a light dusting of additional rye flour on the top surface of the loaf.

Immediately after shaping, score the loaves with a plastic or metal scraper. Hold the scraper at a right angle to the top of the loaf and push it into the dough ½ to ¾ inch to make an "x" that connects opposite corners, crossing in the middle of the loaf.

Cover the loaves and proof for 30 to 45 minutes. Where the cuts were made the loaf will open slightly.

BAKE

During the proof, preheat the oven to 475°F with a steaming system in place. See Baking, page 349, for instructions.

Bake with steam for 20 minutes. After 20 minutes, rotate the loaves.

Reduce the oven to 400°F and bake for an additional 30 to 35 minutes.

After the total baking time of 50 to 55 minutes the loaves should be well colored. Turn off the oven, remove the loaves from the pans, and place them directly on the oven rack. Open the door a few inches and allow them to dry for an additional 5 to 10 minutes.

Our competition day went off about as well as could be expected. We weathered the bumpy arrival and soldiered on, doing our best to proceed with kindness and a little cheer. We finished in the allotted time with the required number of products, and even managed to glue together and patch up the rooster. He was ugly as heck compared with the airbrushed, delicate sculptures others had created, but we were done. In the days following, other national teams, including the Germans, Hungarians, and Israelis, competed. The first day I was content to watch, gleaning what I could, but then, restless with sitting and looking for a way to salvage as much of the trip as possible, I weaseled my way onto a team of bakers from all across Italy. We worked together for two days, baking and selling goods for the benefit of a young persons' baking organization. My Italian was coming back quickly and we laughed, baked, ate, and cleaned, enjoying the opportunity to feel the bond of trade across both language and culture.

The winners were announced on the last day, with the MC bellowing "Italia!" over the loudspeaker to the crack of confetti poppers and applause. We had no hopes for the podium. Only a miracle could have saved the day for us after our late arrival and the smashed sculpture. The twists and turns that followed the medal announcement were a comedy of errors, including a removal of the Italians entirely after some dubious rule bending. We were disappointed, but underneath my sour face a smile was forming. . . . During preparation and also during the competition itself I had felt the improvement in my skills and confidence. My capacity was twitching like leg muscles, ready to flex, to work, to scramble, climb, run, and jump at the bidding of my heart toward something new, something bigger and harder!

COUPE

A few years after I joined the bakers at King Arthur, Jeffrey encouraged me to try out for Team USA, which would compete at the Coupe du Monde de la Boulangerie. The Coupe, as we call it, is the world cup of bread and truly the highest summit in competitive baking. Team members are superheroes in the baking world—we raise them and praise them and they deserve it. Dubbed the "bread Olympics" by my kids, the Coupe occurs every four years in Paris. I knew the multiyear effort required, and when I considered family needs, the time away from home, and, honestly, my own short experience with the trade, I didn't feel ready. But, returning from Italy, I was in a different place; the Coupe felt like the right race, the right motivation to force me to become something bigger and better even if, when I put my toe on the line, I couldn't be sure of finishing.

I quietly submitted the initial application with the required formulas, pictures, and recommendations and a healthy serving of "Who knows," "Why not?" and "Let's see what happens." When asked by friends, family, and colleagues what I was up to, I was sheepish, hesitant even to mention my Coupe bid. It was a long shot of half-court proportions, a bold move that suggested a confidence that did not exist. Still, I threw myself into every detail—I made beautiful breads; Julia Reed took gorgeous pictures; and I received recommendations from Jeffrey, James McGuire, and my friend Richard Miscovich, three of the best bakers in my world. I made a deal with myself, committing to the ideal that, win, lose, or draw, I would come out on top, as the training would force me to continue growing and challenging myself to be a better baker, deepening my relationship with my craft. And so I was off, moving at quite a clip.

I was accepted and scheduled for a slot at the semifinals in Providence, Rhode Island. I became a machine, training as I would for a long race, logging piles of miles each week. I looked everywhere to find inspiration for flavors and shapes, but also worked at the basics, making baguettes every day for weeks on end. I built countless spreadsheets with eight-hour schedules, dividing mock competition days into ten-minute blocks, each booked with overlapping processes. Mix this, scale that, get water for this, divide that, shape those, bake this one, chill this dough, and on and on: eight hours with one four-minute break in order to complete the necessary number of loaves and rolls on time without penalty. I haven't worked in a hospital, but I imagine the complexity there to be something akin to this scenario. Multiple patients ring the call button all at once, all day. I will be right with you! You can wait . . . room three is in arrest! Crap, am I burning something? Managing these separate processes was a new skill set and entirely different from simply making breads with innovative forms and flavors. But it's all part of a successful bid.

I headed to Providence after an ice age of preparation during which my knack for obsessing and working was on full display. By the time I stood in the actual competition space, I had completed enough practice runs that the order of events was second nature. I was organized down to the smallest details; my dough containers and tools were packed like science experiments headed to a space lab, stacked in reverse order of use, with nothing overlooked. The timed one-hour setup went so smoothly that I was sure I must have missed something as I completed it in record time and headed to day two and the full eight-hour period feeling perfect. If I had enjoyed a little celebration after I left that night it would have been good, because after the following full competition day there would be no dancing.

There were mistakes and flubs that I had never made before, I was behind on my timings for the first time since my early practices, and the nail in the coffin was some bum yeast, which left me with baguettes that mostly failed and other loaves that didn't rise well. To say that I felt horrible doesn't quite sum it up. My family, friends, and colleagues had supported me endlessly—a poor performance reflected poorly on the quality of support I had received. I was ashamed. After packing and cleaning I sat dejected in the car for what seemed like hours. The dark lot was empty and windswept, a perfect match for my mood.

But I wasn't the only one who struggled—it is damn hard to walk into a new bakery with different mixers and oven, with a foreign arrangement of benches and sinks, and perform at the top of one's capability. And this is exactly the point—the person chosen for Paris would need to do exactly this, but under even more difficult conditions. This is stressful, even painful—bakers bake for beauty and flavor, and when either one is suffering, so are we. During the six-week wait for the announcement of the finals I decided to pretend (or at least prepare for the possibility) that I was going to them. The time gap between the announcement and the contest would be very short; if any of us wanted to show different breads we would need to begin the long development and practice process immediately in order to have a shot. Names were announced in a bland e-mail that offered thanks to all who had worked so hard, and there, written on the page, was my name . . . I was going on!

If the pace of preparation and focus had been intense before, I turned the dial on the amplifier up to eleven. I needed a new lineup of *more* innovative, *more* beautiful shapes, with flavor combinations that perfectly harmonized grains, fermentation, and additions; and I needed all of this immediately.

Bakers are largely traditionalists. We like our innovation in bits; small bites of change spread on large slices of tradition. I think of the Japanese Kaiseki master, Chef Murata, who advises us to look with one eye forward to innovation and with the other back to tradition. I searched high and low for this balance, but nothing would stick. . . . Everything I created was too cerebral, too planned, too conscious. I found new combinations, techniques, and shapes, but nothing felt honest or truly organic. If my creations were blocks stacked one atop another, the tower always leaned; it was ungrounded and tentative. I was flailing in this space, lost, spinning my wheels, worrying as days fell off the calendar and the time remaining before the finals disappeared rapidly.

Reaching out for help, I called Chef Mitch Stamm, an instructor in the baking and pastry department at Johnson & Wales University. I had known Mitch for years. He had seen me teach and speak to young bakers, he understood my heart's connection to my craft, and he had been one of my judges at the semifinals. It was just like Mitch to recommend *Black Elk Speaks*. He is connected to the heart and soul of what we do. After some coaxing and apologetic hesitancy on his part, he said it; he identified the thing that I was trying to find. In his Alabama drawl he said, "Martin, the breads were good but you weren't in them; they weren't *you*. You need to add *your* heritage, *your* narrative." And that was it. With his simple reminder and direction I saw everything from a different angle. I now had a guide, something to direct me, a mantra, a road sign. We have but one story, you and I. It is the closest, most powerful material we can access; our heart is in this space, it is where we live, it's what we come from. In order to get to this place I tossed everything and began anew.

And when I restarted, I began with home, looking for things that resonated, combining ingredients from long ago with my home of today. There is sweet and there is bitter, whole wheat and white, molasses and salt, all of it going into the bowl. Here is some of what I found.

Frances Harriet Chamberlin, daughter of Martin Chamberlin, was born in the 1880s in Chapin, New York, and wed Samuel Rainey, an Episcopalian priest who was the son of an Irish immigrant from Rhode Island. Momie, as she was known, was the baker, host, and cook that her position required. Ready to soothe or celebrate with a pie or a pot of soup, a loaf of brown bread, or fresh doughnuts, Momie was quite a baker. Momie's daughter, Carolyn, was my grandmother and passed Momie's recipe for brown bread down to me, lines of script from her sweet hand, on a recipe card. Brown bread, a staple in Irish communities in New England, was traditionally made with equal parts of rye, cornmeal, and whole wheat flour with a touch of molasses. It was soda-leavened and steamed in coffee cans. My grandmother preferred it baked rather than steamed, and that is the version I came to know.

powerBROT sits at the junction of Momie's brown bread and German Vollkornbrot. It evolved out of a desire for a hearty, healthy breakfast bread. A high-fiber, stick-to-the-ribs snack with ample seeds and gentle sweetness. Of all the breads I tested and left for our morning bakers to pick over, this is the one that consistently had the least remnants. Perfect with coffee or a smear of cream cheese, or just enjoyed plain. The flour blend for powerBROT is whole wheat, whole cornmeal, and whole rye. To this I add molasses, soaked grains, and dried currants for a tart punch. The loaves are rolled in a mixture of pumpkin seeds, whole teff berries, and rye chops for a crunchy, delicious crust.

powerBROT

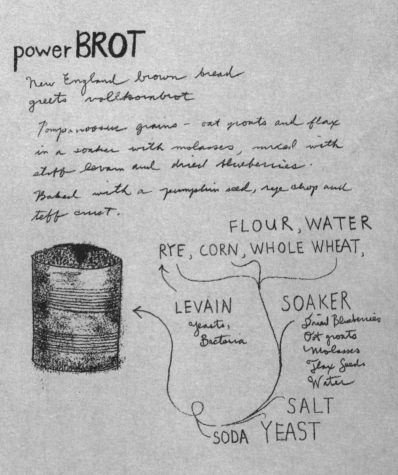

New England brown bread
greets vollkornbrot

Pompanoosuc grains — oat groats and flax
in a soaker with molasses, mixed with
stiff levain and dried blueberries.
Baked with a pumpkin seed, rye chop and
teff crust.

FLOUR, WATER
RYE, CORN, WHOLE WHEAT,

LEVAIN
yeasts,
Bacteria

SOAKER
Dried Blueberries
Oat groats
Molasses
Flax Seeds
Water

SALT
SODA YEAST

POWERBROT **PAGE 268**

POWERBROT

Yield: **Two 3½ by 5½-inch tea loaves**

TOTAL FORMULA
PREFERMENTED FLOUR: 70%

INGREDIENTS	METRIC (GRAMS)	VOLUMETRIC (APPROXIMATE)	BAKER'S %
Whole wheat flour	140	1 cup + 2 tablespoons	55%
Whole rye flour	102	1 cup	40%
Whole cornmeal	13	2 teaspoons	5%
Water	253	1 cup + 1 tablespoon	100%
Salt, fine	6	1 teaspoon	2.50%
Yeast, dry instant	2	heaping ½ teaspoon	0.65%
Sourdough culture	36	heaping 2 tablespoons	14.15%
Baking soda	1	¼ teaspoon	0.25%
Currants, dried	89	½ cup + 2 tablespoons	35%
Oats, thick rolled or old-fashioned	15	2 tablespoons	6%
Millet (can substitute quinoa)	15	heaping 1 tablespoon	6%
Rye chops (can substitute any cracked grain)	15	2 tablespoons	6%
Molasses, blackstrap	13	1½ teaspoons	5%
Pumpkin seeds, raw, green, for the crust (pepitas)	100	scant ½ cup	
Whole teff seeds, chia seeds, or a blend, for the crust	50	2 tablespoons	
Rye chops, for the crust	50	scant ¼ cup	
Total Weight	700	All	275.55%

PREFERMENT

INGREDIENTS	METRIC (GRAMS)	VOLUMETRIC (APPROXIMATE)	BAKER'S %
Whole cornmeal	13	1 tablespoon	7%
Whole rye flour	102	1 cup	57%
Whole wheat flour	64	½ cup	36%
Water	134	½ cup + 1 tablespoon	75%
Sourdough culture	36	heaping 2 tablespoons	20%
Total Weight	349	All	195%

SOAKER

INGREDIENTS	METRIC (GRAMS)	VOLUMETRIC (APPROXIMATE)
Molasses, blackstrap	13	1½ teaspoons
Currants, dried	89	½ cup + 2 tablespoons
Water	81	¼ cup + 2 tablespoons
Oats, thick rolled or old-fashioned	15	2 tablespoons
Rye chops (can substitute any cracked grain)	15	2 tablespoons
Millet (can substitute quinoa)	15	heaping 1 tablespoon
Total Weight	228	All

FINAL DOUGH

INGREDIENTS	METRIC (GRAMS)	VOLUMETRIC (APPROXIMATE)
Water	38	1 tablespoon + 1½ teaspoons
Preferment	349	All
Soaker	228	All
Whole wheat flour	76	½ cup + 2 tablespoons
Salt, fine	6	1 teaspoon
Baking soda	1	¼ teaspoon
Yeast, dry, instant	2	heaping ½ teaspoon
Total Weight	700	All

DAY ONE

PREFERMENT

In a medium bowl, combine the tepid water (75°F to 80°F) and the sourdough culture. Mix with your hands and fingers until the culture is broken up and well distributed in the water, then add the flours and cornmeal.

Mix briefly, then knead until smooth.

Cover and set at room temperature for 12 to 16 hours.

SOAKER

Combine the molasses, currants, water, and grain blend in a medium bowl.

Cover and set at room temperature for 12 to 16 hours.

RECIPE CONTINUES

DAY TWO

Prepare the seed blend for the exterior of the loaf; many options are possible. If you use larger seeds like pumpkin seeds, give them a quick chop in the food processor.

In a small bowl, combine the chopped raw green hulled pumpkin seeds, whole teff, and rye chops.

MIX

Calculate temperatures. See Setting Temperatures, page 320, for instructions. Desired dough temperature: 80°F

In a large mixing bowl, combine the final dough water and preferment. Mix with your hands until the preferment is broken up in the water, then add the soaker, flour, salt, baking soda, and yeast. Stir with the handle end of a wooden spoon until the dough forms a cohesive mass. This wet, sticky dough is easier to handle if kept in the mixing bowl.

BULK FERMENTATION

Because of the large amount of prefermented flour, this dough goes directly to divide and shape.

DIVIDE AND SHAPE

Spray or grease two 3½ by 5½-inch tea loaf pans.

Before dividing, place the prepared seed blend on a rimmed sheet pan. It will be used to coat the surface of the shaped loaves.

This dough is very sticky, almost like a quick bread.

Divide the dough in half (each half about 350 grams). To do so, using a plastic scraper, scoop dough from the bowl and place directly on the scale, then place it on the seed blend and sprinkle and pat the blend on all sides to thoroughly coat.

Roll the dough briefly on the seed pan to ensure a complete coating, then place in the prepared pans and press gently with your knuckles to flatten the dough evenly.

Score the bread after before proofing by cutting an "x" in the top of the rising loaf with a plastic scraper, pushing it about an inch into the top of the loaf.

PROOF

Cover and proof for 60 to 75 minutes at room temperature.

BAKE

Toward the end of the proof, preheat the oven to 425°F with steaming system in place. See Baking, page 349, for instructions.

Bake with steam for 30 minutes. After 30 minutes, rotate the loaves. Reduce the oven temperature to 400°F and bake for another 30 minutes.

At the end of the bake, the sidewalls and tops of the loaves should be firm.

Turn off the oven and remove the loaves from the pans. Place the loaves directly on the oven rack, prop open the oven door a few inches, and allow the loaves to dry for an additional 10 to 15 minutes. Cool the bread for several hours before cutting.

I grew up playing on three hundred acres of red dirt in the Ozark Mountains; hollering could be heard in those hills. That confine of hollows and fields, cloistered by barbed wire and limestone bluffs, filled with forgotten fox traps, drinking springs, and tumbledown log cabins, was our playground.

The Philip boys, four of us, with a sister in tow, would give our rough destination to Mama—back forty, Watson's cabin, bluffs, or something similar—and then disappear, armed to the teeth with air rifles, cow pies, horse apples, and anything else that could serve as a weapon, or projectile. We foraged, stalked, shot, and ran well into the end of the day in our familiar spots: a bluff top for prickly pear cactus fruit, the spring for a drink behind Watson's abandoned cabin, or an ancient mint patch, where we could pack leaves behind our lips and spit until our cheeks caved in.

As we grew, we learned, and sassafras root was quickly a prize. Easily identified, the small trees with three leaves, all different, could be unearthed. The root was quickly harvested from the trunk, and the bounty would later be pulled from a pocket for weeks of sniffing or would be dried and made into a treat of root beer tea. For me, this flavor will always be a potent potion that can transport me through space and time.

The Kvassmiche begins with a brew called *kvass*, a fermented drink common in Eastern Europe, similar in some aspects to kombucha. Warm water is combined with sourdough culture, fresh apples, deeply toasted old bread, and sugar. I add sassafras, fresh ginger, star anise, and vanilla beans to this base and let the mixture work. In 12 to 18 hours the ferment is active and effervescent. I strain the kvass and use it at 75 percent of total hydration in this large miche. The earth notes of whole wheat—mineral, tar, coffee, and chocolate—marry well with the kvass tones, which present as aromatic but not aggressive and transport the sniffer to that sassafras place more easily reached with miles than years.

KVASSMICHE

▸ KVASS IS

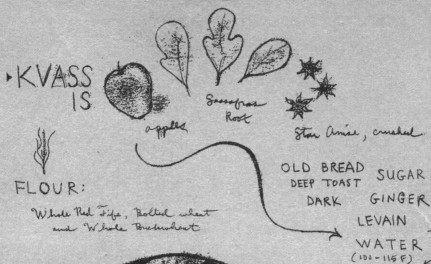

apples

Sassafras Root

Star Anise, crushed

FLOUR:
Whole Red Fife, Bolted wheat and Whole Buckwheat

OLD BREAD
DEEP TOAST
DARK

SUGAR
GINGER
LEVAIN
WATER
(100 - 115 F)

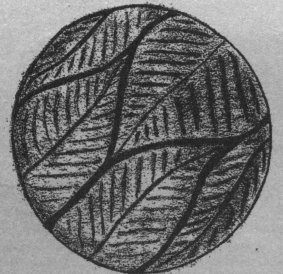

24 - 48 hours,
STRAIN,
CHILL,
Sip

KVASSMICHE **PAGE 274**

KVASSMICHE

Yield: **1 large miche or 2 medium boules**

TOTAL FORMULA

PREFERMENTED FLOUR: 25%

INGREDIENTS	METRIC (GRAMS)	VOLUMETRIC (APPROXIMATE)	BAKER'S %
Whole wheat flour	304	2½ cups	50%
All-purpose flour	304	2½ cups	50%
Kvass (see below)	439	1¾ cups + 3 tablespoons	72.50%
Water	106	¼ cup + 3 tablespoons	17.50%
Salt, fine	15	2½ teaspoons	2.40%
Yeast, dry instant	2	¾ teaspoon	0.25%
Sourdough culture	30	2 tablespoons	5%
Total Weight	1,200	All	197.65%

STIFF LEVAIN

INGREDIENTS	METRIC (GRAMS)	VOLUMETRIC (APPROXIMATE)	BAKER'S %
Whole wheat flour	152	1¼ cups	100%
Water	106	¼ cup + 3 tablespoons	70%
Sourdough culture	30	2 tablespoons	20%
Salt, fine	3	½ teaspoon	2%
Total Weight	291	All	192%

KVASS

INGREDIENTS	METRIC (GRAMS)	VOLUMETRIC (APPROXIMATE)
Water, 115° F to 125° F	992	4 cups
Sugar	64	⅓ cup
Apples, sliced	79	½ cup
Bread, after deeply toasting	99	about ¼ of a loaf
Sourdough culture	20	heaping 1 tablespoon
Ginger, fresh	10	2 teaspoons
Sassafras root, dried	3	1 tablespoon
Vanilla bean (or 1 to 2 teaspoons of extract)	1	1 bean

KVASS CONT.

INGREDIENTS	METRIC (GRAMS)	VOLUMETRIC (APPROXIMATE)
Star anise	2	2 intact "stars"
Total Weight	1,270	

FINAL DOUGH

INGREDIENTS	METRIC (GRAMS)	VOLUMETRIC (APPROXIMATE)
Kvass	439	1¾ cups + 3 tablespoons
Stiff levain	291	All
All-purpose flour	304	2½ cups
Whole wheat flour	152	1¼ cups
Salt, fine	12	2 teaspoons
Yeast, dry instant	2	¾ teaspoon
Total Weight	1,200	All

TWO DAYS BEFORE BAKING

KVASS

Make the kvass (instructions follow) and allow it to ferment overnight before straining and reserving; chill for up to 4 days.

PREPARE THE KVASS

Slice any good loaf of bread (old and stale is fine) and toast in the oven until deep, deep brown, almost black. The bread will lose significant weight during toasting. You will need to begin with roughly half of a medium loaf, or about one-third of a full-size baguette.

Slice the apples, grate the ginger, scrape the seeds from the vanilla bean and reserve the pod, and crush the star anise.

MAKE THE KVASS

Put into a large mixing bowl, plastic container, or pitcher the water (115°F to 125°F), sugar, and sourdough culture. Stir to combine.

Add the toasted bread, sliced apples, ginger, sassafras, vanilla bean (both the pod and the scraped seeds), and star anise. Mix well to saturate the toasted bread and distribute the ingredients.

Cover and place at room temperature for 12 to 24 hours. The kvass is ready when small bubbles are evident at the edges where the liquid meets the sides of the container.

RECIPE CONTINUES

Strain the mixture through cheesecloth or a fine-mesh sieve and reserve until use. The flavor should be slightly effervescent and complex with gentle sweetness. I enjoy chilling the liquid, then sipping any amount that I don't use in the bread.

DAY ONE

STIFF LEVAIN

In a medium bowl, combine the tepid water (75°F to 80°F) and sourdough culture. Mix with your hands and fingers until the culture is broken up and well distributed in the water, then add the flour and salt.

Mix briefly, then knead until smooth.

Cover and set at room temperature for 12 to 16 hours.

DAY TWO

PREPARE

Set the kvass at room temperature 1 to 2 hours before the final mix. It should be room temperature (70°F to 75°F) when used.

MIX

Calculate temperatures. See Setting Temperatures, page 320, for instructions. Desired dough temperature: 78°F

In a large mixing bowl, combine the kvass and stiff levain. Mix with your hands until the preferment is broken up in the kvass, then add the final dough flours, salt, and yeast. Stir with the handle end of a wooden spoon until the dough forms a cohesive mass. If you find it easier, after some stirring, scrape the dough out of the bowl with a plastic scraper onto your work surface and knead briefly with your hands just until the dough comes together. Resist the urge to add more flour. Scrape the dough off the work surface and return it to the bowl for bulk fermentation.

BULK FERMENTATION

Scrape down the sides of the mixing bowl and allow the dough to rise, covered, for 3 hours at room temperature, folding as directed below.

FOLD

Fold after 30, 60, 90, and 120 minutes, then leave untouched for the final hour. See Folding, page 327, for instructions.

As you perform each series of folds, you'll begin to notice that the dough becomes smoother, stronger, and more cohesive.

DIVIDE AND PRESHAPE

If making a single large loaf, preshape as a round. See Preshaping, page 329, for instructions. Cover and let rest for 15 minutes.

For 2 loaves, divide the dough into 2 pieces weighing about 600 grams each. See Dividing, page 328, for instructions.

Preshape as rounds. See Preshaping, page 329, for instructions. Cover and let rest for 10 to 15 minutes.

Shape as boules. See Shaping, page 331, for instructions.

Place the large miche, seam side, up in a banneton or towel-lined bowl, approximately 10 inches wide and 4 inches deep and dusted with whole wheat flour.

Place the two medium boules, seam side up, in bannetons or towel-lined bowls, approximately 9 inches wide and 3½ inches deep and dusted with whole wheat flour.

Cover and proof for 60 to 75 minutes at room temperature.

During the proof, preheat the oven to 450°F with a baking stone and steaming system in place. See Baking, page 349, for instructions.

Transfer the loaves to parchment paper or a baker's peel, gently inverting them so that the side that was against the dusted tea towel or banneton becomes the top.

Score the bread prior to loading. See Scoring, page 339, for ideas and tips.

Bake with steam for 40 to 45 minutes. After 20 minutes, lower the oven to 425°F, and carefully remove any steaming devices, lids, parchment paper, or bowls. Rotate the loaves on the stone.

At 40 to 45 minutes the loaves should be well colored. If making a single large loaf, bake 10 minutes longer than the two medium loaves.

Turn off the oven, prop open the door a few inches, and allow the loaves to dry for an additional 10 minutes.

NOTE: During testing I sometimes wanted to make this bread but didn't have time to brew the kvass. Thinking of the flavors I wanted and options for substitutes, I tried several liquid combinations that worked quite well. My favorite was a blend of unsweetened black tea and ginger beer. Kombucha is also an option, although I've found many store varieties quite bitter.

Here's what I see: down a rusty rail by a weedy factory shell, next to silo cisterns and ripped sections of nowhere track, an old boxcar. A stuck door, unclosing, warped, smoothed with the rubbing of hands and cargo; floorboards unjoined and soiled. If wood could sing from knots, what lyrics would seep out? What tunes were whistled here by gap-mawed ghosts? These characters from Steinbeck's novels train-hopped as the cars rumbled across the South, moving eastward with wheat, corn, and rye from Kansas, trading for pecans in Georgia and sticky treats of tobacco and molasses in the Carolinas. Then, clacking westward, they wound back to the clinking track of Kentucky bourbon bottles to repeat the circle. This antiquity, this marriage of wood, smoke, whiskey, and leather, has flavor.

And so, Boxcar. Cracked corn, rye berries, and smoked barley malt are swelled with whiskey and molasses and mixed with caramelized pecans and whole wheat flour. Searching for a wisp of smoke, I use the smoked Chinese tea, Lapsang souchong, for its intense pine character.

Pecans

The lightly sweet pecans are delicious in this bread, and can also be a crunchy addition to a green salad, used as a garnish on a fall-themed soup (savory roasted apple and potato, or pumpkin, would be nice), or tossed with a mixture of roasted root vegetables. To prepare, put the pecans in a large sauté pan over medium heat. Flick or spray them with a light coating of water (about 1 teaspoon), stirring to coat. Then add 1 teaspoon of confectioners' sugar and stir to coat. Cook them over medium heat, stirring and shaking the pan, until they are dry and brown in spots.

BOXCAR

Yield: 2 large fendu-shaped loaves

TOTAL FORMULA

PREFERMENTED FLOUR: 45%

INGREDIENTS	METRIC (GRAMS)	VOLUMETRIC (APPROXIMATE)	BAKER'S %
All-purpose flour	267	2 cups + 3 tablespoons	60%
Whole wheat flour	178	1½ cups	40%
Water	335	1½ cups	75%
Lapsong souchong tea, brewed and strained	45	¼ cup	10%
Whiskey	22	1 tablespoon + 2 teaspoons	5%
Salt, fine	11	scant 2 teaspoons	2.50%
Yeast, dry instant	2	¾ teaspoon	0.50%
Sourdough culture	13	scant 1 tablespoon	3%
Pecans, chopped	80	¾ cup	18%
Cracked corn or coarse grits (regular or instant)	13	1 tablespoon + 1 teaspoon	3%
Rye chops	13	2 tablespoons	3%
Smoked malted barley (see Note)	13	1½ tablespoons	3%
Molasses, blackstrap	8	1 teaspoon	1.8%
Total Weight	1,000	All	224.80%

Note: Smoked malted barley can be purchased at a store that sells home brewing supplies.

POOLISH

INGREDIENTS	METRIC (GRAMS)	VOLUMETRIC (APPROXIMATE)	BAKER'S %
Whole wheat flour	133	1 cup + 1 tablespoon	100%
Water	167	¾ cup	125%
Yeast, dry instant	Pinch	Pinch	0.10%
Total Weight	300	All	225.10%

RECIPE CONTINUES

STIFF LEVAIN

INGREDIENTS	METRIC (GRAMS)	VOLUMETRIC (APPROXIMATE)	BAKER'S %
All-purpose flour	67	½ cup + 1 tablespoon	100%
Water	40	3 tablespoons	60%
Sourdough culture	13	scant 1 tablespoon	20%
Total Weight	120	All	180%

SOAKER

INGREDIENTS	METRIC (GRAMS)	VOLUMETRIC (APPROXIMATE)	BAKER'S %
Smoked malted barley	13	1½ tablespoons	33%
Cracked corn or coarse yellow corn grits	13	1 tablespoon + 1 teaspoon	33%
Rye chops	13	2 tablespoons	34%
Water	24	2 tablespoons	50%
Whiskey	22	1 tablespoon + 2 teaspoons	46%
Molasses, blackstrap	8	1 teaspoon	20%
Total Weight	93	All	216%

FINAL DOUGH

INGREDIENTS	METRIC (GRAMS)	VOLUMETRIC (APPROXIMATE)
Water	104	¼ cup + 3 tablespoons
Poolish	300	All
Stiff levain	120	All
Lapsong souchong tea, brewed and strained	45	¼ cup
All-purpose flour	200	1½ cup + 2 tablespoons
Whole wheat flour	45	¼ cup + 3 tablespoons
Salt, fine	11	scant 2 teaspoons
Yeast, dry instant	2	¾ teaspoon
Soaker	93	All
Pecans	80	¾ cup
Total Weight	1,000	

RECIPE CONTINUES

DAY ONE

PREPARE

Toast the smoked malted barley on the stovetop over low heat in a dry pan, stirring occasionally.

Make 1 cup of Lapsang souchong tea. Steep at room temperature until use.

Caramelize the pecans (see sidenote, page 278). Chop coarsely before use.

POOLISH

In a medium bowl, stir together the flour and yeast, then add the tepid water (75°F to 80°F).

Mix until smooth.

Cover and set at room temperature for 12 to 16 hours.

STIFF LEVAIN

In a medium bowl, combine the tepid water (75°F to 80°F) and sourdough culture. Mix with your hands and fingers until the culture is broken up and well distributed in the water, then add the flour.

Mix briefly, then knead until smooth.

Cover and set at room temperature for 12 to 16 hours.

SOAKER

In a medium bowl, combine the water, whiskey, malted barley, cracked corn, rye chops, and molasses.

Cover and set at room temperature for 12 to 16 hours.

DAY TWO

MIX

Calculate temperatures. See Setting Temperatures, page 320, for instructions. Desired dough temperature: 76°F

In a large mixing bowl, combine the final dough water, poolish, stiff levain, and tea. Mix with your hands until the poolish and stiff levain are broken up in the water, then add the flours, salt, and yeast. Stir with the handle end of a wooden spoon until the dough forms a shaggy mass. If you find it easier, after some stirring, scrape the dough out of the bowl with a plastic scraper onto your work surface and knead briefly with your hands just until the dough comes together. Resist the urge to add more flour. Scrape the dough off the work surface and return it to the bowl for bulk fermentation.

Place the soaker and the caramelized pecans on top of the mixed dough and fold briefly to begin incorporating. It doesn't need to be homogeneous; these ingredients will fully incorporate during folding.

BULK FERMENTATION	Scrape down the sides of the mixing bowl and allow the dough to rise, covered, for 2 hours at room temperature, folding as directed below.
FOLD	Fold after 15, 30, 45, 60, and 90 minutes, then leave untouched until the divide. See Folding, page 327, for instructions.
	As you perform each series of folds, you'll begin to notice that the dough becomes smoother, stronger, and more cohesive.
DIVIDE AND PRESHAPE	Divide the dough into 2 pieces weighing about 500 grams each. See Dividing, page 328, for instructions.
	Preshape as rounds and cover. See Preshaping, page 329, for instructions.
	Cover and let rest for 15 minutes.
SHAPE, FENDU	Shape as tubes roughly 10 to 12 inches long with tapered tips. Place, seam side down, on a floured surface to rest for 10 minutes.
	After the rest, generously flour the top surface of the shaped loaf with whole wheat flour. Using a transfer peel or thin dowel (½ inch or less), make the fendu shape. See Shaping, page 331, for instructions.
	Place the loaf, seam side up, on a lightly floured baker's linen (couche) or tea towel. Repeat with the second loaf. Pleat the couche between the loaves to support their sides as they rise.
PROOF	Cover and proof for 40 to 50 minutes at room temperature.
BAKE	During the proof, preheat the oven to 450°F with a baking stone and steaming system in place. See Baking, page 349, for instructions.
	Transfer the loaves to parchment paper or a baker's peel, gently inverting them so that the underside, which was against the dusted tea towel or linen, becomes the top.
	Slide the loaves onto the preheated baking stone. I like these loaves somewhat S shaped. You can curve the ends gently before loading to make that form.
	Bake with steam for 30 to 35 minutes. After 20 minutes, carefully remove any steaming devices, lids, or parchment paper. Rotate the loaves on the stone.
	At 30 to 35 minutes the loaves should be well colored. Turn off the oven, prop open the door a few inches, and allow the loaf to dry for an additional 10 minutes.

In 2014, I had an excess of Waltham Butternut squash seedlings, which I decided to plant in our compost as the garden couldn't take their spreading. I plopped them unceremoniously, and left them, nestled in wormy soil, black with potential, and *it* happened. You know the story: *Jack and the Beanstalk*, *George's Marvelous Medicine*, the miracle of five loaves and two fishes. In time, those plants grew, taking over the yard. They became a jungle habitat for chickens, and beneath the large leaves were abundant blossoms where bumblebees could tumble and pollinate, seeding flowers and setting fruit. The epic harvest of 2014 yielded hard, orange-flesh butternuts, which fed us well into 2015.

SunSeed grew out of this excess. To make the bread, I combined roasted squash with sunflower seeds, yellow durum flour, cracked native corn grits, and black pepper. I used some sourdough culture for acidity, and seeded the exterior of the loaves with an apple wood–smoked salt, cracked pepper, and sunflower seeds.

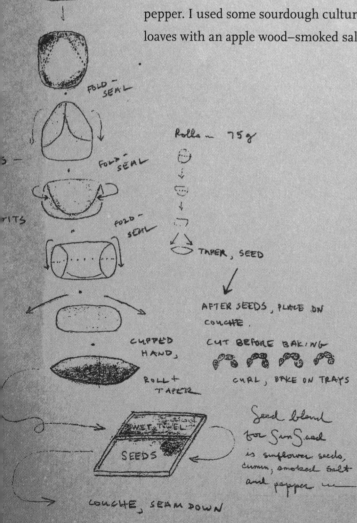

FOLD — SEAL

FOLD — SEAL

FOLD — SEAL

CUPPED HAND, ROLL + TAPER

COUCHE, SEAM DOWN

WET TOWEL

SEEDS

Rolls — 75 g

TAPER, SEED

AFTER SEEDS, PLACE ON COUCHE.

CUT BEFORE BAKING

CURL, BAKE ON TRAYS

Seed blend for SunSeed is sunflower seeds, cumin, smoked salt and pepper

SUNSEED

Yield: **2 medium bâtards**

TOTAL FORMULA
PREFERMENTED FLOUR: 30%

INGREDIENTS	METRIC (GRAMS)	VOLUMETRIC (APPROXIMATE)	BAKER'S %
All-purpose flour	450	3¾ cups	84%
Durum flour	54	¼ cup + 3 tablespoons	10%
Whole wheat flour	32	¼ cup	6%
Water	408	1¾ cups + 1 tablespoon	76%
Salt, fine	13	scant 2¼ teaspoons	2.50%
Yeast, dry instant	3	1 teaspoon	0.50%
Sourdough culture	32	2 tablespoons	6%
Butternut squash, roasted (about 2½ pounds raw; will yield enough to make soup as well)	80	rounded ⅓ cup	15%
Sunflower seeds	80	heaping ½ cup	15%
Pepper, ground black	2	¾ teaspoon	0.30%
Corn grits, regular or instant	46	⅓ cup	8.50%
Total Weight	1,200	All	223.80%

STIFF LEVAIN

INGREDIENTS	METRIC (GRAMS)	VOLUMETRIC (APPROXIMATE)	BAKER'S %
All-purpose flour	129	1 cup	80%
Whole wheat flour	32	¼ cup	20%
Water	93	¼ cup + 3 tablespoons	58%
Sourdough culture	32	2 tablespoons	20%
Total Weight	286		178%

CORN GRITS

INGREDIENTS	METRIC (GRAMS)	VOLUMETRIC (APPROXIMATE)	BAKER'S %
Water	46	¼ cup	100%
Corn grits, regular or instant	46	⅓ cup	100%
Total Weight	92	All	200%

RECITE CONTINUES

FINAL DOUGH

INGREDIENTS	METRIC (GRAMS)	VOLUMETRIC (APPROXIMATE)
Water	269	1 cup + 2 tablespoons
Stiff levain	286	All
All-purpose flour	321	2¾ cups
Durum flour	54	¼ cup + 3 tablespoons
Salt, fine	13	scant 2¼ teaspoons
Pepper, ground black	2	¾ teaspoon
Yeast, dry instant	3	1 teaspoon
Corn grits	92	All
Butternut squash, roasted	80	rounded ⅓ cup
Sunflower seeds	80	heaping ½ cup
Sunflower seeds, for the crust		
Salt, for the crust (table salt, seasoned salt, or smoked salt)		
Black pepper, cracked, for the crust		
Cumin, ground, for the crust		
Total Weight	1,200	All

DAY ONE

STIFF LEVAIN

In a medium bowl, combine the tepid water (75°F to 80°F) and the sourdough culture. Mix with your hands and fingers until the culture is broken up and well distributed in the water, then add the flours.

Mix briefly, then knead until smooth.

Cover and set at room temperature for 12 to 16 hours.

CORN GRITS

In a medium saucepan, slowly toast the grits over medium heat, stirring to heat them evenly.

When they begin to smell toasty and show some color, gradually stir in the water.

Bring the mixture to a boil, then turn off the heat. Cool to room temperature and cover until use.

PREPARE

Preheat the oven to 400°F.

Cut the butternut squash in half lengthwise and roast, cut side down, until fully tender, 50 to 60 minutes. To speed the roasting, add a small quantity of water to the roasting pan.

RECIPE CONTINUES ⅄

Seed, skin, and mash the squash. You will need a rounded ⅓ cup (80 grams) for the bread.

PREPARE
CONT.

Place the sunflower seeds on a baking sheet in the oven. Toast the seeds, stirring them around every few minutes until golden, about 10 minutes.

Alternatively, put the sunflower seeds in a large heavy pan set over low to medium heat. Toast the seeds, stirring them around every few minutes until golden, about 10 minutes.

DAY TWO

Calculate temperatures. See Setting Temperatures, page 320, for instructions. Desired dough temperature: 76°F

MIX

In a large mixing bowl, combine the final dough water and stiff levain. Mix with your hands until the levain is broken up in the water, then add the flours, salt, pepper, and yeast. Stir with the handle end of a wooden spoon until the dough forms a shaggy mass. If you find it easier, after some stirring, scrape the dough out of the bowl with a plastic scraper onto your work surface and knead briefly with your hands just until the dough comes together. Resist the urge to add more flour. Scrape the dough off the work surface and return it to the bowl for bulk fermentation.

Place the grits, roasted squash, and toasted sunflower seeds on top of the mixed dough and fold briefly to begin incorporating. It doesn't need to be homogeneous; these ingredients will fully incorporate during folding.

BULK
FERMENTATION

Scrape down the sides of the mixing bowl and allow the dough to rise, covered, for two hours at room temperature, folding as directed below.

FOLD

Fold after 15, 30, 45, and 60 minutes, then leave untouched for the second hour. See Folding, page 327, for instructions.

As you perform each series of folds, you'll begin to notice that the dough becomes smoother, stronger, and more cohesive.

DIVIDE AND
PRESHAPE

Divide the dough into 2 pieces weighing about 600 grams each. See Dividing, page 328, for instructions.

Preshape as rounds. See Preshaping, page 329, for instructions.

Cover and let rest for 15 minutes.

PREPARE

Prepare the seed blend for the exterior of the loaf. In a food processor fitted with a cutting blade, combine the sunflower seeds, salt, pepper, and cumin. Pulse briefly to break up the sunflower seeds just a little.

To make the sunflower seed crust, fill a sheet pan with a ¼-inch layer of the seasoned crust mixture. On a second pan, place a well-moistened tea towel or dish towel.

SHAPE Shape the dough as bâtards about 10 inches long. See Shaping, page 331, for instructions. Roll them across the moist towel and then through the seed blend before placing, seam side up, on a lightly floured baker's linen (couche) or tea towel. Pleat the couche between the loaves to support their sides as they rise.

PROOF Cover and proof for 40 to 50 minutes at room temperature.

During the proof, preheat the oven to 450°F with a baking stone and steaming system in place. See Baking, page 349, for instructions.

Transfer the loaves to parchment paper or a baker's peel, gently inverting them so that the underside, which was against the dusted tea towel or linen, becomes the top.

BAKE Score the bread prior to loading. See Scoring, page 339, for ideas and tips.

Slide the loaves onto the preheated baking stone.

Bake with steam for 35 to 40 minutes. After 30 minutes, carefully remove any steaming devices, lids, or parchment paper. Rotate the loaves on the stone.

At 35 to 40 minutes the loaves should be well colored. Turn off the oven, prop open the door a few inches, and allow the loaves to dry for an additional 10 minutes.

NOTE: SunSeed bread calls for a small amount of roasted butternut squash. Use the leftover squash to make a soup (see page 290) to accompany the bread.

Start with a medium squash, about 2½ pounds, and you will have plenty of squash for the soup.

CURRIED COCONUT SOUP

INGREDIENTS	METRIC (GRAMS)	VOLUMETRIC (APPROXIMATE)
Olive oil	27	2 tablespoons
Garlic, minced	27	2 to 3 cloves
Onion, minced	113	1 small (½ cup)
Ginger, fresh, about a 2-inch piece, grated	22	2-inch piece
Coriander seeds, whole	1	½ teaspoon
Cumin seeds, whole	2	1 teaspoon
Paprika, smoked (optional)	1	½ teaspoon
Cayenne pepper (optional)	1	½ teaspoon
Tomato sauce	60	3 tablespoons
Butternut squash, roasted	700	3 cups
Coconut milk, full-fat	403	one 13-ounce can
Chicken stock, vegetable stock, or water	227	1 cup
Salt	9	1½ teaspoons
Black pepper, freshly ground	3	1 teaspoon
Whole-fat yogurt or sour cream, for garnish		
Cilantro, fresh, minced, for garnish		
Jalapeño, finely minced, for garnish (optional)		

PROCESS

In a medium pot, heat the olive oil until it shimmers.

Add the garlic, onion, ginger, coriander, cumin, paprika, and cayenne (if using), and sauté until soft and a bronze color begins to form on the bottom of the pot.

Add the tomato sauce.

Stir and reduce until the mixture darkens and thickens.

Add the roasted squash and stir to combine.

Add the coconut milk, stock or water, salt, and black pepper.

Puree the soup until smooth with an immersion blender, stand blender, food processor, or food mill.

Taste and adjust the seasoning with additional salt and black pepper. Reheat and thin as necessary with more stock or water.

Garnish with a spoonful of whole-fat yogurt or sour cream, minced cilantro, and jalapeño if desired.

Chill any leftovers and store for up to 5 days in the refrigerator.

March arrived and I packed everything. The tools, the ingredients, a clean chef's coat, and (I hoped) everything else required. I drove to snowy Providence, Rhode Island, to Johnson & Wales University, where our hosts were again the baking and pastry department. There were four bread candidates in the finals, and we were split up so that each of us had his own bakery with a spiral mixer, benches, and an oven. The requirements, in broad strokes, were three different "freestyle" breads with rolls as well as loaves (all unique formulas with novel shapes and great flavor) and one "healthy" bread with an emphasis on whole grain. We also needed a pain de mie and many, many baguettes, some decorative, some classically shaped and cut. In addition to evaluations for structure, flavor, and innovation for all loaves, the baguettes also needed to weigh 250 grams baked. If loaves fell more than 10 grams outside that range or if they measured outside the range of 54 to 56 centimeters, points would be subtracted. When I arrived, I was confident of my ability to complete the work, preparing almost 200 pounds of dough, and secure in the feeling that I had worked as hard as I could to be ready. I also knew that the other candidates were immensely talented: a baker and miller from California with an astonishing knowledge of niche grains and milling techniques, a French transplant with an amazing résumé and novel flavor combinations, a dark horse from Idaho who had stunned everyone at the semifinals, and me. A hopeful, scrappy boy from Arkansas running on heart fuel and elbow grease.

I would not be telling the whole story if I didn't first say that I was nervous. Yes, I was concentrating on the big picture, the long view of a life of baking and the elusive target of mastery. But I also wanted—*so damn badly*—to be chosen. Every single day, without fail, Arlo, my youngest, wished me luck on my journey to Paris. His small voice chirped as he walked out the door to school, or at bedtime, "Good luck, Daddy, I hope you make it to Paris." I wanted this for him, for my whole family, for my team of bakers, for my company, for anyone, anywhere, who could dream, who could work tirelessly and jump for a height of hope in an attempt to catch something.

From the second we left the starting gate during the sixty-minute period of preparation on day one I was followed by judges and students, who observed my every move. I lined up my containers first, in the order of what I would need, and then taped labels printed with amounts of flour, water, and sourdough culture to the lids. I measured water into containers, then yeast·or sourdough culture, combined them, added flour, and mixed everything by hand. There were more than thirty tasks to complete in sixty minutes. When the timer sounded, I felt confident and relaxed; I had done what I had prepared to do, and took off my apron and headed to the hotel to pretend to sleep. In the darkness of that night I finally dozed off, only to awake a short time later, sick. I had chills and then began to sweat, drenching my clothes as I sat on the tile floor of the bathroom, waiting for the waves of hot and cold to pass. I tried to relax against the onslaught of questions and worry. What had I forgotten? Did I measure things correctly? What the hell was I doing here? In the depths of this mess I looked for some way, some route to a better space.

On a day with the stakes of a high-wire act, performed at the margin of what is possible, some things will go well, and others . . . well, not so much. The room may be cold when doughs need coddling; nerves may cause errors; and you will have to work with curveballs, knuckles, sliders, and fastballs, each one a test to see what you can do. Can you bunt? Will you lean in and take a ball on the shoulder to get on base? My day saw the gamut, from fist pumping to fist pounding; I made mistakes, I tripped, I got back up and ran faster. I pulled myself out of an impossible time deficit and took baguettes from the oven up until the final moments of the allotted eight hours, counting down the seconds until a judge called, "Time!" I loaded everything, hundreds of breads and rolls spilling across multiple cooling racks, and rolled them into a separate classroom where I built my display.

Loaves are like children. They hold the mark of what we do well and also show where we forgot them at soccer practice, weren't patient, or didn't treat them gently. As I picked up each loaf, holding it before placing it on the display table, I saw the stories. The Boxcar was undermixed, with resultant poor volume; some of the

Kvassmiche had been baked in an oven with malfunctioning steam; but, on the bright side, the SunSeed was happier, its deep yellow crumb and salt-seed crust showing the contrast of yellow against mahogany; and the powerBROT was dark, crunchy, seeded, and delicious. For all the breads, I placed the signs that I had made in advance by pressing a stiff dough against the grain of wood from our woodpile before cutting and drying them. I stained the pieces with coffee and made a tiny picture frame for the name of each product, stamped in an old script on aged paper.

And then it ended. It was over, all of it. Nothing more could be done or strived for; years of work, worry, and wishing; all of it, lifted and removed. The corners of my mouth began to lift, curling upward, I felt my heart ache and my throat catch, and all of it rose up and out, forming a smile.

And when I say "smile," I mean my face did things it hadn't done in months and months. I was secure, content, fulfilled, and exhausted—if this was my day to be chosen, then so be it, Team Martin would be part of Team USA. I would prepare endlessly and we would all go to Paris. And if it was my day to simply go home, then that was OK, too. I would leave intact, for I had brought home *with* me. I had used bread to connect my heart to my hands and my soul to my mouth, filling everything with my history, my heritage, my love for my roots and for this craft. It was truly win or win.

It took a few days to receive the final results. People far and wide checked in, hoping, cheering for a positive outcome. I took a few days off in an attempt to un- wind, and then Jeffrey finally called me from King Arthur and asked me to drive in. He wanted to give the results in person rather than have me hear via e-mail or phone. I couldn't tell from his voice whether it was good news or bad. My sense of the day, based on what I had seen and heard, was that I hadn't done anything to either eliminate myself or stand out positively. Jeffrey had helped me endlessly in preparing and knew full well the effort a bid requires. He had been the captain for Team USA in 1996. He had also seen me grow for almost ten years as I worked and improved, building my skills from the basement to the roof. I walked into our office and he stood and, with some formality and a hug, told me that Nicky Giusto, an excellent baker and miller from Northern California, had been chosen. Bummer. I had come to terms with the outcome, whatever it would be, for myself. I would be great with Paris, every aspect of it—the work, the representation of U.S. bakers, everything—and even if I didn't go on, I could see and feel how much I had grown. I had found a connection to my own self, a way to weave what I am, past and present, into what I make. The bummer was that I had to go home and tell my family. Those proudest, most loving, and cheering loudest were also fervent hopers, wishing for a win.

The recovery process continues. I am glad and so fortunate to be exactly where I am, and I am cheering loudly for Nicky, who as I write is in Paris with the rest of Team USA, about to compete.

@ RCW

0% AP

...crease to 30%

...t flour in a

..., malted wheat

...hydration

...% of flour
weight

...% w/ dry yeast

..., toasted and

...toaster

...nd levain

...yeast on

...two minute

...figs

...°F * FF

...w/ 1 fold

...pre-shape

...223 C

HOME AGAIN

Resolutions, taxes, and birth years mark January 1 as the start of all things annual. But the earth here in Vermont says the true season of new things is March. As days get longer, winter's dormancy lifts, raising temperatures from the freezer to the fridge. Sap rises from deep tree roots to feed budding leaves before dropping again during crisp nights. My friends Chuck and Sue had tapped trees and set buckets for sap collection and sugaring at Sunrise Farm when I returned from the Coupe finals. With newfound time to spare, my whole family headed to the farm, where Arlo was offered the ceremonial first match to light the wood-fired evaporator in the sugarhouse. It was stuffed to the throat with four-foot splits of hemlock, white pine, and hardwoods. As the fire caught and sap boiled, the air filled with sticky sweetness, the vapor rising and encircling us in maple syrup clouds.

This place was the best medicine for recovery. I played my banjo while Julie sang and my children sawed on fiddles. The fire raged, pushing searing heat through us and beyond, billowing out the sugarhouse doors into the night, a black pool beyond the reach of light. When the heat became too intense, sweat could be turned to chill with a stint at the woodpile, the crack of the maul in my hands exploding as it ripped through lengths of wood.

I sweated, I froze, and I returned. I was home—home to making, home to the movements of my own hands, transforming flour to bread and then letters to verse. In this space are all the joy, renewal, and beauty I need. Here I will stay, ready to live in my making space. For baking and creating are nothing if not our will, our stories, and our love made manifest. Here I will stay at my home hearth. I am a baker, and flourishing.

Part 2

METHOD

FOUNDATIONS

Salted or unsalted? Whole or 2 percent? Bittersweet or milk? A walk down the aisle of any supermarket is a stroll across a gamut of choices. There are so many options, in fact, that we've had to reduce them to generic categories in order to process them all. Are you going to the store? Yes. Please grab some milk. But in the process of dealing with so many choices, we've stripped something away from food and our eating experience, reducing richness, removing character. We've discarded the very identity of what we eat and where it comes from. Beyond their contributions of flavor and color, form and function, and behind the anonymity of commodities and wheat futures, "low-fat" and "sugar-free," ingredients carry stories. Through the lines they weave from where they grow to where they are enjoyed, ingredients tie eaters to makers, bakers to millers, seeds to farmers, sheaves to dirt, and soil to the earth. Use them with care, look for ingredients that have character, find ways to bake your own narrative, get closer to the "what" and "from whom" of what you consume.

Flour, the milled product of wheat or rye, buckwheat, corn, emmer, chickpeas, and countless other grains, beans, legumes, and nuts, is forever in motion. It appears stable, even immobile, like salt in a shaker, but in fact it is far from inert, far from a commodity. Let's look at the staple flours in my pantry.

Ingredients

WHOLE WHEAT FLOUR: Grind the entire wheat berry, put everything in a bag, and voilà—whole wheat flour. Only a few years ago we had a limited number of national brands to choose from and knew little about what we were buying. These days, bags contain more information ("Hard Red Winter Wheat," for example) and we have many more options for sources (even local or regional farmers) and single varieties like Turkey Red, Red Fife, or Warthog.

Is Whole Wheat Bitter?

Wheat, like other cereal grasses such as barley, rice, sorghum, and corn, is a seed. It grows in nature inside its own package (the mineral-rich outer casing we call "bran"), with its own food source for the early stages of growth (the starchy protein-rich "endosperm") and its own set of instructions for growth (the nucleus of the seed, the vitamin-packed "germ"). As long as the "package" hasn't been opened (milled, in our case), wheat can be stored for a long, long time. However, once it is milled, the clock is ticking—oils contained in the germ will go rancid. This doesn't happen immediately, but the best place to store any whole-grain flour is in a plastic bag in the freezer.

So, what should whole wheat taste like? Whole wheat should taste mildly sweet with a bran-balanced backbone of flavor, which gently heightens its complexity. In the same way, because of the skin, apples, potatoes, grapes, stone fruits, tomatoes, and many other things we eat are made more enjoyable and complex when enjoyed intact. If your whole wheat tastes "bitter," check the expiration date to make sure it hasn't expired.

WHITE WHOLE WHEAT: Wheat comes in colors. White whole wheat, a wheat that contains less pigment in the bran layer and thus has less color, can be substituted for whole wheat in many recipes. The lighter color (and honestly, the more neutral taste) works well in muffins or pancakes and even as a substitute for all-purpose flour in some cases. I rarely use it in bread, however, as I prefer the flavor of hard red winter wheat.

ALL-PURPOSE FLOUR: All-purpose flour is wheat flour that has a moderate level of protein (which can translate to strength in the dough environment) and has been sifted to remove the bran and wheat germ. It does not contain leavening such as baking powder or baking soda (by contrast, "self-rising flour" does contain leavening) and should be unbleached and unbromated. Bleaching is entirely unnecessary—natural carotenoid pigments and vitamins are destroyed in the bleaching process—and bromate has been declared a carcinogen and banned in Europe and Canada (though not in the United States). In addition to all-purpose flour, the world of white flour ranges from "high gluten" to "bread flour" to "pastry flour" and "cake flour," and includes "gluten-free" options. (Note that gluten-free flour blends should be used in recipes designed for gluten-free baking.) The choices are endless and increase almost daily. The recipes in this book use all-purpose flour whenever white flour is called for. High-quality all-purpose is a versatile pinch-hitter with ample strength for bagels, sourdough loaves, pizza, and baguettes and, if handled correctly, has enough tenderness for cookies and biscuits. It is the only white flour I keep in my house, and makes up the vast majority of what we use in the bakery.

WHOLE RYE FLOUR: Whole rye flour, similar to whole wheat flour, is simply the whole rye berry, milled and bagged. Rye, while glutenous, has different proportions and different qualities of the subcomponents (glutenin and gliadin) that combine to form gluten in the moist dough environment. These differing proportions, in combination with other differences from wheat, create very different handling characteristics. Therefore, when mixing, folding, or shaping doughs with a high percentage of rye flour, you will find that they don't feel stretchy or rubbery in the same way as wheat-based doughs. In fact, the first time you make Wood's Boiled Cider Bread (page 196), Citrus Vollkornbrot (page 255), or Pain de Seigle (page 102), you may believe something has gone terribly wrong as the dough will seem more like a stiff quick bread batter than your regular elastic, supple, wheat-based doughs.

Whole Grain and Balance

Have you seen "fat-free" and "sugar-free," "low-carb" and "high-fiber," and the other dietary trends that pass through town, each promising better health and longevity? If you believe the hype, eating less real food and more chemical sweeteners, thickeners, artificial flavors, colors, and additives will make us healthier. But how could that be? Here's an alternative: Buy whole ingredients such as flour, butter, dried beans, rice, quinoa, fresh vegetables, meats, eggs, and cheese. Prepare them yourself and eat in moderation. Foods that are unprocessed and minimally transformed from their living state are full of nutrition, natural fiber, flavor, and beauty. In the summer, a green salad with a side of beans or a piece of sausage from Sunrise Farm and a white flour baguette—this is a balanced meal. I don't have to be a zealot about the fiber content of my bread; it fits within the context of my web of food. If all that I eat is white bread, then, yes, bread should shoulder more of the nutritional burden. White bread fits within my diet, balanced by other sources of fiber. When I use whole grains I don't concentrate on their fiber contribution as much as I think about their flavor. Keep it simple, keep yourself healthy, and stick to the straighter path that passes right through your own hands and homemade products.

Beyond Wheat and Rye

In addition to the old favorites whose names you know, there are a wide variety of niche grains that can be purchased whole, milled into flour, or rolled into flakes like rolled oats. The bulk section of your local food store or co-op can be a great place to find grains such as emmer, spelt, Khorasan, sorghum, einkorn, and others, which may offer new inspiration. You may also find unique local and regional sources. Furthermore, bulk sections often offer grains and flour, and even high-quality spices, at significant savings when compared with a similar quantity of prepackaged flour or spices. So branch out whenever possible—try spelt instead of whole wheat in a scone, try wheat from a local producer, substitute whole rye for whole wheat in pancakes, or mix it half and half with buckwheat flour, and so forth. Not only are these ways to explore new flavors and enrich our palates, but reaching for alternative grains is a way to support farmers and the environment by creating a financial incentive for growing crops that can be planted in rotation with our staple wheat crops.

Sourcing

One could practically traverse the state of Vermont by leaping from farmers' markets to CSAs all the way across. CSA, which stands for "community-supported agriculture," is a system in which consumers pay a farm directly, up front, for a season of produce, meat, eggs, cheese, or even bread. It helps farmers plan and buy seed, and it allows us to get closer to our food providers. In addition to feeding us, the tables of produce at farmers' markets and the distribution bins at CSA pickups offer a learning opportunity. Availability shows what is frost-hardy and what is not. What are early-season greens and what will fill our bellies in June? When can we pick our first bushel of apples or buy winter squash? I moved to Vermont lacking this awareness—we had big gardens when I was growing up, but the years had eroded all but the memory of gathering horse manure and walking behind the tiller. In New York City our supermarkets carried red tomatoes year-round—a constant supply—from Mexico, Florida, or California. Much can be said about whether this system is a problem or not, but it's clear that the tomatoes don't taste better when they are designed for traveling, not eating.

WATER: Our municipal water here in rural Vermont is described as "hard," or mineral-rich. It is chlorinated, but it works fine for starting new sourdough cultures as well as in making all types of bread. If you find some difficulty with starting a sourdough culture, you might try using spring water instead of tap water. Some municipalities treat tap water with chloramine, which will not dissipate and may interfere with the growing culture.

SALT: I don't spend any time fretting about sea salt versus table salt, iodized versus hand-gathered, and on and on. Save the special stuff with the high price tag for sprinkling on fresh tomatoes or other uses where the flavor may be noticed and appreciated. The important thing to know is that different salts—kosher versus table salt, for example—have different densities, so a teaspoon of table salt weighs more than a teaspoon of kosher. For this book, use table salt or fine sea salt for all recipes. Everything has been written and tested with that density in mind. If you must use kosher salt, use the gram measurements for most accurate results.

YEAST: Over the past decade, yeast options and methods have changed. In addition to active dry yeast we now have a version called "instant," which can be mixed with dry ingredients without first hydrating (sometimes referred to as blooming). In the array of things that can push bread from good to better or best, the type of yeast used is actually low on the list. Skilled bakers understand that handling dough, fermentation, shaping, and baking are the components that affect outcomes more than yeast, more than secret recipes, and more than special flour. The most important consideration with yeast is that it be of good quality and within the expiration period. Recipes in this book have been written and tested with instant dry yeast. It is quick to start and needs only dough moisture to activate. Active dry yeast may be used, but it is slower and should be hydrated in a very small amount of warm water before use. Adding it directly to the flour without hydrating is chancy at best.

Sourdough Culture

If one sets a course for flavorful bread, many roads will lead to the land of "naturally leavened," also known as "sourdough" or "levain" bread making. Even among professional bakers, these terms, which essentially refer to bread made with a leavening culture, can be a source of confusion. Let's get a little clarity about what the culture is and then look at the terms.

The leavening culture —which I call "sourdough culture"— that we use in bread begins with a mixture of flour and water. In the fields, many, many strains of yeast and bacteria collect on the surface of grains, then make their way through the milling process into our flour. When flour is hydrated (when water is added) yeast cells wake up and metabolize sugars, producing carbon dioxide (which makes our bread rise!) as well as alcohols and esters as by-products. At this time, bacteria present in the flour also get to work, utilizing the broad range of nutrients present, including maltose, and produce organic acids such as lactic and acetic acid as by-products.

All of this happens naturally; add flour and water to a bowl, stir, wait, and voilà. No hunting parties go out to capture wild yeast in the air; there is no hocus-pocus; the actors are present in the flour, and the stage is set. Over the course of a few days and feedings where a portion of the young fermenting mixture is replaced with fresh flour and water, dominant players will multiply and muscle to the forefront as the culture moves toward stability and symbiosis. The developing mixture can be referred to as a SCOBY, a symbiotic colony (a community really, as there are diverse strains) of bacteria and yeast. Our diet is replete with examples of SCOBYs, from the drink kombucha to vinegars and kefir, a fermented milk drink.

The terms *naturally leavened* (meaning no commercial yeast) and *levain* are also used to refer to sourdough culture. *Naturally leavened* is misleading as bread made with commercially produced yeast isn't necessarily unnatural. *Levain* is the French word for "leaven." The point of all this is that bread made with a leavening culture is more flavorful.

Cultures may be acquired from a variety of sources, including friends who are active bakers, local bakeries, and mail-order websites (many offer a starter culture for $5 to $10). Or, as I describe below, you can make a culture yourself. There are benefits to acquiring an established culture, but a new one can be made cheaply and easily over the course of about a week, so why not start your own? The satisfaction is worth the time and effort. Ultimately, the important thing is that you get the culture whether by mail order, friendship, bribery, or simply stirring and waiting.

If you'd like to try the stir-and-wait method, keep reading.

In basic terms, to build a sourdough culture, combine measured quantities of whole rye flour (I prefer organic) and water, then wait while things begin to grow. You do not need to wave the open container about, hoping to "catch" anything; you do not need to add exotic juice or grapes or sugar or yeast or get any fancier than the product of these two ingredients plus time. Everything you need is already in the flour. Mix the flour and water at regular intervals and discard a portion of the growing culture (to keep it from taking over your kitchen) during the course of about five days. After it becomes active it won't need to be fed with the high-octane rye flour; you will switch to all-purpose for slightly better control and predictability. For starting the culture, I recommend whole rye flour as it contains ample nutrients for the growing culture.

DAY ONE

Combine the rye flour and the tepid water (75°F to 80°F). Mix until homogeneous.

Leave in a warm spot (70°F to 80°F) for 24 hours, covered with a lid.

INGREDIENTS	VOLUMETRIC (APPROXIMATE)	METRIC (GRAMS)	BAKER'S %
Organic whole rye flour	scant 1 cup	100	100%
Water	⅓ cup + 2 teaspoons	100	100%
Total Weight	All	200	200%

Note: To slightly hasten the establishment of your young starter, give it a stir once or twice a day in addition to feedings. This aeration will promote the process of yeast multiplication.

DAY TWO

It is unlikely that the culture will show activity after 24 hours. If it does, the activity will present as very small, pinprick bubbles.

Discard all but 100 grams of the starter and add 50 grams each of rye flour and the tepid water. Mix until homogeneous.

Leave in a warm spot (70°F to 80°F) for 24 hours, covered with a lid.

INGREDIENTS	VOLUMETRIC (APPROXIMATE)	METRIC (GRAMS)	BAKER'S %
Sourdough culture	heaping ⅓ cup	100	200%
Organic whole rye flour	scant ½ cup	50	100%
Water	3 tablespoons + 2 teaspoons	50	100%
Total Weight	All	200	400%

Feeding Sourdough

To make the process of discarding and feeding simpler, here's a trick if you are using a digital scale. When it is time for a feeding, put your container of starter (containing 200 grams) on your scale and tare it (the scale will read 0).

Remove 100 grams of starter (the scale will read -100), then add 50 grams of water (the scale will now read -50) and then 50 grams of flour (the scale will be back to 0). This will save you the trouble of washing the container each time.

DAY THREE TO DAY FIVE (TWICE PER DAY)

By day three, activity should be present. A thriving culture will have small, wispy bubbles (resembling soap bubbles) on the surface; a less active culture will have small pinholes. In either case, continue!

In order to keep up with the activity, the feedings now increase to twice a day.

Discard all but 100 grams at every feeding. Add 50 grams each of rye flour and the tepid water. Mix until homogeneous.

Leave in a warm spot (70°F to 80°F) for 12 hours, covered with a lid.

INGREDIENTS	VOLUMETRIC (APPROXIMATE)	METRIC (GRAMS)	BAKER'S %
Sourdough culture	⅓ cup	100	200%
Organic whole rye flour	scant ½ cup	50	100%
Water	3 tablespoons + 2 teaspoons	50	100%
Total Weight	All	200	400%

After two full days of this routine (the morning of the sixth day after you began the culture), the culture should be bubbly and thriving. When you remove the cover the smell should be slightly sharp, grassy, even sweet. If it is active but still has only pinprick bubbles, continue for two more days with the twice-a-day feeding schedule.

Once the culture is active you will convert it from its diet of whole rye flour over to all-purpose flour. All-purpose flour has fewer nutrients (remember that the bran and germ are removed). As a result, a starter made with all-purpose flour will be slightly less active, and the characteristics of all-purpose wheat flour that enable it to trap gas and rise in a measurable fashion will help you to better determine its activity level.

At home I maintain a stiff sourdough culture, feeding according to the table below. I keep my starter in a jar, which is round with straight sides—an old peanut butter jar, to be exact. To feed, I place the jar on the scale and tare it (the scale will read 0), then remove 80 grams of starter (the scale will read –80), then add 30 grams of water (after which the scale will read –50). Using a butter knife, I briefly stir the water and culture to combine, then add 50 grams of flour (which will return the scale to 0). Then I stir, making sure to incorporate all of the mixture, moving it around until it is homogeneous. Once it is mixed, I push down the starter with the knife to even it slightly and I put a rubber band at a spot that marks the height of the starter in the jar. In 12 hours the stiff starter should at least double. Knowing my starting mark is a great tool and aid for assessing the activity and health of my sourdough.

Stiff starter maintenance amounts:

INGREDIENTS	VOLUMETRIC (APPROXIMATE)	METRIC (GRAMS)	BAKER'S %
Sourdough culture	heaping 1 tablespoon	20	40%
All-purpose flour	¼ cup + 3 tablespoons	50	100%
Water	2 tablespoons	30	60%
Total Weight	All	100	400%

Refrigerating Culture

There are times when it is necessary to pause the sourdough feeding regimen. Maybe life gets in the way, maybe you're going to Hawaii, maybe you can't put the groceries down because BREAD IS COVERING THE WHOLE COUNTER! It happens. It's happened to me. And good news: it's possible to pause.

Culture storage can take a few forms; here are some options.

To store in the fridge, give a normal maintenance feeding, let the culture sit for an hour or so, then chill for up to a week. To revive it, put it on the regular schedule of two feedings per day until it at least doubles in a 12-hour period. For longer storage, thinly spread about 60 grams (¼ cup or so) of ripe culture on a piece of parchment paper and dry it at room temperature. After it's fully dry break it into small pieces and store in a dry place until your money runs out in Hawaii, life stops happening, or people start saying, "Hey, remember when you used to make all that great bread? What happened?" Revive it by soaking the sourdough chips in a small quantity of water until softened, then mix them into the amounts of flour and water called for in the regular feeding schedule and continue, feeding twice per day until fully revived.

One additional long-term option, which Judson Smith of Brimfield Bread Oven says is the fastest way to revive, is as follows. Take 28 grams of ripe culture (2 heaping tablespoons) and knead in flour until the mixture is so dry that it crumbles into small bits. This mixture can be stored in a dry location until mullet hairstyles are cool again, or maybe longer. To revive (the culture, not the mullet), add water to hydrate, forming a dough-consistency mixture. After 12 hours begin normal maintenance feeds until full strength returns (meaning the culture doubles in 12 hours).

Measuring Ingredients

"Well begun is half-done."

Before we can bake, we need to measure ingredients, and the most accurate way to do so is by weight. If ten people scoop a cup of flour, the results will vary wildly. Some will pack the flour, others will sprinkle it into a cup measure, then scrape off the excess; others will fluff the flour in the bag before scooping—no two results will be the same. Can you imagine the problems if approximate measurements were used in woodworking or carpentry, plumbing or surgery? The cup measure is the cubit of baking.

But it is easy to fix this inconsistency. If we measure with a scale that is accurate to the gram (a smaller unit of measurement than the ounce), and ask the same people to measure 500 grams of flour, all will measure 500 grams. No error, no variance. In this sense you and I may have a conversation. I can ask for 500 grams in a recipe and that is what you will measure. Our communication is direct and the scale, the baker's measuring tool, is our $15 communication device.

A few advisories regarding scales: Scales, which are reasonably priced and available for the home market, *can* be inaccurate for very small amounts. Ingredients that fall within this range are high impact. Make a mistake measuring salt, yeast, baking powder, or cayenne, and the results may be disastrous. For these amounts I advise that you check the accuracy of your scale using either calibration weights or, more simply, a nickel. A nickel weighs 5 grams and works well as a calibration weight or as a simple test of accuracy. There are two other options. First, in addition to your scale with a capacity of roughly 5 kilograms (in 1-gram increments), you may want to purchase a second scale that measures in 0.1-gram increments up to 100 grams. Such scales are quite inexpensive and perfect for measuring small amounts of baking powder, salt, yeast, or baking soda. Second, you may switch to the volumetric column for amounts below about 20 grams. A level measure of salt, yeast, baking powder, or baking soda will have little variance when compared with multiple cups of flour, which return a considerable range of variance.

Reading Recipes

Many of the recipes in this book should look relatively familiar, with the possible exception that in addition to cups and teaspoons (what we call "Volumetric" amounts), you will also see metric ingredient quantities in a column labeled "Metric" (Grams). The gram is a metric unit of measurement. To put the gram in perspective, there are 28.35 grams in an ounce and 454 grams in a pound.

In addition to the columns for grams and volumetric quantities you will notice that ingredients are sometimes but not always listed in the order of use. So, for Oma's Pie Crust (page 24) the ingredients list begins with flour and salt; then come the butter and, last, the water. But (and this will require a little explaining—

bear with me!), when we get to bread recipes, the order of the ingredients changes slightly to follow the norms of what we call "baker's math." In baker's math (see Baker's Math on page 314 for an in-depth explanation), ingredients are listed according to a hierarchy that places flour(s) first, then water (or hydration), and follows with the remaining ingredients, in descending order of percentage. For the order of use, simply follow the step-by-step instructions included with each recipe. Further, in the bread recipes in the book, there is an additional column with percentages, labeled "Baker's %," which relates to baker's math. Again, all is explained in the baker's math section, so read on!

Measuring. Baking Is Not Cooking

It's my night to make dinner. Time is limited and I decide on pasta as my kids will eat almost anything that can adhere itself to slippery noodles. I look in the fridge for ingredients. Hmmm . . . some greens . . . a half package of smoked bacon, a bit of cream, walnuts, garlic, fresh herbs from the garden . . . and the journey to dinner begins. On inspection, my greens look best suited for the compost bucket so I step to the garden and snip some broccoli leaves. I toast the walnuts in a dry pan over low heat while I cube and sauté the bacon, add garlic to the sputtering fat and bloom it, then add julienned broccoli leaves and boiled pasta with some of its water. I reduce briefly, add a little cream at the end, and toss in a nice bowl with the chopped herbs and toasted walnuts. Add hard cheese for garnish and a generous grinding of freshly cracked pepper. Dinner. Not a straight line, more riffing than measuring, a side step, a hop and a skip, making it up as I go; I love this.

But this is not baking. Baking is building a stone wall that curves to a row of trees or borders a flower bed. Orderly natural elements marry with measurements as form and order, chaos and proportion combine. Bakers look on function and form the way woodworkers do, delighting in grain and stain, in four legs that kiss the ground evenly. In order for the legs to be equal the woodworker needs precision: measure twice, cut once. Maybe even measure three times and count the sixteenths if you are as accurate as I am with a saw, not in order to be more uptight, but in order to be better. All of the woodworker's love for design, color, wood choice, and texture is irrelevant if the table doesn't stand squarely, for measurements enable creative space. Set a proper foundation, then play. For additional information, see Measuring Ingredients, page 311.

Did you ever forget the salt in your bread or the eggs in chocolate chip cookies? Did you make pizza dough and leave out the yeast, or forget the baking powder in your pancakes? It happens to all of us, professionals and home bakers alike. In working on this book I've been surprised by how challenging it can be to work with focus and accuracy at home. It doesn't take more than a momentary distraction for attention to slip and the next thing you know a batch of bread may be headed for the waste bin or compost. But this is a relatively easy problem to fix (not the dough in the trash, the one before that when you forgot the yeast!).

Here are a couple of tips:

WORK SPACE: Before you begin, clear your countertop or work space of extraneous items. Gather necessary tools and all the ingredients required for what you will make. This *mise en place*, or "putting in place," helps us to set the stage for accurate work.

READ THE RECIPE: Before you begin, read the entire recipe. Some recipes are multiple-day processes; others can be completed in less than an hour. Some contain pointers to other sections that will provide important tips, techniques, or methods for baking your best. Trust me, it's worth the five minutes it will take.

INGREDIENTS: While measuring and adding ingredients do what we do in the bakery and check off each item *as you go*. If you don't want to write in the book place a sheet protector over the page and use a dry-erase marker or grease pen to give a hash mark to each item, checking it off as it is used. Refer to the recipe as you proceed, confirming that you are on track.

Baker's Math

What is "baker's math"? Simply explained, baker's math is a system that helps bakers identify and discuss ingredient ratios. In this system, the total amount of flour in a recipe is weighed and represented as 100%. Against that 100%, the weights of other ingredients are compared, returning a percentage value that is a proportion of the flour weight. If we have 1,000 grams of flour, 750 grams of water, 20 grams of salt, and 10 grams of yeast, we can say that the ingredient proportions (expressed in baker's math) look like this:

FLOUR: 100%
WATER: 75%
SALT: 2%
YEAST: 1%

If we add up these percentages, the sum is referred to as "Total Dough Percentage." In the example, our Total Dough Percentage is 178%.

In the early stages of a baker's growth, the value of baker's math is relatively low. But as we gain experience and compare recipes, we begin to notice differences with our hands and eyes and also on the page. The Poolish Baguette (page 143), for example, has 68% hydration whereas the Straight Baguette (page 147) has 75% hydration. Baker's math will help you compare apples with apples, giving insight into exact differences and similarities. Furthermore, and perhaps most important, learning these ratios and seeing them quantified by baker's math will also enable the baker to make minute adjustments and eventually lead to the ability to write his or her own recipes.

In the bread formulas in the book, the place to see total ratios and quantities is the table, included with each formula, identified as *Total Formula*. The Total Formula is the list of all ingredients and amounts that go into what you are making.

Let me explain. Most breads include subcomponents—a grain soaker or a preferment, for example—that come together with the remaining ingredients in the final mix. The Total Formula allows us to see the big picture. The sub-recipes guide us through the preparation of subcomponents such as the soaker or preferments.

In the SunSeed Total Formula (page 285), we see that the total amount of water is 76% of flour weight, salt is 2.5%, sunflower seeds are 15%, and so forth. These are total amounts of the respective ingredients. Below the Total Formula are sub-recipes for a stiff levain (which uses some flour and water as well as the sourdough culture; all are incorporated as part of the Total Formula) and for prepared grits.

Below the sub-recipes there is another table, called "Final Dough."

In the Final Dough table, remaining ingredients and sub-recipes come together for the mix.

In addition to highlighting ingredient ratios within a formula, baker's math also helps us to identify the amount of "prefermented flour" in recipes. Prefermented flour is flour that is fermented in advance of the final mix, thus the term "preferment." Preferments are discussed more fully in the Fermentation section that follows.

Bad Bread

Most bread produced in factory bakeries in the industrialized world is made without the critical step of fermentation. Instead, fermentation has been swapped out and replaced with chemicals. Dough conditioners, flavorings, processing aids, gums, fats, and additives are all used in an attempt to save one precious thing, time. If measured by output, the factories are quite good at it, even masterful. They mix, shape, and bake a loaf (tens of thousands, actually) in less than one hour, start to finish. A baker using traditional methods and actual fermentation may take up to 72 hours.

But what is the cost of saving this time? It depends on who you ask. My opinion is that fermented foods, from cheese to cured meats, pickled vegetables to soaked grains, are all made more delicious and, in many cases, more digestible and nutritious, with time. Perhaps the dietary trends that have placed bread and other carbohydrates in the crosshairs would lose their targets if more of what we ate was made with time and integrity. That's not to say that the news is all bad—across the country, more and more communities find themselves with bakers and bakeries in their midst, making great bread, which takes longer *and* tastes better.

Fermentation

Setting a proper course for awesome.

Fermentation happens when yeast (tiny single-celled fungi, related to mush-rooms and molds) and bacteria (the most common organisms on earth) break down sugars, producing carbon dioxide gas and alcohol. Historically we have had little view into these microscopic activities, yet we have always been intimately linked to their by-products—in fact, we love them. Grapes, gathered and pressed, will naturally ferment into wine that can be stored without spoiling until next year's harvest. Barley and other grains have a similar eagerness to do something. Once they are moistened, enzymatic processes kick into action and the grains sprout: it is their entire purpose. During sprouting, the sugar content climbs as long starch chains contained in the endosperm of the grain are enzymatically unzipped, freeing food for growth, germination, and fermentation.

Preferments

Well-made bread is a fermented food that often begins with a "preferment," hours before the final dough is mixed. Preferments are made with a portion of the total flour from our recipe, to which we add water and yeast or sourdough culture. Such a mixture ferments, developing flavors that transfer to the final loaf. A preferment acts like a bouillon cube or a marinade. Different ratios of flour and water and different types of leavening make unique flavor contributions; some are forceful, others present themselves with more finesse, but *all* bring complexity and flavor.

The common preferments can be divided into four large categories with "Yeasted" on one side (meaning that fermentation is initiated with commercial yeast) and "Sourdough" or "Naturally Leavened" (meaning that fermentation is initiated with sourdough culture) on the other. The two other categories are formed by a dividing line between liquid and stiff hydrations, with each hydration enabling different flavor profiles and handling characteristics.

PREFERMENTS, HYDRATIONS

	YEASTED	SOURDOUGH, OR NATURALLY LEAVENED
Liquid 100% to 125% hydration	Poolish	Liquid Levain
Stiff ~55 to 88% hydration (see Note)	Pâte Fermentée, Biga	Stiff Levain, Rye Sourdough

Note: Most will fall into the 55% to 66% hydration range, with Rye Sourdough being the exception at 85% to 88% hydration.

POOLISH: Poolish is a yeasted liquid preferment whose origin is attributed to Polish bakers. It is commonly used in baguettes and other French breads. Poolish imparts a yeasty aroma, gentle acidity, and extensibility. In lay terms, extensibility refers to the ease with which a dough can be gently stretched. No stretching—no long, crispy baguettes! Poolish, in baker's math, is hydrated at 100% to 125% hydration. It is "ripe," or ready for use, when its volume has doubled and it is bubbly. You may also notice shallow fissure lines running across the surface.

BIGA: Biga is a stiff yeasted preferment, common in the breads of Italy. Biga contributes strength and a unique floral aroma to breads such as ciabatta. Biga, in baker's math, is hydrated at 55% to 60% hydration. It is ready for use when its volume has at least doubled and the top surface is slightly rounded.

PÂTE FERMENTÉE: *Pâte fermentée*, literally translated from the French as "fermented dough," is a stiff preferment that contains salt. It is essentially dough saved from the previous day's mix. While poolish is mild mannered, pâte fermentée brings a more assertive fermentation flavor and a set of dough biceps for strength. Pâte fermentée, in baker's math, is 60% to 68% hydration. It is ready for use when its volume has doubled and the top surface is convex or rounded.

LIQUID LEVAIN: Liquid levain (*levain* is the French word for "leaven") is a liquid sourdough preferment. Liquid levain adds mild lactic acidity. It is a common preferment in professional bakeries as it is easily mixed and portioned. Large bakeries even have jacketed tank fermenters that agitate the liquid and use time and temperature controls to regulate activity. Liquid levain, in baker's math, is 100% to 125% hydration. It is ready for use when filled with large and small bubbles. The surface will have shallow fissures, and small, sudsy bubbles will be present.

STIFF LEVAIN: Stiff levain is a stiff sourdough preferment. Stiff levain adds strength and acidity and pairs well with the mineral flavor qualities of whole-grain breads and sourdough loaves. Stiff levain, in baker's math, is hydrated at 60% to 68% hydration. It is ready for use when its volume has doubled and the top surface is convex or rounded. I often add salt to a stiff levain that contains whole-grain flour. The increase in fermentation rate that would otherwise be a result of using whole-grain flour in the levain is slowed back down to normal by the addition of the salt.

RYE SOURDOUGH: Rye sourdough is a stiff sourdough preferment that is fed with whole rye flour. Rye sourdough adds strong acidity, a requirement for well-performing breads containing a high percentage of rye flour. It has a unique grassy, bright quality. Rye sourdough, in baker's math, is usually hydrated around 85% to 88% hydration. If hydrated in this range it will be ready when the top is slightly domed but not collapsed. Note that Wood's Boiled Cider Bread (page 196) uses a sourdough with a higher hydration that won't necessarily "dome."

The list of grains that can be fermented and put in bread extends to just about every combination of everything under the sun. The list above addresses common scenarios, traditional hydrations, and leaveners. I encourage you to explore other routes once these elements become familiar. Add whole-grain flour to your liquid levain, make a poolish with rye or buckwheat, try a pâte fermentée with spelt, or ferment rice flour and see how it tastes. Play, invent, create. Sometimes you will stumble across a winner; at other times you will keep moving (as I did after my seaweed bread with sesame-miso crust!). But note: Every change has consequences, a cause and effect that will require all senses. Watch, taste, touch, learn, listen, and enjoy.

Setting Temperatures

Good bakers are much more than just bakers. Before anything can be shaped, baked, or eaten, we guide, coddle, and nurture fermentation through the manipulation of dough temperature. It used to be that "water the temperature of bath water" was close enough, regardless of how hot you like your bath, or how hot the house is, or if your flour is kept in the fridge or freezer. If we want more consistent results, consistent fermentation is key. By starting doughs in a controlled temperature range, we can be on our way to good fermentation and great bread. In order to control fermentation, bakers adjust water temperature. Of all the factors contributing to temperature in the dough environment, water temperature is the easiest to control because adjustment can be made at the tap by selecting hot, warm, or cold and specific temperatures in between. Flour is generally already at room temperature, as are other elements.

In order to determine the proper water temperature, we use a method called desired dough temperature, or DDT. We measure the temperature of three to four factors which, when calculated together, get us close to the water temperature required for mixing. The factors are as follows:

1. Flour (the temperature of all flours that will be included in the final mix; you may ignore salt and yeast)
2. Air (a measurement of ambient conditions where the dough will ferment)
3. Water (the easiest factor for us to adjust, also a major ingredient)
4. Preferments (poolish, biga, liquid levain, etc.)

Most breads in this book have three to four factors. Ciabatta (page 77), which has a biga, might look like this in my kitchen:

FLOUR: 62°F

AIR: 62°F

PREFERMENT: 65°F

Next, check the desired dough temperature, DDT. In the case of Ciabatta, my DDT is 76°F (most doughs in this book and in professional bakeries will fall between 74°F and 82°F). If all factors (flour, air, preferment, and water) measure 76°F and we average them, the average is 76°F. But in our example, in order for the average to equal 76°F, we need to warm the water.

In order to determine the water number, we first:

Multiply 76 times the number of factors (4 factors for Ciabatta). That equals 304.

Next, subtract flour temperature (62), air temperature (62), and preferment temperature (65) from 304. So, 304 – 62 – 62 – 65 = 115°F. Therefore, 115°F is the water temperature required to give us an average of 76°F when we combine all ingredients.

One additional note regarding doughs that have much of their water (even all in some cases) tied up in preferments, soakers, or other sub-ingredients, leaving little water for the final mix. In these cases the final flour, soakers, and other components should be left in a spot that measures as closely as possible to your desired dough temperature. So, on top of the fridge, or in a warm spot in winter and in a cooler location in warm months.

Professional bakers additionally calculate to determine the friction generated by mechanical mixers. However, most of the doughs in this book are mixed by hand only to incorporation, which generates little to no heat.

Dough Temperature and the Goldilocks Zone

If you tried reading Setting Temperatures (page 320) to learn how to guide your dough temperature but all the technical talk was dumping a bucket of cold water on your baking fervor, here is a shortcut that will get you pretty close.

In broad strokes we want your dough to rise at a rate that favors flavor and form; not too fast, not too slow, the Goldilocks zone of yeasted goodness. The easiest way to make this happen is to adjust the water temperature for your mix.

Here's how you do it:

First, find the desired dough temperature (DDT) for your recipe; most are 76° to 78°F. For instance, Mama's Bread (page 31) has a DDT of 76°F.

Next, make an educated guess about the average temperature of the flour and air in your kitchen. Let's say your flour is sitting on the counter and the kitchen is about 70°F. So our average temperature number will be 70°F; it's close enough.

Now, go to the 76°F table below and find your kitchen temperature in the "Average Temperature" column. You'll see that next to your 70°F in the "Water Should Be" column it says 88°F. Therefore, your water for this mix should be 88°F, or if you don't have a thermometer, use water that feels neutral or barely cool to your hand.

DDT 76°F		DDT 78°F		DDT 80°F	
AVERAGE TEMPERATURE	WATER SHOULD BE	AVERAGE TEMPERATURE	WATER SHOULD BE	AVERAGE TEMPERATURE	WATER SHOULD BE
60	108	60	114	60	120
62	104	62	110	62	116
64	100	64	106	64	112
66	96	66	102	66	108
68	92	68	98	68	104
70	88	70	94	70	100
72	84	72	90	72	96
74	80	74	86	74	92
76	76	76	82	76	88
78	72	78	78	78	84
80	68	80	74	80	80

As you grow from basic breads to more complicated recipes, I recommend closely following the instructions in Setting Temperatures for best results.

PROCESS

Gather grain, thresh, winnow, mash, grind, or mill. Mix with water, then stir, form, and bake. These are the timeless, primary steps in bread making. Over thousands of years, our relationship with each step in this process has deepened as we have moved from broadcast seed to cultivars, past hand milling to bagged flour, and onward to wood-fired and commercial baking. But through these changes, the essentials of the bread making process remain intact. We begin with milled grain, most often wheat, chosen for its ability to form gluten; then we add water, salt, and a leavener such as yeast or sourdough culture. This mixture ferments over the course of a few hours before we shape, proof, bake, and eat. Let's add some detail to these steps.

Mixing

Once ingredients are measured and our water temperature is set, we proceed to mixing. Mixing is the process of combining ingredients until homogeneous.

To mix, put the ingredients in a large mixing bowl (12 to 14 inches in diameter) in the order detailed in the steps for each recipe. With hand mixing, this process usually begins with final dough water or other liquids and a preferment, if applicable. Then the dry ingredients, including the flour, salt, and yeast, are added. Using the handle end of a wooden cooking spoon, stir the mass until homogeneous with the spoon held at a right angle to the bowl and counter. The handle end is small and narrow and moves through the mixture quite easily. If it becomes difficult to work, reach in and bring it together with one hand, pressing and kneading while steadying the bowl with the other hand. If you find it easier, after stirring for a bit, you can scrape the dough out of the bowl with a plastic scraper onto a work surface and knead briefly with your hands just until the dough comes together. Resist the urge to use more than a light dusting of flour. Then scrape down and clean the sides of the bowl with a plastic dough scraper before returning the dough to the bowl, where it will rise during bulk fermentation and folding, the period of time before dividing and shaping. If you are making a bread that has soakers, refer to the mixing instructions. Some will be incorporated at the beginning with the final water while others (more commonly) will be added on top of the dough after mixing.

Other Techniques and Further Reading

The dough mixing procedure for breads in this book is purposefully written with the most of emphasis placed on proper scaling (using the digital scale), proper water temperature (through the use of desired dough temperature), a short mix, folds for strength, and long fermentation for further strength and flavor.

In the world of artisan baking there are many, many variations on this theme. As you read and explore you will come across different terms and techniques, all with their own results and benefits. From "Autolyse" to "Slap and Fold" to "No-Knead" and mechanical mixing, there are almost as many ways to make great bread as there are bakers.

When I began to bake seriously I read as much as I could and relied heavily on a few books. Raymond Calvel's *The Taste of Bread*, Jeffrey Hamelman's *Bread,* and *Special and Decorative Bread*, by Raymond Bilheux and Alain Escoffier, which is the bread volume of the Professional French Pastry Series. While I enjoy seeing new books, I still rely most heavily upon these three for inspiration and education.

After mixing, check the dough temperature. When you use the DDT calculations you should be relatively close (within a few degrees). If a dough is too warm—say, for example, it is 82°F and the DDT is 76°F—place it in a cooler spot and consider *shortening* bulk fermentation by 10 to 25 percent. Conversely, if the dough is too cool, do the opposite. If your dough is 72°F and the recipe suggested 78°F, find a warmer spot and consider *lengthening* bulk fermentation by 10 to 25 percent. The important thing is that if you see something—a dough that needs to be encouraged toward a warmer or cooler temperature—do something. If you are off a little, it doesn't mean that you've made a mistake. It's simply a sign that some action needs to be taken. After checking the temperature, cover the dough and set a timer for your first fold. One final note about this. On a recent cool day I did some testing. At the end of mix, my dough temperature was great, 78°F. But after an hour or so in my 62°F kitchen, I found that the dough temperature was plummeting. I turned on the oven for just a few minutes, enough to warm it slightly, and then turned it off. I placed the bowl of dough in the oven to rise and was mostly back on track, lengthening fermentation only slightly. So again, be aware, and change course as necessary.

Stand Mixers

If you want to use your stand mixer, here's what you may do. Put the dry ingredients in the bowl and mix to combine with a dough hook, then add the liquids and any preferments. When the ingredients are fully incorporated (this may take 5 minutes or more on a gentle speed; be sure to check the bottom of the mixer bowl to see that there are no dry bits), shut off the mixer and cover the bowl with a plastic bag (you may leave the bowl attached to the mixer, with the hook also attached; just make sure the bowl is well covered). At each folding interval, remove the plastic bag and turn on the mixer to "stir" (or the lowest setting) until the dough hook has worked its way around the dough mass for one full rotation. Proceed with the normal instructions for dividing and preshaping at the end of bulk fermentation.

Folding

There are many successful methods for folding doughs. A good baker reads the needs of each dough with hands and eyes every time contact is made. A stiff dough requires less folding, a wet dough more; some bakers prefer to dump dough onto a counter for more vigor, others swear by gentle folds in a bucket.

Here's what I do. I call it "cardinal" folding, as I fold the dough from each point of the compass: Using a plastic scraper for wetter doughs (such as baguettes) or wet hands for drier doughs (such as Pain de Mie, page 166; Mama's Bread, page 31; or Jalapeño-Cheddar Bread, page 191), reach under the mass of dough, stretch it upward and press it into the center of the mass, pressing down with your hand or the scraper. Turn the bowl 90 degrees and repeat the process, reaching under, pulling upward, and pressing down. Repeat this process, performing a stretch and fold at each point (north, south, east, and west) of the compass. Some doughs may require a little more than just four stretch and folds. The number varies, depending on the dough, and on the stage of fermentation (a dough in the first hour of bulk fermentation may take more before tightening, whereas a more mature dough in its second or third hour will take only four). In the first hour of fermentation the dough will feel slack and, while smoothing somewhat, will still feel mostly inert. But as the mass wakes up and gluten strands begin to cross-link, you will notice changes. When it's time for a fold, first moisten your fingers (so that they don't stick) and then pull up a section of the dough. You will notice over the course of time how the dough initially shreds or rips rather than stretches; as development occurs, you will see that you can stretch it very, very thinly. A piece gently stretched between the fingers can be thinned until transparent—something we call the "windowpane" test. This ability to stretch is what will allow the loaf to capture gas as the dough rises in the bowl and, eventually, in the oven. I should note that often, even with wetter doughs for which some prefer to use the plastic scraper, I use wet hands. I enjoy touching the dough, and it gives me a better sense of the dough's activity, strength, and weakness.

Dividing

At the end of bulk fermentation dough should be domed, and in most cases it will have risen noticeably. It should feel soft, silky, and active. The transformation that has occurred should be evident—a fragrant mass will be waiting for you.

To divide, begin with a light dusting of flour on your bench or work surface. Using a flexible plastic scraper, gently scrape the dough out onto the dusted surface. All the folding and attention to detail exhibited thus far should continue. Be gentle.

Refer to your recipe to determine the number of pieces for your divide. If you have 1 kilo (1,000 grams) of dough and the baguette weight per piece (in a bakery we say, "scale weight") is 250 grams, visualize the mass divided into the required number of pieces. Visualizing the pieces will help you to have a single, large piece of dough with a small piece on top in case your guess was a little low. A loaf consisting of a single cut of dough has better potential for greatness than a loaf made of many bits. Think of dough as a skein of yarn; long pieces make a more beautiful sweater than many small pieces. With a slight dusting on the top surface of your dough, begin dividing, using your gram scale to ensure accuracy. Don't obsess over a gram or even 5 grams of variance. Place the divided pieces to the side on a dusted portion of the bench and finish dividing. If you find yourself with a small extra portion of dough you may divide it among the pieces. Proceed directly to preshape.

Preshaping

Preshaping is an important step between the dividing and final shaping steps of bread making. It adds strength, removes any large gas bubbles that may remain after fermentation, and gives dough pieces uniformity, which will, in turn, support good final shaping. The most common preshaped form is a loose ball, or what bakers refer to as a "round."

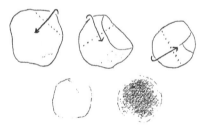

PRESHAPE ROUND: On a lightly floured surface, gently pat the dough to remove any large bubbles, then stretch the outside edge of the dough slightly away from its center. Next, fold the dough back to its center, pressing down to gently seal. Repeat this process, working your way around the entire dough piece in five or six movements.

You will notice that the motion is not unlike the folding motion performed during bulk fermentation. Set the dough to rest on a lightly floured surface, seam side down and covered to prevent a skin from forming, until shaping.

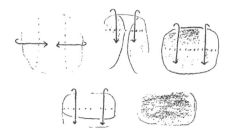

PRESHAPE TUBE: On a lightly floured surface, gently pat the dough to remove any large bubbles and gently stretch it into a rough circular form. Next, fold the sides toward the middle, pressing down to gently seal. Beginning with the side farthest from you, fold the piece one-third of the way toward the leading edge and pat gently to seal. Repeat this process two times, sealing as you go. Set the dough to rest on a lightly floured surface, seam side down and covered, until shaping.

After a rest of 10 to 15 minutes, most doughs will be ready to shape.

Seam Side or Top Side

During preshaping, shaping, and rising, and even when placing loaves in the oven, bakers refer to the unbaked loaf as having two sides. The bottom of the loaf, where seams of dough are gathered during preshaping and shaping, is called the "seam side." The smooth opposite side, containing no seams, is referred to as the "top side." From this point, all the way until the shaped loaf is baked, this orientation will be maintained, with the top side being the surface that will be scored before loading.

We maintain this differentiation because the seam side is structurally the weakest part of the loaf. During baking, when the loaf expands rapidly, it is important that the seam side is against the baking stone or pan, held in place by the weight of the loaf. An exposed seam will open during baking, causing the loaf to deform. If the seam is held in place all the energy of the expanding loaf is directed upward to those parts of the loaf where we create weakness intentionally by scoring, or cutting it. See Scoring, page 339), for more information.

Shaping

There are many paths to the land of beautiful bâtards, boules, and baguettes; here are some steps that I have found helpful.

Shaping Videos

In addition to reading these descriptions I encourage you to look around in the virtual world as there are many resources online where one can see bread shaping. While the steps are important, it is also informative to see how hands move and how the dough responds.

Boule

Shaping the boule, or round form, is very similar to the process of preshaping. Place a preshaped dough piece seam up on a lightly floured surface and, taking the edge of the dough piece, pull upward and outward slightly, then fold toward the center, pressing gently to seal. Repeat this process, working your way around the entire dough piece until the dough tightens noticeably. Next, invert the dough so that the seam side is on the bench and push it forward and backward, tensioning the dough as it adheres slightly to the bench. Avoid the inclination to overwork the dough. If tears or small rips appear, stop—you've reached the stretching capacity of the dough, and further work will only cause harm.

Bâtard

The bâtard shape is an elliptical form, longer than a boule but shorter than a baguette. To form a bâtard, begin with a preshaped round of dough that has relaxed for 10 to 15 minutes. Place the preshaped dough, seam up, on a lightly floured surface and stretch gently to elongate on the north-south axis. Pat gently to remove any bubbles that formed during the rest period. Next, fold the dough from the top down one-third of the way. Then, fold the top left and top right corners of the dough toward the center on a 45-degree angle. Next, fold the top of the dough down two-thirds of the way and seal gently with the heel of your hand. Next, fold the sides toward the middle and pat to seal. Then, fold the dough once more, all the way to the leading edge of the dough, and again seal with the heel of your

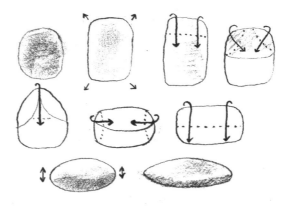

hand. Last, beginning in the middle of the form, roll your hands back and forth, rolling the dough and elongating and tapering it as both hands move away from the center.

Baguette

To form a baguette, begin with a preshaped tube of dough that has relaxed for 10 to 15 minutes. Place the preshaped dough tube, seam up, on a lightly floured surface; stretch gently to elongate on the east-west axis; and pat to remove any bubbles that formed during the rest period. Next, fold the dough from the top down two-thirds of the way and pat with the heel of your hand to gently seal. Next, fold the dough from the bottom up two-thirds of the way and pat with the heel of your hand to gently seal. Next, fold the top down two-thirds of the way and again pat to seal. Last, make a gentle east-west divot in the middle of the dough from end to end, and then fold the dough from the top down to the bottom edge and pat to seal with the heel of your hand.

This is what I call the folding, or origami, phase of shaping, after which you should have a somewhat taut tube that is even in size and shape from end to end. After completing the folding phase, and with the seam side down on the bench, place a single palm in the middle of the dough and roll gently back and forth.

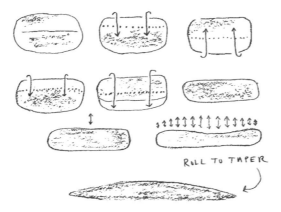

RoLL To TAPER

With light pressure, a depression will form. Next, add your second hand and roll side by side, pushing the dough back and forth, slowly moving hands apart toward the tips, adding pressure in order to taper the tips. If the dough is resistant, go back to the middle and make another pass.

Pan Loaf

The pan loaf is the easiest for the beginner. Doughs that are baked in a pan are generally lower in total hydration. Less hydration (less water) means dough releases from your hands and from the shaping surface more easily, and as it will rise and bake in a pan, the vessel does much of the forming work.

To form a pan loaf, begin with a preshaped round of dough that has relaxed for 10 to 15 minutes. Place the preshaped dough, seam up, on a lightly floured surface and stretch to elongate on the east-west axis and pat gently to remove any bubbles that formed during the rest period. Next, fold the sides toward the middle, pressing gently down to seal. Beginning with the side farthest from you, fold the piece one-third of the way toward the leading edge and pat gently to seal. Next, fold the top down two-thirds of the way and seal gently with the heel of your hand. Finally, fold the dough once more, all the way to the leading edge of the dough and seal again with the heel of your hand. Place the loaf in the greased prepared pan with the seam side on the bottom.

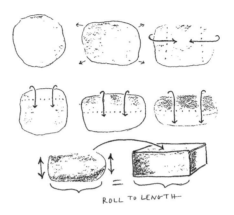

ROLL TO LENGTH

Roll

Rolls may be shaped with the same steps used to shape larger pieces of dough. You may make tiny boules, miniature baguettes, short bâtards; anything is possible.

Fendu

Fendu, literally meaning "split" in French, is not really a shape but more of a finishing technique that can be used with any of the standard bread forms. After shaping, the loaf is set to rest for a few minutes. After the top side of the loaf has been generously floured, insert a dowel, thin rolling pin, or transfer peel is used to press down on the loaf, making a deep impression that will remain through proofing, giving a fissured appearance to the baked loaf. The fendu is most commonly proofed top side down (the top side being the side pressed with the pin) on a floured baker's linen (couche) or tea towel. During baking, the top side, floury from contact with the dusty linen, develops a nice contrast as the loaf opens and expands to reveal the split. It is not necessary to score the fendu shape, as the split creates a natural weakness or expansion point.

Baskets, Linens, and Couches

After shaping, some loaves are set to rise in baskets, which are called *bannetons* or *brotforms*. The baskets support the loaves as they rise, preventing them from spreading laterally under their own weight. Other loaves rise on baker's linen, a sturdy woven material made from flax linen, called a *couche*. Prior to receiving the dough, baskets and linens receive a light but thorough dusting of flour through a sifter. This prevents the sticky dough from adhering to the basket or linen during proofing. It also gives a beautiful contrast and visual appeal to the finished loaf. The amount of dusting flour required is somewhat subjective. Dusting flour should be enough to give the linen coverage during proofing, but not so much that the finished loaf will be caked with raw flour. Remember also to flour the sidewalls of the basket, as the loaf will expand during proofing. The shaped dough is placed in the basket or on the dusted couche with the seam side up. If loaves are rising on a couche, pleat folds of material between them to prevent them from rising into one another. Once the dough is in the basket or set upon the linen, give a small additional dusting to the seam side of the loaf as further insurance against sticking.

A floured cotton tea towel may be substituted for the baskets and baker's linen mentioned above. But note, cotton is much more likely to adhere to a loaf than the sturdy baker's linen. I offer the tea towel, but encourage you to consider the bannetons and baker's linen as early investments. One trick to help the tea towel is to use a blend of 50% rice flour/50% whole wheat flour (or all-purpose flour) for dusting baskets and towels. Rice flour is very resistant to sticking. You can keep this blend in a labeled jar in the freezer for a long time, removing it for use only when dusting. Do not use it for shaping, as the seams of your breads will inevitably open.

Other Shapes, New Shapes, Creating

Finding new shapes and learning and practicing the old ones are sizable areas of play. Almost as long as we've eaten bread, bakers have toyed with its forms, exploring endless possibilities for adding character to it. As you practice shaping, first study the standard forms listed above and then, when your hands are proficient, look around. Available in books and on the Internet are numerous surveys of classical shapes, from the rough, organic forms of Italy, which appear to have split from the earth, to fanciful French shapes, which resemble everything from ballet shoes to horseshoes, to name just a few. Those who are particularly drawn to weaving and textiles will find many ways to play with braided forms of challah as well. And if you run out of inspiration, take the matter into your own creative hands.

Shaping Rye

A couple of things to note about shaping rye doughs: Because a rye dough lacks the extensibility (remember that this is the ability of a dough to stretch) and the elasticity (the snap backward after the stretch) of wheat-based doughs, shaping it is more a process of folding than tensioning. Follow the steps that you would normally use, paying careful attention to the order of folds, but don't expect to feel any dough tension. Furthermore, use enough rye flour on your work surface to prevent the dough from sticking (but not so much that raw flour is pushed into the folds of the loaf). Finally, be brief. Don't overfold; be gentle. A strong hand or fingers, gripping and pulling, will only leave you stuck in the dough, getting stickier and messier. Be deft, and practice!

Rye

There are several recipes in the book that contain a significant portion of whole rye flour (Wood's Boiled Cider Bread, page 196; Pain de Seigle, page 102; Citrus Vollkornbrot, page 255). If you are new to rye flour, you may think that something has gone significantly wrong in your mixing bowl or on your bench. The dough is sticky, even gummy; it adheres to your hands and refuses to unstick itself.... This is normal. Rye does contain gluten, but it largely lacks the elastic characteristics of wheat flour and, if that isn't enough, it also contains starches, which are quite sticky when hydrated. Due to these characteristics, during shaping the dough feels more like cookie dough or modeling clay than a supple, elastic wheat dough. But fear not, all the trouble is worth it. Rye ferments extremely well, has an entirely unique flavor (which has nothing to do with caraway!), and is incredibly nutritious.

Crust Treatments, Seed Trays, and Garnishes

Many breads and rolls are made more delicious and beautiful through the addition of grains, seeds, nuts, or coarsely ground flour to the exterior of loaves and rolls after shaping. During baking, the crust, enhanced with grains and seeds, skyrockets as it toasts and crisps. Our visual enjoyment is heightened as well when we savor the contrast of texture and color.

Almost any crust can be amended. Some consideration should be given to how the loaf will be scored; some loaves with seed crusts (such as pumpkin) must be cut with scissors rather than scored with a utility razor. To apply a crust, follow these steps:

1. Prepare a "seed tray." A seed tray is essentially two small sheet pans, one of which contains a seed blend or grains that will be applied, and another holds a well-moistened towel.

2. After shaping, place the top side of the shaped piece on the moistened towel, then set the moistened top on the seed tray and roll it to coat it. Moisture from the towel, transferred to the shaped loaf, will enable the seeds to stick. For the most thorough coating, leave the loaf on the seed tray for 5 to 10 seconds before placing it on a dusted baker's linen, in a dusted banneton, or in a loaf pan or some other form to proof.

Proofing

Once loaves are shaped and rising for the last time, they enter a phase we refer to as *proofing*. During proofing, fermentation continues and the loaf expands, supported by the network of strength developed during folding and shaping as well as by the basket, linen couche, or pan where it is rising.

In the recipes, I give timings for the final proof that should put you close if your dough is moving at a reasonable rate (remember DDT and all the information in Setting Temperatures) and if the dough has proofed in a moderate ambient environment. Those of you in summertime Arkansas with no air conditioning or in winter wonderland Vermont with a drafty house will need to shorten or lengthen, respectively, your proofing times.

When checking the level of proof, I look for a few things. First, don't wait until the fifty-ninth minute of an anticipated 60-minute proof to see what's happening. Check in after 30 minutes and feel the loaf. With the most sensitive pad portion of your index or middle finger, gently apply pressure to the dough surface. Don't poke with the end near the nail, which has only calluses and no feeling. When pressing, tune in to the resistance you feel. Does the finger depress the dough easily, like pushing into a pillow or cotton candy, or does it meet a slight resistance? Does it spring back immediately? All of this information should be thought of as clues, with each rising loaf giving hints via the resistance felt when you check the proof. With experience, you will see that pan loaves can be proofed until they feel very soft, whereas others, such as baguettes, need to be baked while they still give your fingers resistance.

Scoring

Before loading breads into the oven, we often make light cuts in the top surface of the shaped loaf. This is called *scoring* and the resultant marks are called *cuts*. From a distance, scoring seems a cursory; simply pull a blade across the loaf, and you are done. However, as your skills, knowledge, and experience increase, you may begin to see more nuance, a universe of possibilities for this microspace where blade meets dough. You will notice that blade angle, blade shape, blade speed, the qualities of the shaped loaf, and other factors all affect what comes out of the oven. Scoring is a hand skill not unlike the relationship between the artist's hand and the brush or the sculptor's grip and a chisel. What happens in this connection between the hand and the tool takes time to develop and longer to master.

According to legend, scoring originally evolved as an identification system for large peasant loaves, which were baked in communal ovens. After the bake, one could identify each loaf from the cut and return it to its maker. Whether the tale is true or not, what is important is that scoring serves a function. In the early minutes of baking, yeast and bacteria populations quickly increase their activity as the loaf heats. Moisture in the dough converts to steam, then the loaf expands and springs until the crust sets and yeast and bacteria perish. During this period of expansion, the shaped loaf, unsure which way to move, needs guidance. Scoring is the baker's way of applying guidance, using a razor to "tell" the loaf where to open.

A few things to consider as major components of scoring:

BLADE: As noted in the Tools section (page 357), a double-edge safety razor is best. There are a few (literally fewer than five) doughs that I cut with a serrated knife or scissors; the rest of the time I use the razor. The blade should be sharp and clear of dough bits from prior use. When loading the blade onto the lame, the baker may make a choice of a straight or curved aspect. The majority of bakers use the curved lame for cuts that we would like to open energetically, forming what is referred to as an *ear*; and a straight blade for cuts that we want to open with a flatter, horizontal aspect. Good ears, or *good cuts*, in baker's parlance, signify that the loaf was well shaped, that it was at a proper level of proof when entering the oven, and that the oven had ample heat and steam. This is not to say that good cuts equal perfect bread. Perfect bread should be defined as that which the baker or eater finds most pleasing to see and eat. I have had marvelously delicious bread with bad cuts and poor loaves cut with mechanical precision.

DOUGH SURFACE: The condition of the cutting surface of shaped loaves has an impact related to scoring. I advise placing shaped baguettes on baker's linen with the seam of the shaped loaf up when ambient humidity is high. In other words, the top side of the loaf—the side that will eventually be cut—should be in contact with the dry, lightly dusted linen. This places the top surface away from moist air. Too much humidity guarantees that the cutting surface will be slightly tacky and, when we are cutting, regardless of how well we do with all other aspects of our work, the blade may stick to the loaf, dragging and disfiguring rather than moving quickly, delicately, across the surface.

Many options exist for scoring bâtards and baguettes. Here are a few examples, ranging from a single cut to more involved cross-hatching and chevron forms. For the baguette, I prefer classic options. Baguettes that are sized for the home oven look best with a three-cut. I've included examples of the five- and seven-cut as well, as they are the full-length, bakery standards.

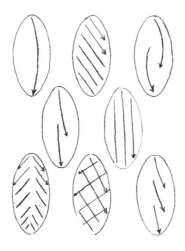

In broad terms, baguettes and bâtards, which should open with energetic cuts, do best when the dough is still youthful, rising, gaining activity, not flabby or overproofed. These breads prefer strong heat and good steam for nice ears to form.

For boules and larger rounds, which we call *miches*, we can push the proof further, as most are cut with a vertical blade angle in anticipation of cuts that will open laterally. Other breads, such as Ciabatta (page 77), the Olive and Rosemary Rustique (page 81), and Pane Genzano (page 69) can be pushed until quite gassy because they are not cut at all. Follow the timings that I suggest in each recipe, and you should be close.

Cross   Cross-hatch   Polka   Box

Circle-cross   Botanical   Leaf   Sunrise

Spiral   Smiley face   Leaves   Swan

Cross

One of the easiest, perhaps one of the oldest, and still one of the best. The cross releases the loaf, allowing it to move in all directions as it expands during baking.

Holding the blade perpendicular to the surface of the loaf, cut first on the north-south axis, then on the east-west axis, so that the cuts intersect.

Crosshatch

Another common and highly functional cut is the crosshatch. Well suited for large rounds or miches, the design works well to fully release the loaf and enable a low profile.

Holding the blade perpendicular to the surface of the loaf, begin with the central north-south cut as you would for the cross, then place parallel cuts on either side. Then apply additional cuts running at a low angle diagonally across the initial lines.

Polka

The Polka cut also releases the loaf well and can be executed with little fuss.

Holding the blade perpendicular to the surface of the loaf, begin with evenly spaced cuts on the north-south axis, then place additional cuts on the east-west axis. As with other cuts, even spacing and consistent cut depth are key to achieving a beautiful result.

Box

I like the Box cut for loaves that I plan to stencil. Cuts are placed on the "shoulders" of the loaf (where the top transitions to steeply sloping sides), leaving a wide-open area for play.

To score, think of the loaf as a clock face and place your blade at twelve o'clock. With a confident, quick cut, move the blade to three o'clock. Then begin the next cut just outside the first cut and move confidently to six o'clock and then continue onward to nine o'clock before ending the journey back at twelve o'clock.

Circle

For the Circle cut, begin a single cut at twelve o'clock on the shoulder of the loaf and proceed all the way around, returning to the starting point. Hold the blade at a low, flat angle (note that this differs from the grip for the preceeding cuts). You may stencil the top surface or keep it simple and cut a cross.

Botanical

The Botanical cut begins with a single north-south cut. Then lighter cuts, which are more decorative than functional, are made, suggesting the veins of a leaf.

Leaf

The Leaf is similar to the Botanical cut, but you may cut the border and center vein of the Leaf with deeper cuts, and then, using light decorative cuts, make the smaller veins.

Sunrise

The Sunrise is one of Jeffrey Hamelman's favorite cuts for a miche. I like it for large rye loaves. Rye, lacking the structural strength of wheat flour, can be a great surface for intricate scores, as loaves containing a high percentage of rye spring less in the oven. The contrast of darkening rye and dusting flour on the exterior is intensely beautiful after baking.

Begin with the longer cuts, arching around the form of the loaf, diminishing and shortening as you proceed.

Spiral

For the Spiral, imagine a small circle at the center of the loaf with arcing lines coming off it. The lines emanate from the center and proceed to the shoulders of the loaf. This cut is best made with a low blade angle, similar to the angle used in cutting baguettes.

Smiley Face

Someone must have a better name for this cut? But regardless of the lack of a better term, it is a favorite for loaves that are strong and expand well in the oven.

The semicircle "mouth" of the smile is made with a low blade angle, the line running along the shoulder line of the loaf. The three additional cuts are made with a vertical blade angle, helping the loaf to expand additionally on the side opposite the more substantial cut. When well executed, the "mouth" will form a large "ear," or *grigne*, which darkens to mahogany as it bakes.

Leaves

Similar to the Botanical and Leaf cuts above, Leaves is a combination of substantial, deeper cuts and light, decorative cuts.

Begin by cutting the outlines of the leaves; the initial cuts will look like two "Y" shapes that intersect. After the outlines, cut the center ribs of each and then, using light cuts that barely break the surface, cut the veins of the leaves.

Oven

Counting backward from when you estimate you will load the oven, preheat it for 45 to 60 minutes. This amount of time is necessary only when you are baking loaves on a baking stone. Everything else (for example, pan loaves or pans of rolls) simply requires that the oven be preheated and set to the proper temperature. For the hearth-baked loaves, which bake directly on a baking stone, preheat the stone on a rack in the lower third of the oven.

Depending on how (if at all) you decide to steam, your steaming system should be in place during preheating. Under the stone, on the floor of the oven, place a roasting pan loaded with lava rocks or a cast-iron skillet with metal scraps or pie weights. If you plan to bake in a cast-iron Dutch oven, a cloche, or some other device that serves as an oven within an oven, rather than on the surface of your baking stone, you should preheat that item during this time period. This is a good time to roast some vegetables or meat, bake a lasagna, etc. However, don't place these items on your baking stone, as it will not fully preheat. Instead, use an empty rack placed above the stone.

Loading

For breads, rolls, scones, biscuits, and anything else baked in or on a pan, *loading* simply means sliding pans onto the rungs of the oven to bake. With loaves that bake directly on a baking stone (we'll call them "hearth loaves"), there are a few steps to learn.

HEARTH BAKING STEPS

FIRST, GATHER THE TOOLS:

- Parchment paper cut to the size of your baking stone. You will eventually graduate away from using parchment paper under the loaf. When you do, a little semolina or whole wheat flour can act like ball bearings, allowing the loaf to slide onto the baking stone.
- Transfer peel or flipping board for moving elongated loaves from their proofing spot to the parchment paper.
- A half-sheet pan, a pizza peel, or any other stiff, thin piece of material that can be used to slide the loaves onto the baking stone.
- Razor and lame for scoring (if the loaves are scored, like baguettes)
- Water for steaming (I like to use a long-necked wine bottle to pour the water into the roasting pan or heated cast-iron skillet)
- Oven mitts

TO LOAD:

- Place the prepared parchment on a pizza peel or an upside-down sheet pan. As I note above, with some practice and experience you can simply sprinkle flour, semolina, or cornmeal onto the peel, aiding the sliding action that will deposit the loaf onto the stone.

- Gently invert the proofing loaf from its basket, towel-lined bowl, or linen couche onto the prepared parchment paper. In some cases (baguettes, for example) you will use a transfer peel or "flipping board" (see Tools, page 357) to move the loaves. Remember that with hearth breads we most often proof the loaf seam side up with the top of the loaf against the floured surface of the proofing vessel. With some recipes that yield multiple loaves (again, baguettes), distribute them on the parchment paper evenly for best baking results.

- Score the loaf as directed or by referring to an example in the scoring diagram (page 342) for options.

- Slide the loaf and parchment paper onto the preheated baking stone. Make any necessary adjustments to the placement of the parchment paper on the stone. Careful, hot!

- Steam the oven and set a timer, referring to the instructions for the recipe.

Loading

If loading the oven is a new process, I would advise a couple of dress rehearsals. One day when the oven is off, practice the loading steps using a 1- or 2-pound bag of beans or rice as a pretend loaf, imaginarily rising on a tea towel or in a proofing basket. Practice inverting this "loaf" onto a transfer peel and then onto a piece of parchment paper cut to the size of your stone. Practice sliding the whole thing into the oven onto the stone a few times, making any necessary adjustments to the placement of the parchment paper on the stone. Remember that when you are actually loading, the stone will be very hot. Be precise with your movements in order to avoid burns. A little practice will go a long ways toward helping you to be smooth and relaxed. You've got this!

Consider the size of the real loaves and their distribution on the parchment paper so that when they rise and expand in the oven they don't touch. I like to place the parchment paper on the underside of a half-sheet pan (18 by 13 inches) and distribute the loaves so that each has the maximum space possible without falling off the stone; this also allows for some flubbing on my part. If the side of the loaf has become tacky or sticky during proofing, dust it slightly with flour so that when you put the loaves on parchment paper you will be able to make some small adjustments with their placement.

Steaming

Steam allows the baking loaf to stretch and expand further in the oven, increasing its volume while also producing a better interior loaf structure and a crisper and well-colored crust.

Here is an overview of common steaming methods proceeding from nothing to complicated:

STEAMING METHODS

NO STEAM: Just skip it. You may feel that the difference between the matte loaf with a little less volume and color and the loaves with shine and a more open aspect is not worth the additional trouble. I understand. One of the best baguettes that I ate this year came from an outdoor wood-fired oven with no steaming mechanism. It baked in just over 10 minutes (fast!) and looked very poor on the outside, but when cut open it revealed a glossy, webbed crumb with the yellow hue of grain held inside the shell of crunchy crust. The simplicity, the honesty, and the smile and pride of the baker more than compensated for the visuals.

SPRAY BOTTLE, PRESSURIZED GARDEN SPRAYER: I tried spray bottles when I first began working with artisan bread at home. The hand sprayer is easy, but it generates only meager steam, much of which flies out the door or vent immediately. A pressurized garden sprayer delivers a significant quantity of moisture if pointed at the oven walls, but the spray often hits the surface of my loaves directly, causing a splotchy crust. Further, if you hit the oven light with water, it will explode. Trust me.

PREHEATED CAST-IRON SKILLET OR BAKING PAN: While the oven is preheating, place a sheet pan or a large cast-iron skillet in the bottom of the oven. After loading, pour a cup of boiling water into the pan or the skillet. For even better results, put scrap-metal objects into the pan or the skillet. Things such as metal cutlery, metal pie weights, blacksmith scrap, and old chain have good surface area and mass which, when heated and then hit with water, will create substantial steam. With an electric oven this method produces ample steam and great results. For gas ovens, I've found that I need some additional tricks to be happy with my bread. The poor results with a gas oven relate to venting. See Oven Types (page 362) for additional information related to the differences between electric and gas home ovens.

Steaming, Scoring, and Ears

I regularly see questions on home baker forums that relate to scoring and "ears." Frequently, scoring, the actual cutting action, is identified as the culprit. In actuality, most of the time when I see a thread with a subject like "HELP! NO EARS?" and I see the picture that is attached, it is clear that the problem is not blade angle, dough strength, proof, flour type, or something hidden under any of the other rocks that have been overturned in the search. The answer is steam. I have seen great ears on baguettes scored from every possible blade angle at many levels of proof and I have never seen great ears on bread that was poorly steamed. Get the steam right and you will be close; mess up the steam, and you will have edible bread but no ears.

At my house I have a gas oven. In the bottom of the oven, hidden from view but within the baking chamber, are a burner and an igniter. The gas burns, heating the air, and the oven's interior and the combustion by-products exit via vents in the top of the oven, near the rear burners. The effluent pouring out of these vents is so hot that if I leave a pan at the back of the range and then try to move it with a bare hand, it will burn me. The gas oven, because of the combustion by-products, must be vented. So, anything introduced to the bake chamber (like wonderful steam!) will be immediately purged. Working around this requires some creativity. Electric ovens, on the other hand, are much tighter—when vents do exist, they are smaller and move much less air.

SELF-STEAMING: Loaves baked inside a cloche, in a Dutch oven, or on a baking stone with a metal bowl on top will essentially self-steam. During baking, in the closed environment (the cloche and the Dutch oven have their lid or cover on during most of baking; the metal bowl placed over the top of a loaf loaded onto a baking stone has the same effect), moisture from the loaf turns to steam. This works quite well for baking boules or a large miche. Remove the lid or the metal bowl approximately one-half to two-thirds of the way through baking to ensure that the loaf properly dries and darkens.

ROASTING PAN, LAVA ROCKS: This method uses two pieces of equipment—once I started following it, I looked no further. Place the baking stone on a rack in the lower third of the oven. Under the stone, on the floor of the oven, place a roasting pan loaded with lava rocks and mostly covered with aluminum foil. Leave a 1-inch channel of exposed rocks along the short side of the pan. Preset a chafing dish on an upper rack. After loading, pour water from a spouted vessel (I use a wine bottle) into the channel, onto the exposed rocks, then place the chafing dish over the loaves with an edge overhanging in such a way as to catch the steam rising from the lava rocks. Having the aluminum foil channel right under the lip of the roasting pan ensures that the maximum quantity of steam is directed to the bread. As with the self-steaming methods, remove the cover two-thirds of the way through the baking.

Be careful when steaming, and protect your hands and arms as you work. Water can cause hot glass oven doors to break. Place a towel over the glass while loading to reduce this risk.

Baking

We have come to the final moment. All that we have controlled and guided, from ingredients to mixing, folding, dividing, shaping, scoring, and loading, has been delivered to hot stones. As the oven is loaded and steam is introduced, our control wanes, our cuts open without us, and the loaves expand, swelling and darkening with chaos and color.

During baking, check to see if the loaves require any shuffling to brown evenly. Do this around two-thirds of the way through the baking. At this time, remove any covers or lids used for steaming as well as parchment paper under the loaf (the bottom will brown better without it). If you are baking your miche with a mixing bowl over it, remove the bowl. If you are baking in a cloche or Dutch oven, remove the lid. If you are trying the roasting pan method, remove the chafing dish (the lava rocks can stay in the oven), and so forth. The steam has done its job; it's now time to set the crust and allow the loaf to dry and color. At the end of the estimated baking time, turn off the oven and leave the door open a few inches to set the crust.

When Is Bread Done?

How do we know when bread is done? In a decade of baking I've pulled millions of loaves and rolls from hot ovens. This repetition and daily practice have refined my senses somewhat. Like many bakers I know, I largely rely upon my eyes to judge when a load of bread is done. With the baker's peel and long handle I can reach deep into the dark oven, scooping up loaves, pulling them into daylight to sense if they are done or need more time. I look for an even color that is appropriate to the bread I'm baking. A buttery pain de mie should be deep golden and toasty with good color and a firm crust on all sides. The Irish Levain (page 112), Kvassmiche (page 274), or Ciabatta (page 77) should be deep mahogany, close to dark chocolate or roasted coffee beans. If my eyes want a second opinion, I pick up a loaf and quickly feel its weight relative to its size. I give a gentle squeeze to sense the firmness of crust and glance at the bottom to check the color on that side as well. Opening the oven door always gets the nose involved, yet another clue to the state of things. All of this information falls into the category of empirical knowledge. Experience collected from the senses, informed and confirmed through repetition, is the best teacher.

Gaining this knowledge and experience as a home baker can be challenging. As in the case of mixing, shaping, scoring, and baking, limited repetitions (how much bread can your family and neighbors actually eat?) can mean a slower learning process. Using the times and temperatures specified in the recipes and, more important, using your senses, you will quickly come into your own.

SO, FIRST, LOOK. Does the loaf have a deep color that is appetizing, not insipid? Deep crust color translates to flavor with bread in the same way that roasted vegetables, caramelized onions, and seared short ribs all benefit from browning. This color, which relates to the Maillard reaction, is important and the first clue to what flavors await.

NEXT, TOUCH. With oven mitts or a pair of work gloves dedicated to oven use, hold the loaf and give it a squeeze. Hearth-baked loaves should be firm and should not yield easily; pan breads should merely give resistance, which indicates that they will remain set after cooling. Holding the loaf will also give some feedback regarding moisture loss during baking. Does it feel light for the size?

I haven't found any success with the use of a digital probe thermometer for judging doneness. Baking loaves (especially those in direct contact with the hearth or baking stone) reach 190°F to 200°F, or, "done," just two-thirds of the way through baking. I promise that the bread is not even close to done. So save the thermometer for use in measuring dough temperature or checking a roast or making jam and leave the heavy decision making to your powerful eyes, nose, and fingers.

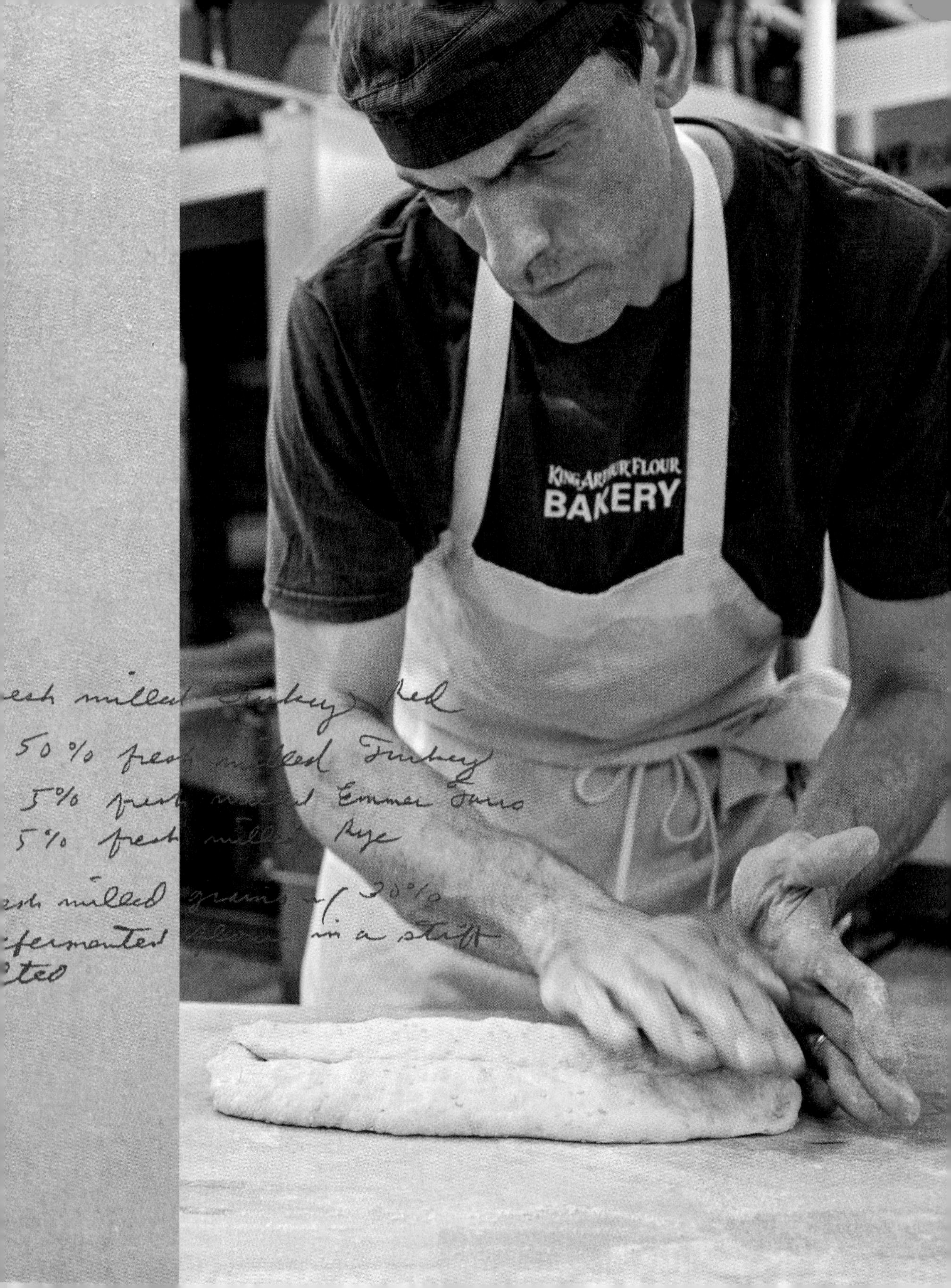

KING ARTHUR FLOUR
BAKERY
esh milled Turkey Red
50% fresh milled Turkey
5% fresh milled Emmer Farro
5% fresh milled Rye
esh milled grains w/ 30%
fermented flour in a stiff
ted

TROUBLESHOOTING TOPICS

With experience comes a sense of how to proceed when things don't go as planned. In the bakery we look for consensus at these junctures. A dough that is too cool is often discussed, and then may go into a warm proof box for the first hour of fermentation, or a dough that is too warm may be parked in the walk-in cooler for a bit. Dough that feels weak may be given extra folds or a stronger preshape and so forth. In reality, everything we touch requires adjustments. Each season brings different ambient humidity, each day a warmer or cooler environment, each dough or each preferment, endless variance. Thank goodness for this daily chaos, which requires our mental presence, our senses, and our skills. Here are a few tips that may help as you develop your own tool set.

STARTER IS OVERPROOFED, FALLEN: A starter that is overproofed or has fallen is not ideal, but it is not necessarily a sign that you should quit and start over. Preferments such as liquid levain and poolish are more prone to collapse than ones held in stiffer mediums. High water content makes their structure especially fragile. In this case you may proceed, taking notes and making adjustments for subsequent attempts. In the bakery environment (with mechanical mixers) I know that a very active liquid preferment will cause a dough to move more quickly and have more strength. At home, with hand mixing, the strength isn't as much of a liability or risk. Nonetheless, if a poolish is collapsed due to overactivity, I will reduce bulk fermentation time slightly or aim for a cooler dough temperature.

DOUGH IS TOO COLD: Place the dough in a warmer location and add 10 to 25 percent to the prescribed bulk fermentation time. If a cool dough is mixed in summer and your kitchen is almost 80°F, be patient. The warmer conditions will naturally encourage it; things will often equal out.

DOUGH IS TOO WARM: Place it in a cooler location and reduce bulk fermentation time by 10 to 25 percent. As with cold dough/summer conditions (example above), if it's winter and the ambient temperature is low, the dough will cool naturally as it rises during bulk fermentation and may solve its own problem.

DOUGH IS TOO LOOSE, UNDERDEVELOPED, OR SOFT: Perform additional vigorous folds and also consider adding 10 to 25 percent to the prescribed time for bulk fermentation, to add strength. When your dough is really, really soft (maybe you accidentally added too much final dough water) you might consider making pizza or focaccia if the dough type is appropriate (meaning a basic white dough—I wouldn't try to make pizza out of a rye bread dough). Occasionally, though very rarely, I will add flour to bring a dough back to a manageable place in the event of a scaling error (yes, this happens in professional bakeries, too). This can be done in a mixer or by kneading in flour on a bench or work surface. It's not ideal, but it's better than discarding dough. If this happens in the bakery, I keep track of the flour added and add salt as well to maintain proper ratios. Doughs are generally salted at 2 percent of total flour weight (see Baker's Math, page 314). If you use 100 grams of additional flour, salt that flour at 2 percent, or 2 grams, in order to make sure that the salt is balanced in the loaf.

DOUGH IS TOO STIFF, TOO STRONG, OR OVERDEVELOPED AFTER MIXING: If a dough feels too tight, strong, or rubbery after mixing, the solutions are in many ways the inverse of the prescription for the dough that is too loose, underdeveloped, or soft. You may reduce the frequency and vigor of folds, reduce bulk fermentation slightly (assuming that the dough temperature and fermentation activity are as expected), or add water. You may add water by simply putting the water on the top of the dough, and then incorporate it during folding. Or you may pour the water on top a little at a time, and then poke and massage it in, briefly kneading the dough until it's incorporated.

SHAPED LOAF IS UNDERPROOFED: The obvious answer is to proof longer, but sometimes that's not an option. If you notice that the shaped loaf is moving slowly, place it in a warmer, moist location to encourage activity. You may also effectively pause (to a certain degree, not entirely) a shaped loaf by covering it and placing it in the fridge. If I am baking at home and know that a dough won't be ready for the oven until too late in the day, I will place it in the fridge, covered, after shaping, and bake it the following day. For more information on this, see the sidebar, "Cold Proofing" (page 339).

SHAPED LOAF IS OVERPROOFED: A shaped loaf that is overproofed to the point of collapse cannot be fixed. If you forgot your baguettes, took the dog for a walk, and then washed your car . . . you will be better served using the dough to make pizza. Loaves that are mildly overproofed can be salvaged with a hotter oven (add 25°F to the prescribed temperature during preheating and lower to the prescribed temperature after loading). If the loaf is scored, like baguettes, for example, fewer cuts will be more successful than aggressive cutting.

TOOLS AND SMALLWARES

As a home baker, I chased tools and flour types, searching for magic skills. In the end, success came from simple, useful tools and experience. Here are some things I use.

SCALE: A digital scale that measures in 1-gram increments up to 5 kilos. Such scales are relatively easily acquired. I have one that I have taken around the world, keeping it in its original little cardboard sleeve; and another that measures in one-tenth of a gram increments up to 100 grams, and is very useful for small amounts of yeast, salt, baking powder, and baking soda. These two scales are almost as essential to my baking as flour, water, salt, yeast, and my hands.

DIGITAL OR INFRARED THERMOMETER: For years I used only the digital probe thermometer—but I have switched to the infrared. Its versatility—whether I'm measuring the temperature of the top of the woodstove, coffee beans I'm roasting, dough, or water—is unbeatable and fast.

MIXING BOWL: I like a large one, 12 to 14 inches in diameter, for mixing and proofing dough. I scale ingredients directly into the bowl, which is set on the scale. I tare the bowl, then add items, using the "tare" function before the addition of each subsequent ingredient. I find that the large bowl is nice, as it is big enough to get my hands in during mixing and folding. It scrapes down and cleans up quite easily. A large metal bowl is also quite useful in baking. See Steaming Methods, page 347.

TIMER: It seems as though every handheld electronic device has a timer on it these days. If you don't mind gumming up yours with doughy hands, it will work. I prefer an inexpensive battery or wind-up variety—even an egg timer will do

PLASTIC SCRAPER: This versatile, cheap tool is very useful for bending against the curved sides of the mixing bowl during mixing, folding, and cleaning.

MEASURING SPOONS: Measuring spoons are useful for small amounts of important ingredients. I have an old set of nesting spoons, which are bound by a metal ring. I like them, as I don't have to search the utensil drawer all day looking for a disappearing eighth-teaspoon measure.

BENCH KNIFE: A bench knife is a flat metal blade, about 4 by 6 inches, affixed to a wooden or plastic handle. Somehow bakers have come to be drawn with rolling pins in hand. I seldom use a pin, but I can regularly be found with a bench knife, a peel, or a razor. The metal blade is best for cleanly dividing dough as well as moving dough around on the bench, scraping surfaces and boards during cleaning, and even cutting cinnamon rolls, if it has a beveled edge.

BAKER'S LINEN (COUCHE): After dividing and shaping elongated loaves, such as baguettes or bâtards, which will be baked directly on a stone, we place them on floured baker's linen to proof. The linen is made from woven flax; its weave naturally resists adhering to sticky doughs. Tea towels may also be used; the ones with a flat weave or limited pile can work relatively well if dusted generously with flour. Baker's linen can be purchased in short lengths (about 24 inches) in a standard width of 26 inches. A single piece will be enough to get you started. Some people also successfully use painter's cloth or tablecloths, cut to size.

BANNETON: A banneton, or brotform, is a proofing basket: it is traditionally made from coiled willow, but can also be made of pressed paper pulp or a plastic weave (essentially a tortilla chip basket). The baskets, which are available in a myriad of sizes and shapes, some lined with flax linen, some unlined, are used to support loaves during proofing. If shaped round loaves are set to proof on a flat surface, they will spread out, rather than rise vertically. The round form helps keep them contained.

TRANSFER PEEL OR FLIPPING BOARD: A transfer peel is used for moving fragile proofed loaves that are elongated (such as bâtards and baguettes) from the linen to the oven peel or baking stone. If you like, precut a sheet of parchment paper that can be slid onto your heated baking stone directly from the peel for less risky loading. At home, rather than use the full-length ones we have in the bakery, I prefer a piece of stiff cardboard cut to roughly 16 by 4 inches. My baking stone is only about 16 inches wide, so I limit my loaves to roughly 13 to 14 inches and generally proof them on a half-sheet pan, lengthwise. Knowing the dimensions of your shaped loaves as well as the dimensions of your stone will help keep things from hanging over.

"LAME" (PRONOUNCED LAHM) OR BAKER'S RAZOR: For scoring loaves right before they enter the oven, I recommend a double-edge razor. To hold the razor, I have a small, thin piece of metal that is called a *lame*, onto which one can thread the razor. This is the way that I cut the first ten thousand loaves that I sent into the oven and I am likely do the same for the next ten thousand. I like the lame, as it allows me to adjust the angle of bend in the blade, and because it is metal, I can attach the blade in a curved or straight fashion (see Scoring, page 339).

CAST-IRON SKILLET: Depending on how you decide to steam your oven for the loaves that require it, you may want to begin with a cast-iron skillet or large stainless sauté pan. Preheating it with the baking stone will ensure that it has plenty of heat.

METAL BAKING PAN: I have a metal baking pan, the cheapest that I could find (I purchased mine new, but I frequently see these pans at thrift stores for about a buck), which I use for steaming (see Steaming Methods, page 347). I fill it with lava rocks and preheat it for 45 to 60 minutes before dumping hot or boiling water on it, producing a large quantity of steam.

LAVA ROCKS: The metal pan will require some lava rocks, which can be found in the grilling section of many hardware stores. A bag of them should set you back only about $10. Rinse them before using. Then cover the metal pan almost entirely with aluminum foil, leaving a hole on one side into which you may pour water. When the water hits the stones, it will vaporize, releasing significant steam.

DUTCH OVEN, CLOCHE: Baking in a Dutch oven, or cloche, can be a very successful technique for making bread at home. This method lowers the difficulty level of shaping, steaming, and, to a certain degree, loading. The bread produced can be quite delicious; if I am traveling and don't have my normal tools or a good bakery, I will often use this method to make a loaf I can live off.

4-INCH CHAFING DISH: If you should decide to go for the most complicated (best results) steaming method, which I describe in Steaming Methods, page 347, you will need a chafing dish. They are available from many sources online—I bought the cheapest one I could find. They do not need to be heavy steel, as they are only holding moisture like a lid.

STENCILS: You may see pictures of my work that show stenciled loaves. In a few cases I have purchased stencils that were the right size for the loaves that I wanted to decorate. More often, I have found or sketched an image that I liked and then drawn it on a sheet called "Quilter's Plastic," which is available at craft stores. I have also carved them from plastic milk jugs and the tops of plastic food containers. Usually I draw the image on paper, trace it with a marker onto the plastic then, put some music on, and get out a very sharp knife (X-Acto brand or similar) and carefully, slowly, cut the stencil against a piece of scrap wood. If the design is intricate and I want it very crisp, I will sometimes pay to have it laser-cut. Etsy has numerous stores offering cutting services. I have had great luck using this method.

BAKING STONE: When I began making artisan loaves, I started with quarry tiles. They are better than a metal baking pan, but they are thin, with little mass; they don't conduct heat very well, and they are fragile. I eventually graduated to a thick baking stone and then improved things further by adding masonry sides and a top, essentially building a masonry box inside my oven. Using this setup, I was able to bake loaves for a portfolio, which helped me to land my job with King Arthur Flour. When I bake at home now, I use the same baking stone that I've had all these years, but with much better steaming methods (see Steaming Methods, page 347), which have made a tremendous difference.

BAKING STEEL: The baking steel is essentially a thick piece of plate steel that can be used in the oven or on top of the stove. Steel conducts heat better than stone; I like it as much for pancakes on top of the stove as I do for pizza under the broiler. If you are using it in the oven in place of the baking stone, be sure to check the bottom of your loaves during baking, as they will bake more quickly on steel than stone.

SHEET PAN: Heavy-gauge half-sheet pans (18 by 13 inches) are indispensable. They won't buckle when you are roasting vegetables, and they transfer heat evenly to cookies, scones, croissants, and crackers. I have a couple of quarter-sheet pans as well; they make great seed trays.

ROLLING PIN: I prefer the straight pins with no handles. I have a few different diameters including some small ones, which I cut from dowels purchased for a couple of bucks at the hardware store. They work, as did the discarded broom handles I used in the early days.

Ovens

Round, burning forms shape the center of our oldest community hubs. Evidence of hominids' use of fire extends back well over a million years. Fire could even be considered a metaphorical womb by modern humans: it brings sustenance, it gathers, and it protects. Perhaps we have evolved more as a direct result of tended combustion than from any other human activity. Our language loves this history. *Focus*, meaning "fireplace" or "home" in Latin, speaks to the centering nature of the space where heart and hearth combine. Home was born here, near the oven, at the source.

Whether we are using a fireplace, fire ring, deck oven, cob oven, or home range, a learning curve exists, a getting-to-know-you, which takes time. First dates and late nights, fumbling, burning, frustration, comfort, success. Heat is not a passive tool; it will let you know when you are doing it right, or wrong. In the world of baking we have many ways to interact with heat. In broad terms, ovens can be divided into categories. Here are a few examples.

Oven Types

COMMERCIAL OVEN: The oven at King Arthur Flour is a five-deck, three-phase, multiton behemoth three times the size of an industrial Dumpster. It has a propane burner that blows more than 450,000 BTUs of superheated air through masonry channels screaming to 250 or more baguettes. It is touch-screen, computer-controlled, and multilingual, and starts on a programmed timer before bakers arrive. It chimes when a baking program is initiated, counting down the seconds and minutes until the breads are ready. If I press the steam button, measured quantities of filtered water hit rippling plates and vaporize immediately in the bake chamber, moistening surfaces, condensing and gelatinizing crusts.

HOME OVEN: A home oven is a hot box that doesn't seal very well. If it is gas, a small gas burner in the bottom heats air and thin metal walls, but much of the hot air pours up the vent as fast as it can be added, or dumps into the room at every opening of the oven door. There is no steam and no ability to retain steam should we add it during baking. My home gas oven is new and yet wildly uneven—anything baked on its lower rungs burns on the bottom. Obsessive rotating can help, but continually opening the door has its own poor outcome. In the steaming section (see Steaming Methods, page 347), I discuss particulars of gas versus electric. The best option for a home oven is electric. One note: An oven thermometer can be very useful for determining if the oven is properly calibrated. Through experience and regular checks I know that my oven runs 25 degrees cool and that I should adjust accordingly.

MASONRY OVEN: A retained-heat wood-fired masonry oven has no knobs, dials, thermostats, or steaming apparatus. Heat is applied by burning wood, slowly firing over the course of a day, giving unquantifiable heat to the masonry mass in order to draw it back out during baking. Temperature may be roughly judged by how long an arm extended fully into the bake chamber can be held there, or by the length of time it takes for a handful of flour to smoke, then burn, if cast onto the hot baking surface. Before baking, the oven is swept clean of ash and coals and briefly swabbed. There are many great references written on wood-fired oven baking and construction, including Richard Miscovich's comprehensive *From the Wood-Fired Oven*; *The Bread Builders,* by Dan Wing and Alan Scott; and Kiko Denzer's approachable *Build Your Own Earth Oven*. Wood-fired ovens did not originally have a steaming function. When fully loaded they will self-steam during baking. As moisture in the loaves exits (bread loses more than 10 percent of its weight while baking) it enters the bake chamber, moistening the surface of the loaves and eventually billowing out.

I will admit that when I returned to home baking after years of working with professional tools, there was some frustration. And I will say (from the other side of this experience) that over time I have developed a relationship with what tools and means I have. The results are not always what I get with professional tools but I am proud of what I make. I sincerely hope that, using the recipes, tips, and guidance offered here, you might find yourself in this satisfied place, proud of your wares, encouraged to proceed.

A Note on Volume and Metric Measurements

Some of the more experienced bakers and mathematicians using this book may notice that the grams and volume measurements do not always correspond perfectly. The recipes began with grams, ensuring great accuracy. Then we converted the recipes to volume measurements, using weights that have been established, or that we determined by having several people measure and remeasure, keeping track of the weights to determine an average weight per cup.

The gram weights were divided by the yield per cup; this led to a decimal format, which was rounded to the nearest measurement in cups and tablespoons. In some cases, the volume amount is slightly more, or slightly less, than the actual gram weight. Based on the author's best judgment, a few recipes may have more water or less water in the preferment or soaker to ensure a convenient amount to measure by volume. Finally, the recipes were tested at home with only volume used, and readjusted only if the results were significantly different or discouraging. The ultimate difficulty arose in using liquid measuring cups. We tested several brands, with huge discrepancies. Use a graduated beaker for the closest results. If you're making a particular loaf by volume and the dough doesn't feel quite moist enough after a fold or two, use a French technique called *bassinage* (*doppio impasto* in Italian). Add a few teaspoons or tablespoons of water over the top of the dough, and fold it in. As you perform the folds, the dough will absorb the water, correcting the hydration.

Overall, the recipes work using volume, so please feel free to use this method if that is all you have, but a scale will make your life much easier, your time will be used more wisely, and the baked goods will be consistently delicious.

—LAURIE FURCH

ACKNOWLEDGMENTS

We were so close. The due date of the book, no longer a mirage in the distance, was fast approaching, and I was set to finish on time when Julie found a lump in her breast. Early appointments led to follow-ups and more tests, and then she texted me from the hospital after a biopsy. "Please come. Now." I wheeled into the parking lot with a stomach full of dread—is this happening? She was at the curb, waiting for me, arms crossed, clutching herself with her own hands. As our eyes met, her legs gave away, unable to bear the weight of what she had just heard. Cancer. We were leveled, broken with the worry of worst-case scenarios and life-threatening concerns.

The events of the days and months after the diagnosis—telling our children, trips to Boston for surgeries, home nurse visits, meal trains, and recovery—now exist as chunks of memory set in healthy tissue; seams where my mind stops, as it feels its way through those difficult days. Yet there is also a feeling of richness. It was abundant with grief and worry, but also layered with care, overflowing with the compassion and support, and was deep, deep with luck. Almighty luck.

And there is good news. Julie is in excellent health, fully with us, as abundant and life-filled as ever. Without her, there would be no abundance. Julie, thank you for being the center of our world, our star, the source of our family, all that we care for. Thank you also to my sweet children, Clementine, Anthem, and Arlo. Be nothing more than you are: You are everything, and perfect.

Giving thanks is not a thing to begin or end. It's a state, an awareness—it is gratitude in motion. But I need to write some names and places here, so let me make a start, knowing that the list is incomplete, and growing.

To my family, my roots. To the places where I began. Without you there are no limbs to grow, no fruit to bear, no seasons, nothing to come from or become. Thank you, Mama and Daddy. Thank you to George, Michael, Carolyn, Samuel, Angela, and others, named and unnamed, long past. Each of you has shaped me; I love you all. Thank you also to your spouses and children, who also have a close seat on this great tree.

Thank you also to my wife's family, which I now consider my own. Thank you for your daughter and for your unending support and celebration of our union, our lives and our children.

To the employee-owners—founding, past, and present—of King Arthur Flour who have cheered, held, supported, and tolerated me in everything that I pursue. It is no wonder that our great company has achieved so much under the early guidance of Frank and Brinna Sands and then under the passionate and wise direction of my good friend Steve Voigt. To our caring and committed leadership team of Karen Colberg, Suzanne McDowell, and Ralph Carlton; to Jeffrey Hamelman, who hired me and continues to inspire through his kinship with bread; to our team of bakers who live the life, walk the walk, and shimmy the daily baking dance; thank you, one and all!

When I began this project I needed a team—a support system that could help navigate the gaps between where I was and where I needed to go. I asked my friend James Sturm, the celebrated cartoonist, if he knew anyone who might be a good fit as a writing coach. James sent me to our mutual friend, the author Sarah Stewart Taylor. It is intimidating and awkward to open your heart and write. Sarah took my words and work in stride, finding the perfect balance between encouragement and asking for better. She fostered a place where I could take risks without judgment, letting things unfold naturally. What a gift you have, Sarah. Thank you.

For my mind, stress, and guidance, I found my way to Paul Caver. I saw Paul twice a month. His office became a place where I could share my upset, worries, and foibles and also talk at length about writing, cancer, the mindful practice of running, meditation, the creative process, or whatever else moved me. In doing so, it helped me find my way to a better place. Thank you, Paul.

I owe many bakers a large debt of gratitude. Judson Smith of Brimfield Bread Oven is that friend to whom I can send an expletive-laden rant at any hour of the day and know that he will understand, or at least laugh his ass off with me. We are bread brothers, sharing a passion for crusty and dark, buttery and crisp, and a deep love for time in the woods. He is a baker of the very best order. Thank you, brother. James MacGuire is a font of curiosity and connection to the historical context of what and how bakers have worked for centuries. Jeff Yankellow gets the final say on everything bread-related. If I need definitive and accurate, "do this, not that," Jeff is where I turn. Susan Miller—thank you for always caring, always listening, understanding and cheering. It has meant so much. Allison Reid of Scratch Baking Company and Toast Bar, you are the skilled, engaged, active person that I hope to be. Now teach me to surf? Roger Gural of Arcade Bakery in New York and Mike Zakowski (the Bejkr) were endless sources of inspiration in the years of preparation leading to the Coupe process. I studied galleries of their work and also the formulas they shared with complete willingness.

There is a Fantasy Island in Peterborough, New Hampshire. A jewel in a hemlock forest, crisscrossed with pine needle trails that connect still ponds to studio havens where one may make art, write, or simply nap. This magical place where power and inspiration can be gathered and channeled is called the MacDowell Colony. I was able to spend two weeks as a fellow in the summer of '16. Two weeks in "MacDowell time" is equal to six months in real life, for one can live faster, experience more, and dream more deeply there than in any other place on earth. MacDowell cracked me open, exposing something in the process, and what came out of that fissure, leaving the old shell behind, was a person more connected to his true nature and story. To the MacDowell Colony, the fellows, the librarians, the director, the board, thank you. I'm forever changed and twice as grateful.

I've known Jodi Picoult for more than a few years. We met when her children came to our house for voice lessons with Julie. While they sang, she settled in at our kitchen table among the mess of toys, block crayons, and bread crumbs, completely unfazed by our chaos. Somewhere along the way she asked me to share some baking with her as research for a book, and we spent an afternoon making challah, bagels, and bialys; chatting, laughing, and fully stuffing ourselves. When I thought that I might have some pieces of a book, I asked Jodi if she would review them. Within a few hours, I received an e-mail from Jodi, introducing me to her agent—and so it began. Jodi's reputation for generosity is legendary and well deserved. Thanks for all the support, Jodi!

Soon after the e-mail from Jodi I scheduled a face-to-face in Boston with Laura Gross and then, only a few weeks later, the country boy baker from Arkansas and Laura, a British expat, went to New York to meet potential publishers. Laura is drawn to meaning, justice, good stories, and connections with family and place. She's never expressed anything but confidence and support for me, for my voice. I can't imagine anyone doing this better. Thank you for the onion picture.

Our first stop in New York was Harper Wave, Karen Rinaldi's imprint at Harper Collins. As Karen and I talked, I felt understood. She stopped, she listened, and she cared. If Karen and the team at Harper had initial doubts or question marks around what I could do as a writer, I never sensed it. I received nothing but support and space to do my work without anyone looking over my shoulder. I don't know how this process normally unfolds, but it was all Karen and Hannah Robinson, keeping me in line, fielding my newbie questions and cheering as I ran around, trying to make something respectable. Thanks are also in order to Leah Carlson-Stanisic for her beautiful design and layout, and also to the entire production and marketing team at Harper.

On paper we live a long way from family . . . but there is this thing called community and it can be a damn good stand-in. We are so fortunate to live near many, many people who have been adopted into our fold. Especially helpful for me this year were Sue Krincich and Chuck Wooster. Thank you for all the gifts of time, hospitality, and music.

Thanks to Julia Reed for the gorgeous pictures, which capture everything with texture, richness, and beauty. She finds the things that we all want to see and frames them for our delight. Thank you, Julia.

There are home bakers, serious home bakers, and people who would have been professional bakers if they hadn't found a bunch of other things to master first. Whenever I needed the insight of a bread expert who could think as a professional *and* a home baker, simultaneously, I went to Steve Brandt. I can't think of an example where Steve suggested a change that I didn't make—not a single one. Steve, you worked tirelessly and accurately, reading my words, baking the recipes, and even doing some line editing. Thank you for everything.

Laurie Furch converted all my grams to volumetric amounts, and helped to conform instructions and tie everything together with clarity along the way. Her assistance and testing were timely and infinitely helpful. Thank you, Laurie. Now go write your own book!

Last, but not least, a sincere thank-you to the staff, patrons, and members of the Howe Library in Hanover, New Hampshire. I wrote the whole book on a couch in the poetry room. Our public spaces, which encourage reading, learning, and insight into the lives and worlds of others are more valuable than ever. Thank you!

INDEX

Page reference in *italics* refer to illustrations.

A

all-purpose flour, 303
    switching sourdough culture from rye flour to, 307, 309–10
almonds, in Romesco, *222*, 225
alternative grains, 304–5
anchovies, in Tapenade, *50*, 51
Anise-Fig Scones, 188–89
Appalachian Trail, 246
apple(s):
    Bread, Carrie's, 200–203
    cider, in Wood's Boiled Cider Bread, 195–99, *197*
    dried, in Spiced Honey Bread, 208–10
    Kvassmiche, 271, *272–73*, 274–77
Apple Bread, Carrie's, 200–203

B

artisan baking, author's introduction to, 94–96
Artisan Baking Center, Long Island City, 116

Baba Ganoush, 228–29
Bagels, 88–89, *90*, 91–93
baguettes, 140, *141–42*
    baking, 153
    Basic French Dough, 52–54
    chilling shaped loaves, 146
    Country, 149–52
    Poolish, 143–45
    scoring, 340–41, *341*
    shaping, 135, 140, 332–33, *333*
    Straight, 146–48
    transfer peel or flipping board for, 359
baker's linen, 335, 359
baker's math, 313, 314–16, 318–19
baker's razors, 340, 359–60

baking, 349–50
baking pans, metal, 347, 360
baking powder, measuring, 312
baking soda, measuring, 312
baking steels, 361
baking stones, 361
    baking directly on (hearth baking), 345–46
Balthazar Bakery, New York, 111
Banana-Pecan Muffins, 109–10
bannetons, 335, 359
baskets, proofing, 335, 359
bassinage technique, 364
bâtards:
    Basic French Dough, 52–54
    Cranbuck, 242–45
    Durum-Rosemary Bread, 234–37
    Poolish, 143–45
    scoring, 341
    shaping, 140, 331–32, *332*
    transfer peel or flipping board for, 359

From the Wood-Fired Oven
(Miscovich), 208

G

garbanzo bean flour, in Socca,
 230, 230–31
garden sprayers, pressurized,
 347
garlic, roasted, in Romesco,
 222, 225
gas ovens, steaming in,
 347–48, 362–63
Genzano, Italy:
 Pane Genzano from, 64,
 66–68, 69–71
Genzano da Roma, Italy, 64
German Citrus Vollkornbrot,
 254–57
ginger:
 -Infused Pastry Cream,
 126
 Kvassmiche, 271, *272–73*,
 274–77
 Scones, 182–84, *183*
Glaze, Cinnamon Roll, 172,
 173
glazing, with egg wash,
 181
gluten-free baking, 303
Goldilocks zone, 322
grains:
 adding to exterior of loaves
 and rolls, 337–38
 alternative, 304–5
 whole, balance and, 304
 *see also specific grains and
 flours*
Great Chefs, 52
grits. *See* corn grit(s)

H

half-sheet pans, 361
Hamburger Buns, Brioche,
 118–19, 120–22
Hamelman, Jeffrey, 116–17,
 129–30, 261, 293–94,
 326, 343
hearth baking, 345–46
Hoecakes, Corn Grit, 17, *18*, 19
Homeboy Industries, 190
Honey Bread, Spiced, 208–10
Hummus, 226–27
hydration, correcting, 364

I

Indian foods:
 Lentils, *218*, 219–20, 222
 Pickled Onion, *218*, 220
 Raita, *218*, 221
 Roti, 216–17, *218*
infrared thermometers, 358
ingredients, 302–6
 baker's math and, 313,
 314–16
 checklist technique for addition of, 314
 listed in order of use,
 312–13
 measuring (*see* measuring
 ingredients)
 sourcing, 305–6
Institute for Culinary Education, New York, 116
Irish Levain, 112–15
Italian breads:
 biga in, 318
 Ciabatta, 76–79, *78*, 320–21

Filone di Sesame, 72–74,
 74–75
Focaccia, 46–49, *47, 48*
Pane Genzano, 64, *66–68*,
 69–71
see also pizza

J

Jalapeño-Cheddar Bread,
 190–94, *193*
Jalapeños, Pickled, 194
jam, 12
 checking temperature of, 14
 Lemon-Blackberry, 16
 Plum Port, 12–13, *15*

K

King Arthur Flour, 5, 190, 200
 author hired by, 129–30, 361
 author's first days working
 at, 134–35
 author's studies at, 116–17
 daily routine at, 153–55
Kvass, 274–76
Kvassmiche, 271, *272–73*,
 274–77

L

lames, 340, 359–60
lapsong souchong tea, in Boxcar, 278–83, *281*
lava rocks, 349, 360
lavender flowers, in Beekeeper's Pain de Mie, 211–15
Leaf cut, *342*, 343
leavening culture. *See* sourdough culture

masonry, 363
preheating, 344–45

P

Pain de Mie, 166–69
  Beekeeper's, 211–15
  Cinnamon Rolls, 166–68,
    170, 170–72, 173
  options for batch sizes,
    120
  Pull-Apart Rolls, 164–65,
    166–68, 167, 169
  Sandwich Loaf, 166–69
pain d'épices, 208
Pain de Seigle, 101, 102–5,
  103
Pain Quotidien, 100–101
pain rustique, 80
  Olive and Rosemary
    Rustique, 80–84, 83
pancakes:
  Corn Grit Hoecakes, 17,
    18, 19
  fluffier, tips for, 174
  Risen, 177, 177–79
  Socca, 230, 230–31
  Wheat, 174, 176
Pane Genzano, 64, 66–68,
  69–71
pan loaves, forming, 333–34,
  334
parchment paper, for loading
  loaves into oven, 345, 346,
  359
Pastry Cream, Ginger-In-
  fused, 126
pâte fermentée, 318
PBS cooking shows, 52
Pears, Poached, 128

pecan(s):
  Banana Muffins, 109–10
  Boxcar, 278–83, 281
  Pie, 27
peels, transfer, 359
peppers, bell:
  red, in Romesco, 222, 225
  Tapenade, 50, 51
Pickled Jalapeños, 194
Pickled Onion, 218, 220
pie crusts:
  ingredients kept cold for, 10
  Oma's, 22–23, 24–26, 25
pies:
  Molasses, 20–21, 22–23
  Pecan, 27
pizza, 55–57
  Napoletana, 56, 58–60, 59
  Red Sauce for, 61–62
  using soft dough for, 354
plastic scrapers, 358
Plum Port Jam, 12–13, 15
Polka cut, 342, 342–43
poolish, 318
  collapse of, 353
poolish, breads and baked
  goods made with:
  Bagels, 88–89, 90, 91–93
  Boxcar, 278–83, 281
  Durum-Rosemary Bread,
    234–37
  Poolish Baguette, 143–45
Poolish Baguette, 143–45
Port Jam, Plum, 12–13, 15
powerBROT, 265, 266–67,
  268–70
preferments, 96, 317–20
  baker's math and, 315, 316,
    318–19
  categories of, 317–18

  getting creative with,
    319–20
  pâte fermentée, 318
  straight dough and, 146
  swelling followed by, 242
  see also biga; liquid levain;
    pâte fermentée; poolish;
    rye sourdough; stiff
    levain
preheating oven, 344–45
preshaping, 329–30
pressurized garden sprayers,
  347
proofing, 338–39
  cold, 339
  tools for, 359
  troubleshooting under-
    proofed or overproofed
    shaped loaves, 355
proofing baskets (bannetons),
  335, 359
Pudding, Bread, 34–35
Pull-Apart Rolls, Pain de Mie,
  164–65, 166–68, 167,
  169
pumpkin seeds, in power-
  BROT, 265, 266–67,
  268–70

Q

quarter-sheet pans, 361
quick breads:
  pain d'épices, 208
  Roti, 216–17, 218
  Spiced Honey Bread,
    208–10
  Wheat Pancakes, 174, 176
  see also biscuits; muffins;
    scones

R

Raita, *218*, 221
ratios of ingredients, baker's math and, 313, 314–16
razors, baker's, 340, 359–60
recipes:
  baker's math and, 313, 314–16
  ingredient lists in, 312–13
  reading, 312–13, 314
  sub-recipes in, 315–16
  Total Dough Percentage, Total Formula, and *Final Dough* in, 315–16
Red Sauce, 61–62
Reed, Julia, 261
Rhodes, Michael, 246–48
Rhubarb-Strawberry Compote, 207
  Shortcake Biscuits with, 204–7, *206*
rice flour, in dusting blend, 335–36
Risen Pancakes, *177*, 177–79
rising, in baskets or on linens, 335, 359
Roasted Corn–Chive Scones, 185–86, *187*
roasting pans, steaming method with, 349
rolling pans, 361
rolls:
  Cinnamon, Pain de Mie, 166–68, *170*, 170–72, *173*
  Jalapeño-Cheddar, 190–94
  Pull-Apart, Pain de Mie, *164–65*, 166–68, *167*, 169
  shaping, 334

Romesco, *222*, 225
rosemary:
  Durum Bread, 234–37
  and Olive Rustique, 80–84, *83*
Roti, 216–17, *218*
round preshape, 329–30
rum, in Spiced Honey Bread, 208–10
Rustic Walnut Ciabatta, 248–53, *250–51*
rustique. *See* pain rustique
rye, freshly milled, in Fresh-Milled Miche, 159–62, *161*
rye chops, in Citrus Vollkornbrot, 254–57
rye flour, whole, 303, 337
  Citrus Vollkornbrot, 254–57
  Irish Levain, 112–15
  Pain de Seigle, 101, 102–5, *103*
  powerBROT, 265, *266–67*, 268–70
  Spiced Honey Bread, 208–10
  starting sourdough culture with, 307–9
  Wood's Boiled Cider Bread, 195–99, *197*
rye loaves:
  shaping, 336–37
  Sunrise cut for, 343–44
rye sourdough, 319
rye sourdough, breads with:
  Citrus Vollkornbrot, 254–57
  Irish Levain, 112–15
  Pain de Seigle, 101, 102–5, *103*
  Wood's Boiled Cider Bread, 195–99, *197*

S

salt, 305–6
  added flour and, 354
  measuring, 312
  in preferments, 318, 319
Sandwich Loaf, Pain de Mie, 166–69
sassafras root, 271
  Kvassmiche, 271, *272–73*, 274–77
Sauce, Whiskey, 35
savory dishes:
  Baba Ganoush, 228–29
  Black-Eyed Peas, 38–40, *41*
  Curried Coconut Soup, 290
  Hummus, 226–27
  Raita, *218*, 221
  Tapenade, 50, *51*
Savory Tart, 120–21, *122–23*
scales, 357–58
  checking accuracy of, 312
  "tare" function of, 358
SCOBY (symbiotic colony of bacteria and yeast), 307
scones, 180–81
  egg wash for, 181
  Fig-Anise, 188–89
  Ginger, 182–84, *183*
  ingredients kept cold for, 10
  Roasted Corn–Chive, 185–86, *187*
scoring, 324, 337, 339–44
  baguettes, 340–41, *341*
  blades for, 340
  chilled loaves, 339
  dough surface and, 340–41
  function of, 340

ABOUT THE AUTHOR

MARTIN PHILIP is the head bread baker at King Arthur Flour in Norwich, Vermont. He holds a degree from Oberlin Conservatory and is a MacDowell fellow. He lives in the hills of Vermont with his wife, Julie Ness, his three sweet children, and two chickens.